IEG
Independent Evaluation Group

WORLD BANK GROUP
World Bank • IFC • MIGA

# World Bank Group Assistance to Low-Income Fragile and Conflict-Affected States

## AN INDEPENDENT EVALUATION

new deal
rule of law
hunger
impoverishment
low capacity
transformation
destruction
refugees
reintegration
conflict
displacement
country ownership
grievances
peacebuilding
local economic
fragility
institutional
human capital
development
justice
political settlement
infrastructure development
civil society development
equitable social contract
inclusion
security
youth unemployment
gender equity
gender-based violence
legitimacy
citizen voice
poor infrastructure
revenue mobilization
resilience
violence
corruption
fear
trust
accountability
insecurity
political risk
weak institutions
jobs
reconstruction
inclusive growth
access 2 opportunities
statebuilding
donor harmonization
access 2 services
transition
reconciliation
transparency
resource curse
patronage
elite capture

JANUARY 20

**IEG** | INDEPENDENT EVALUATION GROUP

**WORLD BANK GROUP**
World Bank • IFC • MIGA

# World Bank Group Assistance to Low-Income Fragile and Conflict-Affected States

## AN INDEPENDENT EVALUATION

new deal
rule of law
justice political settlement
infrastructure development
civil society development
equitable social contract
inclusion

hunger
impoverishment
low capacity
refugees
displacement
grievances
transformation
reintegration
country ownership
peacebuilding
local economic
institutional
human capital

destruction

conflict

fragility

development

security

youth unemployment
gender equity
citizen voice

gender-based violence
legitimacy
resilience

revenue mobilization
accountability

violence corruption
fear
trust
jobs
statebuilding
access 2 opportunities
inclusive growth
transparency
reconciliation
transition
access 2 services
donor harmonization

insecurity

weak institutions

reconstruction

resource curse

elite capture

Design: Crabtree + Company
www.crabtreecompany.com

**Library of Congress Cataloging-in-Publication Data**
World Bank Group assistance to low-income fragile and
conflict-affected states : an independent evaluation.

pages cm
Includes bibliographical references and index.
ISBN 978-1-4648-0218-8 (alk. paper)
ISBN 978-1-4648-0219-5 (ebook)

1. Economic assistance—Developing countries.
2. Poverty—Developing countries. 3. Economic
development—Developing countries. I. World Bank.

HC60.W667 2014

332.1'532—dc23                    2014020558

# Contents

## Appendixes

*The appendixes are published online as a separate volume*
*http://ieg.worldbankgroup.org/Data/reports/chapters/fcs_appendix.pdf*

# Abbreviations

| | | | |
|---|---|---|---|
| AAA | analytical and advisory activities | DPO | Development Policy Operation |
| ADB | Asian Development Bank | EITI | Extractive Industries Transparency Initiative |
| AfDB | African Development Bank | | |
| AfDF | African Development Fund | ESW | economic and sector work |
| AGEI | Adolescent Girls Employment Initiative | EU | European Union |
| AS | advisory services | FCS | fragile and conflict-affected states |
| CAFEF | Conflict-Affected and Fragile Economies Facility | FCV | fragility, conflict, and violence |
| | | FDI | foreign direct investment |
| CAS | country assistance strategy | FPD | Financial and Private Sector Development Network |
| CASA | Conflict Affected States in Africa | | |
| CASCR | Country Assistance Strategy Completion Report | GAVI | Global Alliance for Vaccines and Immunizations |
| | | GDP | gross domestic product |
| CCSD | Center on Conflict, Security and Development | GTFP | Global Trade Finance Program |
| CDD | community-driven development | HIPC | heavily indebted poor countries |
| CPA | Comprehensive Peace Agreement | IBRD | International Bank for Reconstruction and Development |
| CPIA | Country Policy and Institutional Assessment | | |
| | | ICR | Implementation Completion Report |
| DAC | Development Assistance Committee | ICRR | Implementation Completion and Results Report |
| DDR | demobilization, disarmament and reintegration | | |
| | | ICT | Information Communications and Technology |
| DFID | U.K. Department for International Development | | |
| | | IDA | International Development Association |
| DOTS | Development Outcome Tracking System | IDA15 | IDA Fifteenth Replenishment |
| DPL | Development Policy Lending | IDA16 | IDA Sixteenth Replenishment |

| | | | | |
|---|---|---|---|---|
| IDA17 | IDA Seventeenth Replenishment | | PEFA | Public Expenditure and Financial Accountability |
| IEG | Independent Evaluation Group | | PFM | public financial management |
| IFC AS | IFC Advisory Services | | PIU | Program Implementation Unit |
| IFC | International Finance Corporation | | PPP | purchasing power parity |
| ISN | Interim Strategy Note | | PRI | political risk insurance |
| ISR | Implementation Status and Results Report | | PSD | private sector development |
| LICUS | Low-Income Countries Under Stress | | SDN | Sustainable Development Network |
| MDG | Millennium Development Goal | | SFD | Social Fund for Development |
| MDRP | Multicountry Demobilization and Reintegration Program | | SIP | Small Investment Program |
| MDTF | multi-donor trust fund | | SMEs | small and medium enterprises |
| MIGA | Multilateral Investment Guarantee Agency | | SPF | Statebuilding and Peacebuilding Fund |
| NGO | nongovernmental organization | | TDRP | Transitional Demobilization and Reintegration Program |
| ODA | official development assistance | | TF | trust fund |
| OECD | Organisation for Economic Co-operation and Development | | UN | United Nations |
| OPCS | Operations Policy and Country Services | | UNDP | United Nations Development Programme |
| PAF | Poverty Alleviation Fund | | WDI | World Development Indicator |
| PCPI | Post-Conflict Performance Indicators | | WDR | World Development Report |

All dollar amounts are in U.S. dollars unless otherwise indicated.

# Acknowledgments

This evaluation of World Bank Group support to fragile and conflict-affected states (FCS) was prepared by an Independent Evaluation Group (IEG) team led by Anis Dani. The evaluation was carried out under the guidance of Nick York (Director) and the direction of Caroline Heider (Director General, Evaluation, and Senior Vice President).

Members of the core team included Victor Eduardo Macias Essedin, Ann Elizabeth Flanagan, Amnon Golan, Catherine Gwin, Hiro Hatashima, Shoghik Hovhannisyan, Lauren Kelly, Ali Khadr, Christopher Nelson, Nestor Ntungwanayo, Judith O'Connor, Jack van Holst Pellekaan, Inder Sud, Stephan Wegner, Emily Harwit Whewell, and Disha Zaidi. The case studies in six countries were undertaken by three- to four-person teams from among the core team to prepare background papers on each country.

The desk research team for the portfolio analysis, thematic reviews, and staff and stakeholder surveys included Jacqueline Andrieu, Samia Ausaf, Houqi Hong, Jane Margaret Olmstead-Rumsey, Daniel Palazov, Aida Tapalova, Hrachaya Topalyan, and Kathryn Steingraber. The econometric analysis of portfolio outcomes was undertaken by Kenneth Chomitz. Program assistance for the evaluation was provided by Carla F. Chacaltana, who was assisted by Cecilia Jade Kern in preparation of the evaluation report.

Thanks are also due to Anila Kuka in HR Analytics, World Bank and to Svetlana Greenberg and Thomas Williams of the International Finance Corporation for their help in analyzing the human resources data relevant to work in FCS.

The team also acknowledges the advice received from Geeta Batra on the recommendations and Management Action Record, and the help from Barbara Rice in editing the report.

IEG is grateful to the numerous government representatives and development partners who provided valuable insights into the program in the case study countries. The team is also thankful to World Bank Group management and staff, in particular the staff of the Center on Conflict, Security and Development and the FCS Community of Practice who provided valuable feedback during the course of the evaluation. Thanks are also due to the management and staff in the case study countries for the information they provided and their support to the evaluation team.

The report has benefited from the council of the External Advisory Panel which was comprised of Minister Emilia Pires, Minister of Finance, Timor-Leste, and chair of the g7+ (Panel Chair); Mr. Jordan Ryan, Assistant Secretary General and Director, Bureau of Crisis Prevention and Recovery, United Nations Development Programme; Dr. Ahmed Mushtaque Chowdhury, Vice Chair, Board of Governors, BRAC; and Dr. Ashutosh Varshney, Sol Goldman Professor of International Studies and the Social Sciences, Brown University. Peer reviewers for the evaluation were Soniya Carvalho (Lead Evaluation Officer), Phil Keefer (Lead Economist), Louise Walker (Private Sector Development Adviser, U.K. Department for International Development), and Ted Kliest (Policy and Operations Evaluation Department, U.K. Department for International Development, Netherlands Ministry of Foreign Affairs).

# Overview | HIGHLIGHTS

About 370 million people live in low-income fragile and conflict-affected states (FCS). They have higher poverty rates, lower growth rates, and weaker human development indicators than other low-income countries. The World Bank Group has identified support to FCS as a strategic priority, critical to achieving its mission of poverty alleviation and shared prosperity. Progress is evident in several areas, but Bank Group engagement in FCS is clearly a long-term agenda with several challenges and constraints yet to be overcome.

This review of International Development Association (IDA) countries establishes that the World Bank's portfolio performance in low-income FCS has improved since 2001 compared to low-income countries that are not fragile. The evaluation finds that:

- Country assistance strategies have lacked tailoring to fragility and conflict drivers and realism, and do not currently have contingencies based on political economy and conflict risks to adjust objectives and results if risks materialize.

- The Bank has been relatively effective in mainstreaming gender within the health and education and community-driven development portfolios, but has paid insufficient attention to conflict-related violence against women and economic empowerment of women in low-income fragile and conflict-affected states.

- Community-driven development has been a useful vehicle for short-term assistance to local communities in fragile and conflict-affected states; but in the absence of a mechanism to ensure sustainability their long-term viability remains questionable.

- The World Bank Group lacks a realistic framework for inclusive growth and jobs that is based on economic opportunities and constraints in fragile and conflict-affected states and effective coordination and synergies across World Bank Group institutions.

- The global shift in aid flows toward fragile states has not been matched by IDA, and fragile and conflict-affected states receive less aid per capita from IDA than do other low-income countries.

To enhance the relevance and effectiveness of its assistance to FCS, this evaluation recommends that the World Bank Group adjust its strategy, approach, and product mix by:

- Developing a more suitable and accurate mechanism to classify FCS;

- Tailoring country strategies to fragility and conflict contexts;

- Supporting institutional capacity building at national and subnational levels;

- Enhancing the institutional sustainability of community development programs;

- Addressing the effects of violence against women;

- Developing a more realistic framework for inclusive growth and jobs; and

- Adapting the business models, incentives, and systems of the International Finance Corporation and the Multilateral Investment Guarantee Agency to the needs of FCS.

# Introduction

Fragile and conflict-affected states (FCS) have become an important focus of World Bank Group assistance in recent years as recognition of the linkages between fragility, conflict, violence, and poverty has grown. Addressing issues of recurring conflict and political violence and helping build legitimate and accountable state institutions are central to the Bank Group's poverty reduction mission.

The evaluation focuses on IDA-only countries, which are deemed to have certain characteristics such as very low average income and no access to private finance, making them eligible for special finance tools and programs. As the benchmark for measuring results, Bank Group performance is evaluated in 33 fragile and conflict-affected states against that of 31 IDA-only countries that have never been on the FCS list (i.e., Never FCS). The 33 countries include 21 that have always been on the Bank Group's FCS list (i.e., Always FCS), and 12 that were on the list for part of the review period (i.e., Partial FCS).

Among IDA-only countries, fragile and conflict-affected states are much poorer, grow more slowly, and have higher population growth rates than those that are non-FCS. Using the measure of $1.25 a day, poverty is 57 percent in the 21 Always FCS, compared to 43 percent in the Never FCS. The population within the 33 FCS IDA-only countries alone is 370 million. Another 88 million live in FCS that are International Bank for Reconstruction and Development (IBRD) or blend countries; some of them will be covered by a separate Independent Evaluation Group (IEG) evaluation of fragile and conflict-affected situations.

# Evaluation Approach

This evaluation assesses the relevance and effectiveness of World Bank Group country strategies and assistance programs to FCS. The operationalization of the *World Development Report 2011: Conflict, Security, and Development* (2011 WDR) is also assessed, to see how the framework has been reflected in subsequent analytical work, country assistance strategies (CASs), and the assistance programs. The evaluation framework has been derived from the concepts and priorities articulated in recent WDRs, policy papers, and progress reports issued by management, based on past experience, to draw lessons from FCS. The framework is organized around the three major themes emerging from the 2011 WDR: building state capacity, building capacity of citizens, and promoting inclusive growth and jobs.

The evaluation comprises six new country case studies; analyses of Bank Group portfolios; human resources and budget data; secondary analysis of IEG evaluations; background studies including those on aid flows, gender, private sector development, and jobs; and surveys of Bank Group staffs and stakeholders.

## Country Assistance Strategies in FCS

While Bank strategies in FCS have been relevant in the early stages of post-conflict reconstruction, they have generally not been designed appropriately for medium- and long-term development. The Bank is most responsive to FCS in the immediate aftermath of conflict. Relevance of the Bank's medium-term strategy has been lower because of a lack of adequate strategic underpinning and focus. The need for selectivity and strategic sequencing, while important for all countries, is particularly critical in FCS because of the severe limitations in state capacity. In practice the distinction between the Interim Strategy Note (ISN) and the CAS has been blurred with prolonged use of ISNs over several strategy cycles and much longer duration than prescribed in the policy. Lack of realism and selectivity in most FCS country strategies evaluated has resulted in lower outcome ratings for CAS Completion Reports.

Recent CAS's show much more sensitivity to fragility and conflict drivers. However, in most of the FCS inadequate attention was given to dividing up areas of focus among donors and harmonization in practice in order to reduce demands on the limited capacity of the government and to allow donors to have a greater impact. And there is little evidence yet of the 2011 WDR's impact on Bank Group operations. CASs are not the key determinants of engagement in FCS by the International Finance Corporation (IFC) and the Multilateral Investment Guarantee Agency (MIGA) since their activities are based on alignment with corporate strategies and the availability of clients. The piloting of Bank Group Joint Business Plans for several FCS appears to be a useful mechanism to foster more collaborative approaches.

There is a significant variation in total annual per capita official development assistance (ODA) to the FCS, and IDA and grant allocations by the World Bank largely mirror the distribution of overall ODA. Development policy lending (DPL) has been a significant part of support to FCS, averaging 15 to 25 percent of total IDA commitments. DPLs have helped to support institution building and policy reforms in FCS.

## Portfolio Performance in the FCS

In commitment amounts, IDA financing to the FCS more than doubled since FY01. During the FY07–12 period, total commitment to all of the 33 FCS was $11.5 billion from IDA and $4.4 billion from trust funds. During the same period, total commitment to the 31 IDA countries that were not FCS was $32.9 billion from IDA resources and $5.2 billion from trust funds. The sectoral composition of new commitments in FCS during FY07–12 shows the dominance of infrastructure sectors ($5 billion), followed by the human development sectors ($3.8 billion). Bank support for analytical and advisory activities has increased more substantially, with a five-fold increase in spending on technical assistance to build institutional capacity within FCS.

Direct financial support for private sector development (PSD) remained modest over the period FY01–12. Lending and grants from the Finance and Private Sector Development Network to FCS totaled $1.1 billion during FY01–12, but Bank support to other sectors, including infrastructure and mining projects, which are also relevant to PSD, has been more substantial. IFC approved $1.7 billion between FY01 and FY12, of which $1.3 billion was invested during FY07–12. Investments in FCS are on average smaller and riskier than investments in other IDA countries. IFC's investments in FCS are highly concentrated in telecommunications, transportation, oil, gas, and mining. Advisory Services (AS) are more focused on FCS than investment projects, fragile states absorbing 14 percent of AS expenditures.

MIGA guarantees in FCS have been $1.3 billion between FY01 and FY12, of which about $1.1 billion was in FY07–12. But among providers of political risk insurance in FCS, MIGA played a modest role.

Since FY09, the World Bank's portfolio in FCS has had better outcome ratings than other IDA countries. FCS ratings are now comparable with Bankwide ratings. Outcome ratings lagged in the Africa Region, but by FY10 they had caught up with other FCS.

Although the number of observations is small, IFC investments in FCS have low outcome ratings, and are somewhat lower than those in non-FCS. IFC's Advisory Services in Always FCS perform at par with IDA-only countries that were not fragile. Despite higher country risk, MIGA's portfolio in FCS has not proven more risky than its overall portfolio.

The FCS portfolio is riskier, but this risk has to be taken on and managed if improvements are to be sustained because they are central to delivering the Bank Group's strategic goals on poverty.

## Building State Capacity

Building the capacity of the state in FCS requires a particularly strong understanding of conflict and fragility drivers. Understanding the criteria through which an effective, responsive, and accountable state can be supported is essential for successful World Bank engagement in FCS. Measures to build state capacity in FCS need to be sequenced and paced realistically. Priorities need to be based on the needs of governments, the needs of donors, the expectations of citizens, and the major political economy risks in the country.

World Bank support to public expenditure management in FCS has been good, but progress has been uneven across countries and reform areas. Procurement issues in Bank operations within FCS continue to face challenges, despite attempts to provide technical capacity in this area.

Overall, the performance on the efficiency of revenue mobilization in FCS has been good. Recognizing that mismanagement of mineral resources had contributed to conflict in several FCS, the Bank Group focused its support on reforming the regulatory framework in the mining sector. The World Bank has been effective in strengthening the regulatory framework in natural resource sectors but less effective in assisting its clients in FCS to accurately value and negotiate resource contracts. Monitoring and transparent reporting can lead to better revenue valuation, collection, and management of extractives, however, FCS countries perform less well than non-FCS in compliance with the standards set by the Extractive Industries Transparency Initiative.

The World Bank has made considerable effort, but there has been a lack of traction on civil service reform. Decentralization is widely recognized as an important means to improve service delivery and enhance citizen accountability. In FCS, where government responsiveness to citizens has been relatively weak, finding the right modality for reaching people with services is vital to avoiding further fragility and conflict. Decentralization is an important element to this approach. While some effort and results were recorded in the African Region, in other regions the Bank has been reticent to engage with decentralization until recently, despite substantial interest by other development partners.

## Building Capacity of Citizens

Poverty reduction and shared prosperity among citizens are the strategic goals of the World Bank Group and the raison d'etre of its engagement in reconstruction and development. Countries that are FCS typically suffer from some or all of the following traits—absence of political settlement, regional inequality, social exclusion, weak administrative capacity, risk of corruption and elite capture, absence of the rule of law, and lack of accountability of citizens. Each of these traits affects citizens adversely by trapping them in vicious cycles of fragility, conflict, and violence that undermine their capabilities to demonstrate resilience in response to these crises. For that reason, assistance for human and social development is a critical dimension of Bank Group support to FCS.

Despite the concerns raised by the 2011 WDR, most fragile and conflict-affected IDA countries are likely to achieve at least one Millennium Development Goal target. Outcome ratings for the health sector have improved while those for the education sector have declined in FCS. Health projects were more likely than education projects to use innovative implementation arrangements through hiring service providers from the private and nonprofit sector, and to utilize performance-based contracting.

Community-driven development (CDD) projects have grown by number and commitment volume much faster in FCS than in IDA countries that were not FCS. They have been effective in providing essential short-term development assistance to local communities, but they have not evolved over time and lack institutional sustainability.

The Bank has little to show in FCS on the 2011 WDR priority of enhancing work on justice reforms. The evaluation team did not find any evidence of demand for a more proactive role by the Bank in the justice sector, nor did stakeholders feel the Bank had a comparative advantage in the justice sector.

## Promoting Inclusive Growth and Jobs

In the FCS context, a focus on inclusive growth and employment is highly relevant to address drivers of fragility, with important linkages to state-building and peace-building activities. Vulnerability caused by low per capita income and high unemployment is a major driver of conflict.

Growth and job creation have been slow and face challenges in FCS. The sectors driving economic growth in FCS are not necessarily labor intensive, and in many cases growth has not been inclusive. Promoting inclusive growth and jobs needs sequencing and prioritizing customized to FCS contexts.

The private sector is constrained by lack of infrastructure, a business friendly environment, bankable projects, and skills. World Bank Group support for private sector development has been focused on investment climate reform.

In infrastructure, the Bank prioritized transport, urban, and energy and mining sectors, while IFC invested more in telecommunications infrastructure. There is huge demand for infrastructure services, and a perception that the lack of infrastructure, especially in power and transport, remains a leading constraint to PSD and for growth. The telecommunications sector has attracted private sector investments early in conflict- affected countries, with catalytic support from IFC and MIGA, and is considered "transformational" due to its potential to spur growth, entrepreneurship, and service delivery.

Investment climate reforms are necessary but not sufficient for private sector development. Results of IFC and Bank support for investment climate reform have been mixed, with challenges in implementation.

In some FCS, the World Bank Group was effective in helping establish commercially oriented microfinance institutions and in supporting institutions lending to small and medium enterprises. The Bank's lending to financial sector development in FCS was $270 million. IFC supported small and micro finance institutions in Afghanistan, Cameroon, the Democratic Republic of Congo, Haiti, Nepal, and the Republic of Yemen. MIGA also supported a micro finance institution in Afghanistan. Bank Group support for the financial sector in Afghanistan was an example of effective coordination and synergies.

The share of MIGA's guarantee volume in FCS has reached 10 percent in the FY07–12 period and is more highly concentrated in infrastructure. MIGA's Small Investment Program appears to be relevant to supporting smaller size manufacturing, agribusiness, and services projects typical for FCS, but those projects in FCS have performed poorly.

Bank Group support for skills development has been limited and remains insufficient to address long-term human capital constraints.

Agriculture is the largest sector in IDA countries, accounting for one-fourth of gross domestic product on average in FCS and Never FCS but for a much larger share of employment in FCS. Bank Group support for agriculture has not been commensurate with its effects on food security and employment in FCS. Lack of clarity on land rights can be a major cause of conflict, fragility, and stagnation in rural areas, and is a major constraint to private sector development.

Many FCS economies are highly dependent on extractive industries, yet the Bank Group has paid more attention to legislation and regulatory reform and less attention to the distribution of benefits and local economic development. The fragility risks associated with natural resource management have not been sufficiently addressed.

The Bank Group lacks a strategic and effective framework for inclusive growth and job creation in FCS: Bank Group support for long-term jobs has focused on investment climate reforms, which are necessary but not sufficient for private sector development. Synergies across the Bank Group are lacking, and fragmented interventions reduce the potential effect on long-term employment generation.

The Bank has focused targeted support for jobs mainly on short-term jobs through projects supporting community-driven development and public works programs over the FY01–12 period. International migration is another important livelihood strategy in many IDA countries—especially in the short-term when the local economy cannot provide a sufficient number of jobs.

## Gender

In several conflict-affected countries, women and girls have been targeted as a tactic of war. The CAS documents that were reviewed recognize gender disparities but not necessarily in an FCS context. Most of the demobilization, disarmament, and reintegration programs were not gender sensitive and focused primarily on ex-combatants, with few programs for victims of violence. Women in FCS affected by gender-based violence could benefit from targeted programs for economic empowerment.

## Bank Group Inputs and Processes

Bank Group classification of FCS has not been consistent. The assumption that the Country Policy and Institutional Assessment (CPIA), which was designed primarily as an instrument to determine entitlements under the Performance-Based Allocation system, works equally well for FCS classification has proved to be problematic in recent years with the emergence of new drivers of fragility and conflict.

The World Bank has enhanced its capacity to engage in FCS through significant increases in administrative budgets and in-country staff resources.

The Bank has redeployed administrative budgets for country and operational expenditures in favor of FCS compared with non-FCS. In real terms preparation and supervision expenditures per project have increased since FY07 in the Always FCS group. Projects in these countries have received 9 percent more on average in real terms for project preparation and 19 percent more for supervision than projects in IDA countries that were Never FCS.

World Bank staff numbers in FCS country offices have increased by 68 percent from FY06 to FY12. Internationally recruited staff in FCS grew by 100 percent globally and by 150 percent in the Africa Region. Half of all new international hires to FCS between FY06–12 were women. However, the staff working in FCS remain unconvinced about the adequacy of human resources incentives.

IFC deploys its standard instruments with little adaptation or product innovation in FCS contexts; its conventional products may not be conducive to work with the largely informal economies of FCS. IFC has increased its staffing in FCS, as part of internal reforms intended to align its organizational structure, processes, and incentives with its strategic priorities. Staffing in FCS doubled in FY06 to 124 by FY13. Most of the staff in FCS are from Advisory Services. Nevertheless, IFC performance incentives are not well aligned with supporting its strategy of increasing engagement in FCS.

## Aid Flows and Donor Coordination

The share of overall ODA flows in IDA-only countries has changed in favor of FCS; however, the share of IDA flows to FCS remains much lower than that to non-FCS IDA countries. Since 2002, overall ODA per capita to FCS has exceeded per capita ODA to other IDA countries, and ODA to FCS continued to grow. Despite the exceptional allocations that supplement Performance-Based Allocations, FCS IDA-only countries still receive less ODA per capita from IDA than countries that are not FCS.

The evaluation also assesses the World Bank's management of multi-donor trust funds (MDTFs) in FCS. MDTFs with active involvement of recipient governments, clear governance protocols and responsibilities, and complementarity with Bank country programs were more effective. The main conclusion from the analysis is that the Bank should look more carefully at the contribution of multi-donor trust funds to FCS development beyond the financial contribution. They can also be a highly effective tool for government engagement, harmonization, and strategic alignment, but these outcomes require structures and skillful management to ensure the process is not compromised by unrealistic expectations.

## Conclusions and Recommendations

The World Bank Group has made significant efforts in understanding fragility and conflict drivers, enhancing its capacity to address these issues in some of the poorest and most challenging environments among its client countries. The response to the FCS challenge in IDA-only countries has included scaling up of investments and technical assistance, larger investment of staff and administrative budget resources since 2007, and greater managerial attention leading to improvements in quality of the World Bank's portfolio. It has also included strategic commitments by IFC and MIGA to scale up their support to FCS, the production of the 2011 WDR, and the establishment of the Center on Conflict, Security and Development as well as the Hive, a knowledge-sharing platform designed to connect practitioners, researchers, policy makers, and organizations working on issues of fragility, conflict, and violence around the world.

This evaluation finds the efforts and results to date to be commendable and moving in the right direction. But this is clearly work in progress, with several challenges and constraints identified by this evaluation that are yet to be overcome. In terms of operationalizing the 2011 WDR, the evaluation finds that progress has been made in enhancing support to country teams and achieving greater Bank inputs and improvement in portfolio quality in the FCS, but at least at two levels more clarity and work is needed. First, there is a need to clarify the

Bank Group's role on security, justice, and jobs. Second, while considerable efforts have been made to undertake and draw on fragility and conflict analyses to formulate country assistance strategies, the insights and lessons have not yet been applied to Bank Group operations.

On jobs, there was unanimity among clients and development partners that the Bank Group needs to play a leading role. But there was also agreement that a jobs strategy appropriate to high-risk FCS environments has yet to be developed. The evaluation found demand for specialized services such as public expenditure reviews of the security sector conducted in partnership with United Nations (UN) agencies but little demand for Bank work on justice from clients or country departments, and concludes that partnerships are likely to be the principal means of engagement in these two areas.

The Center on Conflict, Security and Development (CCSD) was established by the World Bank in 2011 to strengthen corporate support to the FCS agenda. Progress has undoubtedly been made in the two years since the 2011 WDR but this effort needs to be sustained and in some areas even intensified. CCSD has successfully raised the profile and visibility of Bank Group support to FCS and established a community of practice for FCS work.

At the corporate level, both in preparing the 2011 WDR and during subsequent implementation, the relationship on FCS issues between the World Bank Group and the UN appears to have improved. Significant challenges remain at the country and operational level. A recent independent review concludes that progress in strengthening the UN–World Bank Partnership in FCS has been mixed. CCSD could help to clarify with its UN counterparts the respective roles and boundaries of work, especially on governance and rule of law, and on security and justice.

## Lessons

The World Bank Group has made significant efforts in understanding fragility and conflict drivers, in enhancing its capacity to address these issues in some of the poorest and most challenging environments among its client countries. The evaluation finds the efforts and results to date to be commendable and moving in the right direction. A few key lessons have emerged from the evaluation:

• Country assistance strategies are more relevant and realistic when they integrate analysis of fragility and conflict drivers which often persist in FCS for many years, making it imperative that country teams draw on these analyses and adapt to them in the design and implementation of assistance programs.

- Bank Group operations in FCS are more resource intensive, but enhanced financial and staff resources and greater managerial attention can lead to better performance outcomes in FCS.

- Fragile and conflict-affected states are constrained by a lack of capacity, weak infrastructure and services, and social tensions that weaken the effectiveness of public sector reforms. To be effective, Bank Group support for state-building needs to be sustained through careful sequencing, better use of political economy analysis, and prioritization of long-term reforms. This is best achieved by a mix of predictable, programmatic budget support, investment projects and technical assistance to build country capacity and country ownership for reforms.

- Community-driven programs have played an important role in providing local benefits and services in FCS. In the absence of attention to ensure the institutional and financial sustainability of CDD programs, the viability of the community institutions and benefits will remain at risk.

- Inclusive growth and jobs has been constrained by the absence of clearly prioritized and sequenced support for a focused medium- to long-term strategy. Linkages and synergies across the World Bank Group were not systematically developed in critical areas, such as linkages between education, skills development, infrastructure, and private sector development. Many FCS lacked adequate analysis of the conflict and fragility drivers and of the binding constraints and opportunities for the private sector.

- Mainstreaming of gender in country programs is feasible in FCS, but in countries where the conflict affects women disproportionately, deliberately targeted programs by the Bank Group can help to address the social and economic consequences of conflict.

- When the private sector adapts its product mix—as it has done with microfinance—to the social and institutional conditions in FCS, it can provide services relevant to the needs of those countries.

- Multi-donor trust funds are more than a source of finance in FCS and play a central role in donor coordination, policy dialogue, and institution building. MDTFs with active involvement of recipient governments, clear governance protocols and responsibilities, and complementarity with Bank country programs, as in Afghanistan and Liberia, were more effective than those in Haiti and Sudan.

## Recommendations

The following recommendations are put forward to strengthen these efforts.

- The Bank Group should develop a more suitable and accurate mechanism to define FCS status. This would involve, at a minimum, integration of indicators of conflict, violence, and political risks within the current system that serves as the basis for FCS classification.

- Country assistance strategies should be tailored better to FCS, with clear articulation and monitoring of risks and contingencies for rapid adjustment of strategic objectives, implementation mechanisms, and results frameworks if those risks materialize.

- To enhance state-building outcomes, the Bank should provide increased support to reform-oriented FCS for capacity building at national and subnational levels through predictable, programmatic budget support, complemented by technical assistance, and investment lending.

- The Bank should develop and implement a plan to ensure the institutional sustainability of the community-driven development programs through which large volumes of investments have been channeled within FCS.

- In post-conflict countries, programs addressing gender issues need to be more responsive to the conflict context and help the government address the effects of violence against women and the legal constraints on economic empowerment.

- The World Bank Group should develop a more realistic medium- to long-term framework for inclusive growth and jobs in FCS and ensure synergies and collaboration across the three Bank Group institutions.

- IFC and MIGA should adapt their business models, risk tolerances, product mix, sources of funds, staff incentives, procedures, and processes to be more responsive to the special needs of FCS and to achieve their strategic priorities of increasing engagement in FCS.

# Management Response | INTRODUCTION

World Bank Group management welcomes this Independent Evaluation Group (IEG) review of World Bank Group assistance to low-income fragile and conflict-affected states (FCS), focusing on International Development Association (IDA)-only countries and covering the period FY2001 to FY2012. This report could not have come at a better time. The World Bank Group recently designated fragility, conflict, and violence as a cross-cutting solutions area to accelerate learning, collaboration, and support to FCS. Given the high poverty levels in many FCS, more effective support to development efforts in FCS is critical to achieving the World Bank Group goals of eradicating extreme poverty and promoting shared prosperity and consistent with the World Bank Group Strategy.

International Finance Corporation (IFC) management notes that the report coincides with the implementation of a new strategic approach to FCS and its plans to increase IFC's engagement in this group of countries through transformative investments. IFC is also pleased to note that its new initiatives for FCS are closely aligned with the report's recommendations for IFC.

FCS has been a strategic priority for the Multilateral Investment Guarantee Agency (MIGA) since 2005 and has become even more important with the (FY13) launch of the multi-donor trust fund Conflict-Affected and Fragile Economies Facility (CAFEF). MIGA's own survey of foreign corporate investors has shown political risk to be their principal concern when investing in FCS.

# World Bank Group Management Comments

▶ Broad Concurrence with Analysis and Conclusions. Management broadly concurs with the findings and conclusions of the evaluation and welcomes the overall conclusion that progress has been made in operationalizing the World Development Report (WDR) 2011: Conflict, Security and Development, though many challenges remain. In particular, management concurs that (i) Country Assistance Strategies (CASs) in FCS could have better incorporated an understanding of drivers of fragility and conflict as well as contingencies based on political economy and conflict risks, though concerted support to FCS country teams in the last two years has resulted in substantial improvements; (ii) there has been a notable increase in the quality of the overall FCS portfolio associated with significantly enhanced investments in staffing and budget resources for project design and supervision in FCS (the overall FCS portfolio is now performing on par with other IDA countries, despite the considerably higher risks); (iii) the Bank has made considerable efforts in support of building state capacity, especially in areas of the Bank's comparative advantage, such as public financial management, public sector management, and decentralization, although the results have been uneven across regions; (iv) the Bank has made considerable efforts in support of human development outcomes through community-driven development (CDD) projects, although the sustainability of these delivery mechanisms remains a challenge; (v) World Bank Group attention to gender issues in FCS has improved, but requires more concerted action, especially gender-based violence and economic opportunities for women, in both strategies and programming; and, (vi) the World Bank Group needs to do more in the area of jobs, particularly to more effectively adapt to and utilize World Bank Group instruments in addressing the specific challenges of job creation and livelihoods support in FCS contexts.

▶ IFC's focus on FCS. IFC management recognizes FCS as an urgent development priority and following the publication of the WDR 2011 has further increased emphasis on FCS. As part of this increased focus, in 2012 IFC formed an FCS Coordination Unit led by two directors representing both Advisory and Investment Services, and has developed a formal strategy for increased investment in FCS. IFC's latest strategic document, IFC's Roadmap FY14–16, outlines plans to increase the volume of investments in FCS by 50 percent compared to the FY12 levels, and the share of its advisory expenditure to at least 20 percent of total. The report acknowledges these developments and provides a very useful overview of IFC's activities in low-income FCS.

IFC management is pleased that the report recognizes the high value of many programs, such as IFC's support for small and micro finance institutions in FCS and the role that IFC played in transformational impact of telecommunications in many FCS, including Afghanistan. The report also accurately reflects IFC's efforts to improve its presence on the ground, which resulted in doubling of its staff based in FCS between FY06 and FY13. In 2013, IFC rolled out a new approach designed to reduce these barriers and increase investments and development impact in FCS.

▶ MIGA's contributions to FCS. MIGA management welcomes the report and agrees with its findings and conclusions. However, it finds that the overall analysis and discussion in the report provides only a partial analysis of MIGA contributions in FCS. The report notes that MIGA's guarantee volume in FCS has increased significantly since FY11. MIGA's guarantee volume of $1.3 billion during the FY01–12 period is concentrated in infrastructure (74 percent) and agribusiness, manufacturing, and service (21 percent). MIGA notes that the discussion in the report on the infrastructure projects is limited, presumably due to the lack of evaluative evidence.

The report acknowledges correctly that too few guarantees have been evaluated to draw conclusions, since there are only five completed Project Evaluation Reports (PERs), of which four had Satisfactory Development Outcomes. MIGA notes that the report makes no further reference to the evidence presented in the PERs, though they provide important lessons and insights into the Development Outcomes of MIGA-supported projects in Low-income FCS as well as MIGA's effectiveness. For example, the Dikulushi Copper-Silver Mining Project in the Democratic Republic of Congo was the first mining project in the country following the civil war. Overall, MIGA played a critical role in facilitating foreign direct investment (FDI) which supported the country's post-conflict reconstruction and development. The project also provided important knowledge transfer benefits to employees from local communities.

On the other hand, the report discusses the performance of projects supported by the Small Investment Program (SIP) in some detail, even though the underlying data is not presented, nor has the assessment been shared with MIGA. As noted in the report, SIP projects made up only 3 percent of the guarantee volume, but 49 percent (17/35) of the number of projects.

▶ **Strong Alignment with the proposed IDA17 Commitments and World Bank Group Change Management Agenda.** Since the publication of the WDR 2011 and associated operationalization paper, Bank management has launched a series of measures to address the main issues covered in the evaluation; Bank management recognizes that it is still too early for this IEG evaluation (which covers FY01 to FY12) to measure the impact of many of these interventions. Moreover, the World Bank Group's enhanced commitment to FCS is reflected in the proposed IDA17 commitments on the special theme of fragility and conflict and the related financing scenarios, which could significantly increase the share of IDA resources invested in FCS. The proposed IDA17 commitments are closely aligned with the key recommendations of the evaluation. The planned establishment of a cross-cutting solutions area on fragility, conflict, and violence as part of the global practices reform—based on the recently created Fragility and Conflict Hub in Nairobi and the FCS Unit in IFC—may ensure effective implementation of these commitments across the World Bank Group. The IDA17 Results Management System (RMS), along with regular reporting to the Board on progress on operationalizing the WDR, will allow for close monitoring of the implementation of these commitments

▶ **World Bank Group Engagement on Fragility, Conflict, and Violence beyond IDA.** Though the evaluation focuses exclusively on IDA-only countries, management would point to some important innovations and results on fragility, conflict, and violence in other client segments that have implications for the World Bank Group's overall engagement in these areas. There is an increasing demand for the World Bank Group to address issues of violence and insecurity in low-income and middle-income countries, especially in the Latin and Central America region, often as part of a broader agenda related to urbanization or security sector reform. Many International Bank for Reconstruction and Development (IBRD) and blend countries are also seeking World Bank Group assistance to confront the drivers of conflict and violence at a sub-national level as part of a broader agenda on decentralization and shared prosperity. While these developments are outside of IDA countries, they form an important part of the broader fragility, conflict, and violence focus within the World Bank Group and lessons from these engagements need to be considered together with the experience in working in IDA countries.

▶ **World Bank Group Promotion of Private Sector Development and Jobs in FCS.** Management agrees that inclusive economic growth and creation of employment opportunities is the most important pathway out of poverty in FCS. Furthermore, management welcomes the findings on private sector development and agrees with IEG that "investment climate is necessary but is not a sufficient condition for the growth of private sector and of jobs." World Bank Group support to private sector development reflects the complexity of this important area for poverty reduction and shared growth. As the report states, the inclusive growth and jobs agenda encompasses infrastructure, private sector development, natural resources management, agriculture, skills development, and support to both the private and public sectors. World Bank Group interventions have been designed in this vein and have therefore included many interventions, including development policy operations, skills development, and trade, as well as IFC advisory and investment, and MIGA guarantees. Management has recently initiated activities supporting job creation (e.g., WDR 2013 on jobs, which is only mildly referenced in the report, a new Cross Cutting Solutions Area on Jobs) and welcomes the recommendation to develop a more realistic medium- to long-term framework for inclusive growth and jobs in FCS.

IFC's approach—as highlighted in IFC's FCS strategy—focuses on alleviating the barriers to business growth, specifically access to power, access to finance, access to markets, enabling environments for business, and transparency/rule of law. In particular, access to power—identified as a number one constraint for firms operating in most FCS—holds a transformational potential and can play a key role in unlocking the economic potential and can help lead to the creation of employment opportunities in FCS.

The IEG report also recommends development of a framework for inclusive growth and jobs in FCS. Both the recent WDR 2013 on Jobs and IFC's 2013 Jobs Study focused on this issue, and the World Bank Group is working on implementing the findings from both. This process is now likely to be accelerated and facilitated through the implementation of the Cross-cutting Solutions Area on Jobs. IFC's FCS Coordination Unit will work closely with the Cross-cutting Solutions Area on Jobs and the Cross-cutting Solutions Area on Fragility, Conflict, and Violence to formulate the FCS-specific angle of the World Bank Group approach to inclusive growth and job creation. In the interim, IFC had already started implementing the findings of the WDR 2013 and the 2013 Jobs Study by forming a Global Partnership to create more and better private sector jobs—"Let's Work." Part of the work program under "Let's Work" includes applying a jobs lens at the country level, in collaboration with other partners across the World Bank Group and beyond (e.g., private sector companies, international financial institutions (IFIs), donors, and other stakeholders). FCS will be one of the areas of focus of this program, and the initiative will be piloted in selected FCS.

The report states that the private sector in FCS countries presents different types of opportunities and challenges to MIGA. It also states that MIGA has approached doing business in FCS in much the same way as in non-FCS countries. However, MIGA notes the absence of any underlying evaluative evidence in the report and feels that a more detailed discussion of these aspects would have been helpful.

MIGA has taken a number of steps already to address the challenges that are unique to FCS (i) introducing the SIP program in 2005, with streamlined procedures for clients and MIGA, which the IEG report has acknowledged as being useful and relevant in FCS, despite challenges; (ii) managing the Japan-MIGA Trust Fund for environmental and social support and capacity building in Africa, which has a high concentration of FCS, and (iii) the new Conflict-Affected and Fragile Economies Facility (CAFEF) initiative and previous FCS-focused trust funds (Afghanistan, West Bank and Gaza, and Bosnia-Herzegovina).

▶ Determinants of Success in the FCS World Bank Portfolio. Bank management welcomes the finding that there has been a notable increase in the quality of the FCS portfolio associated with significantly enhanced investments in staffing and budget resources for project design and supervision in FCS. Bank management also considers that there are other factors that could have contributed to this improved portfolio quality. These include reforms of the enabling World Bank Group policy framework for FCS operations (e.g., the adoption of OP8.0 or new policies on small grants, restructuring, additional financing, and risk), increased reliance on country systems, increased emphasis on the simplification of project design and implementation arrangements, and greater focus on definition of achievable results recognizing the long time frames for institutional change in such contexts. Further work is needed to deepen the analysis of the factors affecting quality in FCS to ensure that recent trends are maintained and strengthened as well as to draw lessons for the rest of the World Bank Group portfolio. Of particular concern is the finding that improvements in performance at the project level have not yet been reflected in improved outcomes at country level as indicated in CAS completion reports. Bank management intends to carry out further analysis of the determinants of success in the FCS portfolio to build upon the work in the current evaluation.

▶ Recent IFC Initiatives. IFC notes that there are recent significant developments that were outside of the report's review period. Firstly, IFC has already recognized that investment opportunities in FCS are often smaller than in non-FCS, and face higher risks, longer gestation periods, and more complex due diligence processes. Accordingly, in 2013 IFC has rolled out a new approach designed to reduce these barriers and increase investments and development impact in FCS. The program will support projects of $10 million or less in FCS, primarily in the manufacturing, agribusiness, services, and financial markets sectors. Secondly, IFC is actively exploring new ways to address inadequate access to power—the number one constraint for private sector development in most low-income FCS countries—through World Bank Group collaboration and exploring blended finance solutions with donors. Thirdly,

IFC continues to undertake other initiatives including: the Joint World Bank, IFC, and MIGA business plans in FCS, dialogue on private sector investment with the g7+ group of fragile states, and increased networking and knowledge-sharing.

▶ MIGA's Share of Political Risk Insurance (PRI) Coverage. Based on Berne Union data, the report states that MIGA's share of political risk insurance coverage provided in FCS was 6 percent vs. 10 percent in Never-FCS and therefore concludes that MIGA played a more modest role among PRI providers in FCS. MIGA disagrees with this conclusion and finds the analysis simplistic. MIGA notes that it targets a market segment different from Export Credit Agencies and the private sector, in particular the longer end of the PRI market in FCS.

MIGA also notes that its role in FCS is always likely to be "modest" compared to the public sector Export Credit Agencies, with larger balance sheets and distinct mandates to support national interests, as well as lighter administrative processes and policies. In addition, there are specific sectoral (e.g., extractive industries) and country factors (e.g., resource-rich) as well as policy considerations that create opportunities for the private sector in FCS.

MIGA's analysis of Berne Union data shows the Export Credit Agencies share of PRI coverage in FCS to be 60 percent (with the share of one Asian export credit agency referred to in the report at 44 percent) and the private sector's share, 34 percent. On the other hand, the share of Export Credit Agencies in Never-FCS is only 27 percent, compared to 62 percent for the private sector. Given these considerations, MIGA notes the need for a deeper analysis to understand better the structure, conduct, and performance of the PRI market in FCS.

MIGA also notes the need to recognize the longer tenor it provides compared to other PRI providers, in the context of MIGA's FCS role discussion. For example, an IEG evaluation of a mining project in an African country found that very few insurers provided 10+ years PRI insurance and the investor regarded MIGA's participation as critical. Also, IEG's evaluation of a telecom project in another African country showed that the host country ranked near the bottom of the Doing Business report at the time of the MIGA guarantee and was the only PRI provider in the country and served as a catalyst for facilitating investments in the country's telecom sector. In addition, the investor made MIGA's guarantee a condition precedent for its equity investment in the project, based on its good experience with MIGA elsewhere.

The report states that even though FCS have higher country risk profiles than Never FCS, in practice, MIGA's portfolio in FCS has not proved to be more risky than the overall portfolio. The report therefore concludes that the perception of high risk was not borne out by actual portfolio risk. MIGA would note that the primary reason for the lower-than-expected portfolio risk is MIGA's superior project-level risk management, alluded to in the report, as well as the MIGA deterrence effect. MIGA agrees with the analysis in the report regarding the mediation function—the ability to resolve investment disputes related to insured risks—distinguishing MIGA from other PRI insurers and a central element of MIGA's value-added proposition for long-term investors.

▶ Bank Support in Building State Capacity. Bank management welcomes the focus on building state capacity, a key step toward eradicating poverty and managing conflict. Bank management agrees with the recommendation to support reform-oriented FCS for capacity building at national and subnational levels through predictable, programmatic budget support, complemented by technical assistance, and investment lending, in response to client demand and when conditions are conducive to such an instrument. At the same time, there is need for caution in drawing definitive conclusions on key areas of state capacity building that remain subject to considerable debate. On the use of parallel structures in the civil service, these can be very heterogeneous in their design with different impacts on performance and sustainability. Bank management takes a differentiated view on the topic of parallel structures and commits to continue to more actively and consciously manage the challenge of balancing and integrating parallel structures with sustainable institution building, in line with the World Bank Group commitment to use, or build capacity toward the eventual use, of country systems. On decentralization, Bank management has pursued a nuanced approach. The report describes the Bank's stance as "ambiguous" and in this regard there is need to recognize that there is still insufficient evidence on the impact of decentralization in FCS contexts to draw definitive conclusions for practice. Decentralization is a fundamentally political decision—and often one that is at the center of the conflict. In these situations, the Bank has focused on facilitating sub-national service delivery within the prevailing political settlement.

▶ IFC Advisory Services in FCS. IFC is continuing the delivery of targeted Advisory Services to clients in FCS, focusing on greater alignment of Advisory Services with investments in priority sectors that hold transformational potential. In Sub-Saharan Africa, where most IDA FCS exists, IFC Advisory Services will continue working through its Conflict Affected States in Africa (CASA) program. IFC would also like to note that the report underestimates the reach of its Advisory Services to offer firm-level capacity building to non-investee companies. In fact, a large majority of Advisory Services engagements at the firm level in FCS are with non-investees. However, when working with individual firms IFC finds greater synergies as they are more likely to implement our advice and they have the resources to implement to scale. Finally, IFC would like to point out that because of the methodology used by the report, the data and numbers presented in the report vary from those typically reported by IFC for FCS.

For example, the investment commitment numbers that IFC is reporting are higher than the numbers quoted in the report, as they also include short-term finance (Global Trade Finance Program), rights issues and swaps

▶ Community Driven Development in FCS. Bank management agrees that there is need to strengthen the link between community driven development (CDD) and local governance structures. It should be noted that in most FCS contexts, CDD is used as quick and visible delivery mechanism that bolster public confidence in the context of extreme institutional weakness or active conflict. CDD programs can directly reach down to local communities to provide access to public goods and a point of contact with the state. The opportunities to develop linkages with local government structures are often limited, given the nascent status of these institutions. Bank management appreciates IEG's examination of CDD from the perspective of the sustainability of the program, results, and institutions and World Bank notes that CDD operations are not the only ones that face challenges of sustainability and use of country systems, especially in FCS.

▶ Gender. Management appreciates the report's examination of World Bank Group responses to gender issues in FCS, which is focused on the impact of various issues on women and girls and focuses on gender-based violence, economic empowerment of women and legal constraints. Management notes that the Bank's record in addressing gender issues in FCS is strong. The IDA 16 Mid-Term Report shows that the share of gender-informed operations in FCS has been at least as high as those in non-FCS. In the Sub-Saharan Africa region almost nine out of ten World Bank operations in FY12 were gender-informed, which include gender analysis or consultations, specific actions to narrow gender disparities, and gender-specific monitoring and evaluation. Management also recognizes that the substantial efforts to enhance the analysis and awareness of gender issues in Bank operations in FCS have not had the expected impact on outcomes of the FCS portfolio. Management is proposing under the IDA 17 replenishment to further integrate gender issues into country strategies, drawing on and discussing the findings of gender assessments. Management is also enhancing the integration of gender in projects, so that IDA operations go beyond gender analysis in project design and include the tracking of follow-up actions (in terms of project activities and/or monitoring and evaluation). Furthermore, management is proposing to strengthen its efforts to address gender-based violence during IDA. 17. While the IEG evaluation focuses on women and girls, it is important to address both sides of gender. The World Bank program addresses issues such as young men at risk and conflict-related impacts on health, education, voice, and participation that are not fully recognized in the report. Management notes that although gender sensitive programming in disarmament, demobilization and reintegration programs (DDR) has been limited, progress has also been made in, for example, the on-going Burundi and Rwanda DDR programs where differentiated needs of male and female ex-combatants have been addressed, partners of ex-combatants included in reintegration training, and sensitization on Gender Based Violence (GBV) offered.

▶ Justice. Bank management considers justice as essential to achieving the new World Bank Group strategic goals of eradicating extreme poverty and boosting shared prosperity: economic growth without equity and justice does not necessarily benefit the poorest or translate into shared prosperity. While justice is a cross-cutting issue in development practice, the IEG discussion considers only judicial reform and law enforcement, excluding other World Bank Group engagement aimed at promoting justice. While justice projects, as stand-alone initiatives, are limited in number, the themes of justice and rule of law are integrated in a range of public administration areas as well as water, transport, health, and other programs. By this count, there have been at least 48 operations in the 33 FCS countries reviewed in the report since 2000 (including ESW and TA work) that incorporate substantial justice or rule-of-law activities. Since the WDR 2011, the Bank's justice team has worked to define a strategic approach to justice in FCS, focusing on three key business lines: strengthening justice service delivery; criminal justice and citizen security; and mitigating and managing justice stresses arising from land and natural resource management. Bank management believes and demand shows that the Bank has a significant comparative advantage in several areas related to justice: capacity for high quality analytics; ability to apply broad public sector expertise toward a more comprehensive institutional approach; modalities of client engagement that promote ownership; ability to integrate justice and grievance management in a range of sectors; and global knowledge and convening power. These comparative advantages account for partner and client requests for Bank engagement on justice and have indeed led to concrete partnerships on justice in FCS.

▶ Security Sector Work. Bank management agrees with IEG that there could be greater clarity on the Bank's ability to engage in the security sector and with security actors where there is country demand. Bank management would caution about the finding that there is little demand from clients or country departments for Bank work on security. Given that the IEG evaluation is limited to IDA-only countries, the report draws this strong conclusion but only briefly discusses the Bank's work on the security sector in three paragraphs, two of which are on disarmament, demobilization, and reintegration (DDR). Due to the narrow scope on IDA countries, the report does not consider the well-established citizen security program in Latin and Central America region. An increasing number of IDA and non-IDA clients are demanding technical support in policy dialogue around security and justice, particularly through the public expenditure and public financial management AAA instruments (e.g., in El Salvador, Mali, Niger, and Central African Republic). This work has typically been carried out in partnership with United Nations (UN) agencies given the sensitivity in this area and in order to stay within the World Bank Group mandate. The Bank through the Legal Vice Presidency, has been providing guidance as needed to teams on addressing security issues in a way that is consistent with the Bank's mandate, in the context of fragile and conflict situations, and emphasizing the importance of partnerships with other agencies in undertaking support for security sector reforms.

The report refers to a MIGA-supported project experiencing local conflict heightening the need for MIGA to include security and conflict risks in its due diligence. However, MIGA notes that conflict and security issues are explicitly considered in the risk analysis of the War and Civil Disturbance cover. This aspect was also recognized in the CAO report on the project. MIGA agrees with the need for deepening security and conflict risks analysis and notes that this is a key element of the CAFEF initiative.

▶ Disarmament, Demobilization, and Reintegration Programs. A key area in security-related issues where the Bank has established leadership is in support of disarmament, demobilization, and rehabilitation (DDR) programs, always in partnership with government and other agencies, such as the UN. The report's analysis of Bank support to DDR programs focuses exclusively on gender, while the core development objective of DDR is a focus on ex-combatants rather than victims. Project beneficiaries of DDR programs are often linked to national policies guiding eligibility for rehabilitation. If these policies focus on armed combatants, the programs by nature will focus on disarmed ex-combatants. Addressing issues of other community members, such as victims, including women and girls, should be considered in broader post-conflict programming. The key issue is not if victims of conflict are included in DDR, but if overall programming in a country addresses these issues.

▶ Multi-Donor Trust Funds (MDTF) and FCS Operations. Given that MDTFs now channel more funds to FCS than IDA, Bank management would have welcomed a deeper and more detailed analysis of the role, results, and risks of MDTFs in World Bank Group support to FCS. Bank management considers MDTFs a strategic tool that is critical to World Bank Group support to FCS beyond financing. MDTFs have helped advance frontier work—both analytic and operational—on FCS issues, including piloting operational approaches that have later been scaled up through IDA financing (e.g., CDD, land rights, justice issues); allowed the World Bank Group to continue its engagement in economies such as Somalia, Sudan, Zimbabwe, and West Bank and Gaza, where IDA is inactive, and in new states or countries emerging from isolation, such as Myanmar, South Sudan, and Timor Leste. While this is not evident from the evaluation report, it is important to note this holistic role of trust funds in the World Bank Group's engagement with FCS given their critical importance relative to IDA. Bank management would have welcomed an assessment that distinguishes MDTFs in terms of size and function recognizing important differences between global MDTFs, such as the Bank's State and Peace-building Fund, which was recently evaluated, and country-focused MDTFs.

▶ IFC Donor Engagement in FCS. IFC has also been working closely with donors to diversify sources of funding available for investments in FCS allowing IFC to do projects in higher risk environments. In 2012, IFC launched a $200 million investment in the new Global SME Finance Facility, the first global platform of its kind to blend donor funding with funding from international development institutions to expand lending to small businesses in emerging markets. The United Kingdom's Department for International Development (DFID), with an investment of $63 million, was the facility's first donor. The facility is supporting high-impact projects with higher risk profiles, such as in conflict-affected areas of Africa and South Asia and women-owned businesses. Similarly, the private sector window of the Global Agriculture and Food Security Program (GAFSP)—available to all IDA FCS that are not in non-accrual status—brings together IFC and five donors (Canada, Japan, the Netherlands, the United Kingdom, and the United States) to support increasing the commercial potential of small and medium-sized agri-businesses and farmers by connecting them with local, national, and global value chains.

▶ Recommendations. Management broadly agrees with all seven recommendations, with the caveats described in the attached Management Response matrix. As the evaluation notes, work undertaken in the last two years has improved the attention CAS/ISNs give to drivers of fragility and conflict and has led to the formulation of more realistic country strategies. These initiatives, among others, are part of management follow-through on World Bank Group-wide post-WDR 2011 commitments to dramatically improve support to FCS. Management commits to continue this process and welcomes further systematic review. Management will develop specific approaches to operationalize the report's recommendations, building on the ongoing implementation of the WDR 2011 Operationalization Paper and taking into account the new World Bank Group strategy and the establishment of global practices and cross-cutting solutions areas to spearhead integrated support for FCS. Consistent with the report's recommendation, IFC has embarked on a number of special initiatives to adapt its business model to better serve its clients in FCS. MIGA management agrees with the overall spirit of the last recommendation for MIGA to do more in FCS, but notes the various initiatives that have been taken and are ongoing, as noted above. In particular, MIGA's focus on FCS has sharpened in recent years, with an emphasis on large transformative projects in the infrastructure and energy sectors.

▶ Conclusion. Management shares IEG's commitment to maximize the World Bank Group's relevance and effectiveness in operating in FCS, and believes that by working effectively together in FCS, the World Bank Group can make a great contribution to achieving the goal of eliminating extreme poverty and promoting shared prosperity for all.

# Management Action Record

## Definition of FCS Status

With the evolution in the nature of fragility and conflict drivers over the last few years, the reliance on Country Policy and Institutional Assessment (CPIA) ratings to determine FCS status results in considerable errors of exclusion and inclusion in FCS classification. The Bank applies a set of Post-Conflict Performance Indicators (PCPI) to determine the size of exceptional allocations to countries deemed eligible for this support. However, the PCPI indicators are applied ex-post, after countries have been deemed eligible for exceptional allocations, rather than to determine if countries should be eligible for them. Indicators of conflict, violence and political instability are not currently used to identify fragile and conflict status.

### IEG RECOMMENDATIONS

**The Bank Group should develop a more suitable and accurate mechanism to define FCS status.** This would involve, at a minimum, integration of indicators of conflict, violence and political risks within the current system that serves as the basis for FCS classification.

### ACCEPTANCE BY MANAGEMENT

World Bank Group: Agree

### MANAGEMENT RESPONSE

World Bank Group management agrees that the present mechanism to define FCS status and to determine eligibility for IDA Exceptional Allocations presents challenges.

Rigorous conflict indicators are important for robust decisions. In this regard, management is continuing to invest in indicator development and statistical systems that support monitoring and evaluation of relevant indicators, including through the PCPI process, and continued support to the g7+ in developing peace and state-building indicators.

In order to capture aspects related to conflict and violence that might otherwise be excluded from the selection of FCS, management currently complements harmonized average CPIA country rating of 3.2 or less with the presence of a UN and/or regional peace-keeping or peace-building mission during the past three years. It is to be noted that the list excludes IBRD only countries for which the CPIA scores are not currently disclosed.

World Bank Group management commits to review the criteria for classification of FCS and work to develop improved methods for FCS classification that are relevant to the Group. Such a review would need to engage with a wider range of actors, including the UN, other MDBs, OECD/INCAF, and the g7+.

## Tailoring of Country Assistance Strategies
### IEG FINDINGS AND CONCLUSIONS

Project level outcome ratings have improved in FCS. However, lack of realism and selectivity in most FCS country strategies evaluated has resulted in lower-outcome ratings for Country Assistance Strategy Completion Reports (CASCR). Most FCS strategies have not been underpinned by systematic analysis of the drivers of fragility, conflict, and violence. Recent CAS documents in FCS make greater use of fragility and conflict analysis but even so, FCS strategies do not include scenarios based on political economy and conflict risks, with built-in contingencies to adjust objectives and results if risks materialize.

### IEG RECOMMENDATIONS

**Country assistance strategies should be tailored better to FCS, with clear articulation and monitoring of risks and contingencies for rapid adjustment of strategic objectives, implementation mechanisms and results frameworks if those risks materialize.** This would enable formulation of more realistic country strategies and tailored performance assessments when risks that are monitored lead to changes in strategic objectives.

### ACCEPTANCE BY MANAGEMENT

WB: Agree

Implementation of this recommendation is already underway. Recent analysis by the Bank shows that strategies finalized after the publication of the 2011 WDR performed better in integrating sensitivity to drivers of fragility, conflict, and violence than those finalized prior to the WDR.

Additionally, within the framework of IDA 17, management is proposing to incorporate commitments leading to better understanding of the underlying drivers of conflict and fragility in new FCS strategies, including through the analysis of the new country diagnostic assessments.

Management will actively track in CASs, the analysis of drivers of fragility and conflict and ensuring strategy documents are responsive to such analysis.

Likewise, due regard will be given to contingency planning to adjust development objectives and results expectations as opportunities and risks materialize in FCS.

## Enhancing State-Building Outcomes
### IEG FINDINGS AND CONCLUSIONS

The Bank has made considerable effort on civil service reform but there has been lack of traction due to political economy interests which weaken client ownership. In several FCS, Bank attempts to build capacity of the civil service reform have been adversely affected by the substitution of civil servants by externally-funded advisers who function as a "second civil service," the recruitment of civil servants to project implementation units implementing donor-financed projects, and the competition for skilled national staff among donor agencies and international nongovernmental organizations (NGOs). These measures are often necessary to provide urgent humanitarian and reconstruction assistance, and to rejuvenate the government and the economy in the immediate aftermath of conflict. However, in the medium term, unless they are absorbed within the public sector, they also weaken, rather than strengthen the capacity of the civil service. Building sustainable civil service capacity is in keeping with the g7+ objective of aligning donor assistance with national programs and country systems under the New Deal.

Regular and predictable budget support has been found to be correlated with improvements in policy and institutional reforms, especially when the reforms have been complemented by related investment lending and technical assistance. Among the CPIA indicators, regular budget support is most highly associated with improvement in the ratings for governance reforms in public sector management.

IEG RECOMMENDATIONS

**To enhance state building outcomes, the Bank should provide increased support to reform-oriented FCS for capacity building at national and subnational levels through predictable, programmatic budget support, complemented by technical assistance, and investment lending.** This would involve more systematic dialog with other development partners to reach agreement on measures to build capacity and sustain reforms.

ACCEPTANCE BY MANAGEMENT

WB: Agree

MANAGEMENT RESPONSE

In relation to the findings, management would like to point out that the debate on how to balance reliance on parallel structures (including PIUs) with efforts to strengthen government systems in FCS is complex and highly controversial. Parallel structures are very heterogeneous in their design and impact on performance and sustainability. Management takes a differentiated view on the topic of parallel structures and commits to continue to more actively and consciously manage the challenge of balancing and integrating parallel structures with sustainable institution building, in line with the World Bank Group commitment to use, or build capacity toward the eventual use, of country systems.

In relation to the recommendation, management commits to consider the appropriate use of programmatic development policy operations to support the country policy and reform priorities, in response to client demand and when conditions are conducive to such an instrument.

On the recommendation to improve donor-coordination in public administration reform, management action is already underway. A proposal has been developed to pilot a joint UN-WB diagnostic framework for (re-) establishing core-government functions in post-conflict situations.

Management will continue to encourage coordination at the country level as part of the broader post-WDR 2011 commitment on greater partnership with UN agencies. To this end, the Bank and UN operate a Partnership Trust Fund that supports joint work, a Partnership Framework, and the UN-WB Fiduciary Principles that allow for close coordination in implementation, including execution of each other's projects.

## Community-Driven Development Programs

### IEG FINDINGS AND CONCLUSIONS

Community-driven development (CDD) programs have been a major feature of Bank assistance to FCS and have been effective in providing essential short-term development assistance to local communities. However, these programs have not evolved over time and institutional sustainability has not received adequate attention. In FCS these programs are still projectized and not joined up with local government, and do not receive regular fiscal transfers. Nor has the Bank instituted alternate financing and governance mechanisms to ensure their viability beyond the life of the projects supporting them. As a result, their institutional sustainability is questionable.

### IEG RECOMMENDATIONS

**The Bank should develop and implement a plan to ensure the institutional sustainability of the community-driven development programs through which large volumes of investments have been channeled within FCS.** This could involve either more systematic linkages between CDD programs and local government organizations, or the development of an alternative time-bound plan for financial and institutional sustainability of CDD programs.

### ACCEPTANCE BY MANAGEMENT

WB: Agree

### MANAGEMENT RESPONSE

Management agrees that there is need to strengthen the link between community driven development (CDD) and local governance structures. However, in many FCS, local governments and the national/sub-national systems necessary for sustainable service delivery at community level often do not exist.

While working to build government capacity, the Bank focuses increasingly on helping local communities and citizen-beneficiaries become effective stakeholders for poverty reduction.

Thus, management commitment to this recommendation is limited to making sure that the Bank's approach to sustainability will include more knowledge generation and learning on reinforcing state-citizen linkages and durable structural connections between local government institutions (where they exist) and CDD operations.

## Gender Programs
### IEG FINDINGS AND CONCLUSIONS

Gender issues in FCS are often even more acute than in other IDA countries. Women are more vulnerable to gender-based violence and often also face greater economic burden than in more stable societies. The Bank has been relatively effective in mainstreaming gender in FCS within the health and education portfolios and in CDD projects. But gender analysis has often been delayed, and the Bank has not responded adequately or in a timely manner to conflict-related violence against women. The Bank Group as a whole has paid insufficient attention to legal discrimination against women and economic empowerment of women. Both conflict-related violence and legal constraints on business activities of women are more acute in the Africa Region.

### IEG RECOMMENDATIONS

**In post-conflict countries gender programs need to be more responsive to the conflict context and help the government address the effects of violence against women and the legal constraints on economic empowerment.** This would involve timely gender analysis in FCS to assess the effects of conflict and violence, and implementation of measures to address, conflict-related violence against women and the legal constraints against women's engagement in economic activities.

### ACCEPTANCE BY MANAGEMENT

WB: Agree

Management concurs that strategies for FCS should indeed be more responsive to gender disparities and specific gender issues related to conflict in both analysis and programming, including addressing the effects of violence against women and legal constraints on economic development.

Implementation of this recommendation is already underway. The IDA 16 mid-term report shows that the share of gender-informed operations in FCS has been at least as high as that in non-FCS.

Under IDA 17, management is proposing to deepen integration of gender considerations into country strategies drawing on and discussing the findings of gender assessments. In addition, management is now raising the bar for the integration of gender in projects, requiring that IDA operations go beyond gender analysis in project design and include the tracking of follow-up actions (in terms of project activities and/or monitoring and evaluation).

Management welcomes the recommendation to pay more attention to Sexual and Gender Based Violence (GBV) in the context of conflict as well as specific actions to address the legal constraints against women's engagement in economic activities. Management will carry out the following: (a) proposing an IDA policy commitment on GBV for FCS for IDA 17; (b) planning to conduct a systematic review of what the Bank is currently doing related to GBV; and (c) planning to launch a cross-regional strategic initiative on GBV aimed at building on lessons learned from experiences in FCS (including in AFR, ECA, EAP, and SAR) to strengthen the delivery of services to survivors of GBV and prevention of GBV.

## Inclusive Growth and Jobs
### IEG FINDINGS AND CONCLUSIONS

The 2011 World Development Report (WDR) identified jobs as one of the priority areas to break the cycles of violence in FCS; however, Bank group support has not been effective particularly in creating long-term jobs in FCS. Direct World Bank support for job creation has been primarily in the form of short-term jobs through CDD, DDR (demobilization, disarmament, and reintegration), and public works programs and microfinance programs. Employment in agriculture, which absorbs 50-80 percent of the FCS workforce, has received inadequate attention, and the potential for leveraging natural resources management and migration toward job creation remains untapped.

World Bank Group support was not clearly prioritized and sequenced around a focused medium- to long-term agenda specifically on jobs and growth. It did not systematically develop the linkages and synergies across World Bank Group entities and activities for effective engagement by the World Bank Group in FCS. The Independent Evaluation Group (IEG) found that a lack of Bank Group coordination in critical areas, such as linkages between education, skills development, infrastructure, and private sector development, weakened its effectiveness in achieving the Bank Group's poverty reduction objectives. Many FCS lacked adequate analysis of the conflict and fragility drivers and of the constraints and opportunities for the private sector. When analyses were available, it was often not utilized by staff from other Bank Group entities.

### IEG RECOMMENDATIONS

**The World Bank Group should develop a more realistic medium- to long-term framework for inclusive growth and jobs in FCS and ensure synergies and collaboration across the three Bank Group institutions.** Such an approach should be based on sound country diagnostics of conflict and fragility drivers, and should address the main constraints and opportunities for job creation, including the role of the private sector. It should systematically explore linkages and synergies among Bank Group activities for job creation in order to accelerate progress toward the Bank Group's strategic goals of poverty reduction and shared prosperity.

### ACCEPTANCE BY MANAGEMENT

World Bank Group: Agree

### MANAGEMENT RESPONSE

Management agrees with the report findings about the centrality of private sector growth and jobs creation for development in FCS. It also agrees that World Bank Group management should strengthen collaboration across the organization and promote systematic linkages and synergies to enhance growth and job creation in FCS.

The new Cross Cutting Solutions Area on Fragility, Conflict, and Violence will further strengthen the efforts in the FCS context. Additionally, with the creation of a new Cross Cutting Solutions Area on Jobs, management has signaled a serious commitment to World Bank Group-wide action to support job growth globally, including in FCS. Finally, management continues to promote concrete Joint Business Plans in individual sectors between the World Bank, IFC, and MIGA to focus on policy action and investments that accelerate growth, a prerequisite to shared prosperity.

## Private Sector Engagement
IEG FINDINGS AND CONCLUSIONS

The private sector in FCS countries presents different types of opportunities and business challenges to the International Finance Corporation (IFC) and the Multilateral Investment Guarantee Agency (MIGA). IFC and MIGA have approached doing business in FCS in much the same way as in non-FCS countries even though sponsor quality is lower and capacity is weak; project risks are higher than in IDA countries. IFC projects that integrated tailored capacity building for clients into project appraisal, design, and implementation of investments to account for the weak capacity environment tended to have a better chance of success. But IFC lacked the resources to offer firm-level capacity building to noninvestee companies which have the potential for local private sector development or future IFC financial engagement.

IFC and MIGA's products are not specifically tailored to needs and conditions in FCS; IFC's business model as a development financier may not be conducive to reaching private firms in FCS, which are on average smaller, with weaker capacity, and more informal compared with other types of organizations. IFC and MIGA lack flexibility similar to the Bank's OP 8.0, and appraisal and approval processes are perceived as cumbersome and lengthy.

Staff incentives and performance measurement systems linked to project performance and volume targets are not aligned with increasing IFC engagement in FCS. Similarly, results measurement frameworks may not be fully adapted to FCS contexts. IFC has relatively few investment officers deployed to country or regional offices dedicated to working on FCS; and MIGA has not developed specialized staff expertise with knowledge of FCS markets for business development and risk assessment and underwriting. Both IFC and MIGA have little specialized training and knowledge management products to support learning from experience and, over time, improving portfolio performance.

IEG RECOMMENDATIONS

**IFC and MIGA should adapt their business models, risk tolerances, product mix, sources of funds, staff incentives, procedures, and processes to be more responsive to the special needs of FCS and to achieve their strategic priorities of increasing engagement in FCS.**

IFC: Agree

MIGA: Agree

IFC recognizes that FCS face different types of challenges than other client countries, and since 2012 it has embarked on a number of special initiatives to adapt its business model to better serve FCS. In October 2013, IFC management rolled out a new approach designed to reduce these barriers and increase investments and development impact in FCS. This pilot program consists of an allocation of $70 million in economic capital and up to $250 million in nominal capital depending on investment product type to support projects of $10 million or less in FCS, primarily in the manufacturing, agribusiness, services, and financial markets sectors. It will enable IFC to take more risk in FCS by funding projects that fall outside the organization's typical risk tolerance. The program will also provide operational flexibility needed to complete investments in the challenging conditions of FCS, such as streamlined procedures and documentation. As an additional aspect of the program, IFC will be creating dedicated support within legal and credit teams to guide and facilitate these investments, and aligning Advisory Services with investee companies to increase the development impact of these projects. .

IFC is also making concerted efforts to address inadequate access to power, the number one constraint for firms in most FCS, as highlighted by the World Bank Group's Enterprise Surveys. IFC has identified numerous barriers to attracting private investment in the power sector in FCS, including: lack of a creditworthy off-taker; lack of operational competence (such as poor collection rates); low tariffs that prevent cost (investments plus operating) recovery; lack of adequate regulatory environment enabling private sector investments in the power sector; lack of ability to regulate effectively, in many cases; and lack of government buy-in or private sector champions, which are necessary for tariff increases and sector planning. To address these challenges, IFC is now working in conjunction with the World Bank Group to identify opportunities for private sector power investments in FCS, and to develop the solutions necessary to enable these investments. IFC also realizes that in some situations, the additional risk involved in power projects may need to be covered through a separate funding source. IFC is actively exploring ways to work with development partners and donors to develop the funding stream that can address the factors that contribute to the lack of commercially viable power projects in FCS.

In addition, Advisory Services will continue to support the CASA program, currently present in eight Sub-Saharan African FCS. The second phase, CASA II, has just commenced and will expand the program to additional FCS in the region and focus on delivery of advisory services in alignment with investments in priority areas.

IFC will also continue exploring additional staff incentives to encourage greater staff engagement in FCS.

MIGA already recognizes that FCS face different types of challenges than other client countries, and since FY05 has embarked on a number of special initiatives to adapt its business model to better serve FCS. In 2005 MIGA rolled out the Small Investment Program (SIP) with streamlined processes to specifically cater to smaller investors, many of which are operating in FCS.

The Agency's support of projects in FCS has grown significantly due to proactive business development, increased risk appetite, and the comfort provided by MIGA as a multilateral institution. Over the five year period ending in June 2010, MIGA averaged approximately US$50 million of new guarantees (5 projects) per annum. However, MIGA's new guarantees in FCS increased to US$ 228 million (8 projects) in FY11, and US$327 million (12 projects) in FY12.

MIGA has historically used country-specific trust funds to help provide first loss cover for MIGA, and facilitate greater engagement in specific FCS. Trust Funds are (i) Bosnia and Herzegovina Investment Guarantee Fund (1997); (ii) West Bank and Gaza Facility (1997) (iii) Afghanistan Investment Guarantee Facility. In fact MIGA has recruited a Business Development (BD) officer in Jerusalem for the West Bank Gaza Trust Fund, with specific knowledge of investors in this area.

The 'Japan-MIGA Trust Fund to Address Environmental and Social Challenges in MIGA-Guaranteed Projects in Africa' (2007) – helps companies in Africa (many of which are FCS) to meet MIGA's Environmental and Social Performance Standards.

In FY13 MIGA launched the multi-country Conflict Affected and Fragile Economies Facility (CAFEF) to further expand our operations in FCS.

MIGA has recently developed a BD strategy for FCS, which will be rolled out over the next few years with the help of CAFEF. MIGA is planning to place a BD officer in Africa and to further strengthen our partnership with IFC/WB in FCS.

MIGA will continue to use evaluations (self-evaluations & IEG evaluations) to generate lessons of experience from FCS operations.

MIGA already has incentive programs in place to recognize work in FCS. The EVP Award program (non-monetary) recognizes challenging projects which address MIGA's strategic goals, including working in FCS. MIGA also has a Staff Incentive program, which does have a monetary component, which is used by MIGA to recognize Staff who has delivered on departmental initiatives above and beyond expectations, and this includes working on FCS initiatives. MIGA will also continue exploring additional staff incentives to encourage greater staff engagement in FCS.

# Chairperson's Summary:
# Committee on Development Effectiveness

On October 21, 2013, the Committee on Development Effectiveness (CODE) met to discuss the evaluation entitled World Bank Group Assistance to Low-Income Fragile and Conflict-Affected States: An Independent Evaluation and Draft Management Response.

## Summary

The Committee welcomed the Independent Evaluation Group's (IEG) evaluation on the relevance and effectiveness of World Bank Group assistance to International Development Association (IDA)-only low-income and conflict-affected states (FCS), and expressed appreciation for the constructive engagement between IEG and management. The committee agreed with the findings and recommendations, noting that the evaluation will provide valuable inputs for the IDA17 discussions and the implementation of the World Bank Group strategy. Members were pleased that progress is being made in operationalizing the World Development Report (WDR) 2011.

Members agreed that the World Bank Group was moving in the right direction but acknowledged that there is room for improvement. They noted that the World Bank Group should ensure a long-term perspective for World Bank Group engagement in FCS. Members welcomed the integration of FCS work into the Global Practices (GP), and the potential for collaboration of the cross-cutting solution area on fragility, conflict, and violence with other cross-cutting solution areas; they concurred that this should help the World Bank Group deliver better operational solutions to clients. They underscored the need for more in-depth fragility and conflict analysis during the Systematic Country Diagnostics (SCD) to identify impediments and strategic areas of intervention for success in FCS. The committee urged management to better incorporate fragility and conflict drivers, contingency provisions, jobs, and gender in Country Partnership Frameworks (CPF). Furthermore, members called for a review of the mechanism defining fragility status to incorporate conflict, violence, and other pertinent criteria.

Members highlighted the importance of enhanced synergies within the World Bank Group, greater donor coordination, more effective use of partnerships, and a more strategic division of labor to efficiently address the drivers of fragility. They underscored the need to build institutional capacity in FCS to foster sustainable delivery of services through legitimate public institutions. Members urged increased attention to gender issues and improved performance and impact in the area of jobs and inclusive growth. The committee appreciated that management intends to continue strengthening and aligning staff incentives, and addressing staffing and career development issues, to ensure the right mix of staff on the ground. They agreed that this could go a long way to improve the institution's performance in FCS.

Members looked forward to the future IEG evaluation that will review other client countries affected by situations of fragility, conflict, and violence.

Juan José Bravo
CHAIRPERSON

# Statement of the External Advisory Panel

The External Advisory Panel welcomes this evaluation of the World Bank Group's assistance program over the last 12 years in low-income fragile and conflict-affected states (FCS). We found the Independent Evaluation Group (IEG) report exhaustive and candid. The report acknowledges the World Bank's efforts, especially in recent years, and notes the progress made in seeking to contribute to FCS recovery and development. The report, then, points to inadequacies that have marked the World Bank Group's work in the FCS, and identifies ways of moving forward. The Advisory Panel discussed the earlier draft of the report on September 10, 2013. Since the IEG has agreed to incorporate most of our suggestions, this final statement is brief.

Let us first call attention to the significance of the FCS in international development. Not only is it true, as the report notes, that poverty rates are significantly higher in the FCS than in countries not affected by fragility and conflict, it is also highly likely that as poverty rates rapidly decline in countries and regions, which used to have the largest concentrations of the poor (e.g., India, China, Indonesia, Bangladesh), poverty in the FCS will acquire even greater significance for development agencies in the coming years. This report, thus, deals with a set of countries and problems, which are not simply of current significance. Their importance is likely to increase in the future. We know from the available research that the risk of conflict is highest at low levels of income. Conflicts can surely exist at higher levels of income, but their incidence is significantly greater at lower incomes.

Traditionally, development and conflict were viewed as two separate fields of inquiry and practice, with a distinct set of experts in each, who rarely overlapped. The two fields are increasingly connected in many parts of the world. In the FCS, restoration of order and development must go together. In non-FCS settings, order is less of a factor. Unlike the United Nations (UN), the World Bank Group was set up to deal with economic reconstruction and development, not with issues of conflict and political settlements. The nature of development challenge in the FCS, therefore, requires fresh and deep thinking on the part of the World Bank Group.

Based on our discussions, we would like to draw attention to nine issues.

**Partnerships.** For effective development interventions in the FCS, three kinds of partnerships are necessary: with the UN, with governments and inter-government groupings (like the g7+), and with civil society. UN agencies have greater experience dealing with conflict than the World Bank Group; governments have intimate knowledge of their societies and need to co-own World Bank Group programs in order for the programs to be successful; and the nongovernmental organizations also have a lot of on-the-ground experience in conflict settings, which can be leveraged not only for health projects, which the report mentions, but also in the field of education. Special mention should be made of national ownership of projects and programs. Right after the conflict, the FCS may not have the capacity to undertake analysis and implement programs, but the World Bank Group can help build such capacity as a partner. As conflict becomes progressively distant and normalcy deepens, less help is necessary. Partnership with governments is critical for country ownership, which in turn is a vital determinant of program success. Synergy at the operational level between donors is also crucial.

**Classificatory Scheme.** As the report rightly points out, how the World Bank Group defines fragility and classifies countries as FCS remains problematic. The current classification is primarily a function of the Country Policy and Institutional Assessment (CPIA) except when UN peacekeeping forces are deployed in a country. This is supplemented by Post-Conflict Performance Indicators (PCPI) for countries deemed eligible for exceptional allocations. CPIA is an indicator of aid effectiveness, not of fragility and conflict. FCS classification should be based on, or should at least include, direct indicators of violence and conflict, which exist in the field of conflict research but have not been used by the World Bank Group. The absence of countries like Nigeria, Pakistan and Sri Lanka from the FCS list is hard to understand, given how the world of research has classified them over the last decade or so. The World Bank Group should investigate alternative ways of defining fragility, including those being used by the g7+. Essentially, classificatory criteria should rely heavily on conflict data.

**Security and Justice.** Two different kinds of comparative advantages can be combined for better results. The UN and bi-lateral government partnerships have a comparative advantage in the fields of security and justice. Except in very specialized areas like demobilization and reintegration of armed combatants, or contract law, the World Bank Group does not have much prior experience in, or great current expertise on, how to think about security and justice. As an institution created primarily for economic development, however, it does have expertise in public expenditure analysis, optimal budgeting, and infrastructure investments and should continue to work in these areas. The external panel recommends that the Bank consider formulation of a specific plan relating to how its areas of comparative advantage can apply to the security and justice sector. If the UN and the World Bank Group can work together with governments on the basis of their respective expertise, the outcomes are likely to be better in the FCS.

**Growth and Jobs.** As the report notes, improving investment climates might kick off the growth process, but that on its own may not generate sufficient employment in the short run. Post-conflict years are often marked by huge unemployment. World Bank Group projects need to pay special attention to strategies that enhance productive skills and employment. This too is an area where partnership opportunities abound, including with the UN and international financial institutions, which can draw on the World Bank Group expertise.

**Gender.** Given that women are often special targets of sexual violence in conflict and given also that due to the high mortality of men in wars, female-headed households are very common in post-conflict settings, special attention needs to be paid to women's needs, participation, and welfare in World Bank Group projects. The report notes this, and we would like to underline its significance.

**Analytic Capacity.** Historically, the World Bank Group has not had expertise in conflict analysis. However, as the report puts it, an analysis of the drivers of fragility and conflict is absolutely necessary in developing projects and assessing their viability and impact in the FCS. The World Bank Group needs to develop, or have access to, this expertise, so conflict analysis can be brought into country assistance strategies more systematically to make them more effective. With the establishment of the Center on Conflict, Security and Development (Nairobi), perhaps the World Bank Group will start addressing this analytic gap seriously.

**The ISNs.** The Bank's use of Interim Strategy Notes (ISNs) is perfectly understandable in immediate post-conflict years, when the situation is fluid, the knowledge base limited, and strategic planning inherently difficult. However, since the ISNs, as opposed to the Country Assistance Strategies (CASs), are not subject to evaluation, the World Bank Group should limit their use, or they should be subject to evaluations like other country assistance programs whenever ISNs are used repeatedly beyond the initial crisis period of 2–3 years. Furthermore, the CASs and ISNs should be aligned with the government's own development strategy where it exists.

**The MDTFs.** The evaluation team rightly points out that its terms of reference with regard to the multi-donor trust funds (MDTFs) did not include the impact of World Bank Group MDTFs on other partners such as the UN. However, given the importance of the MDTFs, we do believe that such an examination is necessary. The MDTFs need to leverage the comparative advantages of all partners concerned, reduce transaction costs, and speed up delivery. While the MDTFs have been useful short term tools, the panel notes that as government capacity increases, governments ought to be given greater voice in decisions about how to use these funds.

**Capacity Building.** The evaluation team felt that capacity constraints of the FCS are a problem that needs to be resolved. There needs to be a gradual phasing out of PIUs with the staff being integrated into the government structure. For that to happen the challenges of the government structure need to be thoroughly analyzed and solutions developed. The need for flexible civil service regimes that allow for the retention of local talent is a problem that the donors and governments can jointly solve in a partnership.

To conclude, we are greatly in accord with the IEG's report, and we hope that its recommendations will be given the attention they deserve. Since the report is about working in fragile states, where things need to be implemented quickly, it will be vital for the World Bank Group to develop a credible plan of how these recommendations will be operationalized.

Minister Emilia Pires
MINISTER OF FINANCE, TIMOR-LESTE (CHAIR)

Mr. Jordan Ryan
ASSISTANT SECRETARY-GENERAL AND DIRECTOR,
BUREAU OF CRISIS PREVENTION AND RECOVERY,
UNITED NATIONS DEVELOPMENT PROGRAMME

Dr. Ahmed Mushtaque Chowdhury
VICE CHAIR, BRAC BOARD OF GOVERNORS, DHAKA

Dr. Ashutosh Varshney
SOL GOLDMAN PROFESSOR OF INTERNATIONAL STUDIES
AND THE SOCIAL SCIENCES, BROWN UNIVERSITY

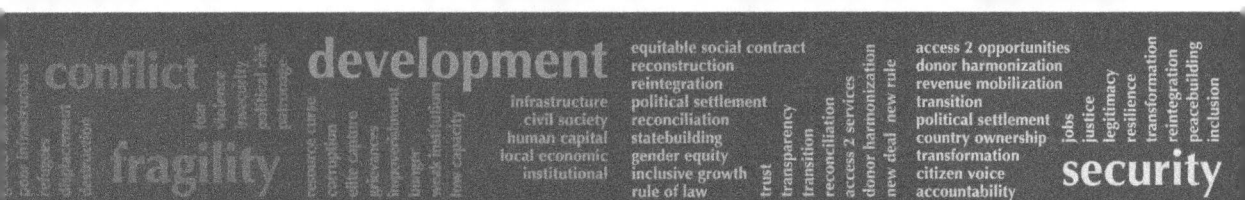

# 1

## Introduction and Methodology

### CHAPTER HIGHLIGHTS

- An estimated 370 million people reside in fragile and conflict-affected states among low-income countries, while over 1.25 billion live in countries facing fragile and conflict-affected situations.

- Fragile and conflict-affected states among IDA-only countries (IDA FCS) are much poorer, grow more slowly, and have higher population growth rates than non-FCS countries.

- This evaluation assesses the relevance and effectiveness of World Bank Group country strategies and assistance programs to IDA FCS.

- Support to projects in FCS has been a strategic priority for the Multilateral Investment Guarantee Agency since 2005. In FY10, the International Finance Corporation added support to FCS to its strategic priorities.

Fragile and conflict-affected states (FCS) have become an important focus of World Bank Group assistance in recent years as recognition of the linkages between fragility, conflict, violence, and poverty has grown. Understanding the root causes of fragility and conflict and identifying pathways out of this vicious circle have been a concern of scholars (Collier and Hoeffler 1998, 2004; Collier and Sambanis 2005; Fukuyama 2004; Migdal 1998), practitioners (Ghani and Lockhart 2008; Hoff and Stiglitz 2008), and development agencies (DFID 2010; World Bank 2012). Bank Group assistance has evolved from post-conflict reconstruction to broader state- and peace-building. As part of its effort to align its assistance with that of other development partners, the Bank Group has replaced the term "low-income countries under stress," introduced in 2003, with the more broadly accepted term for fragile and conflict-affected states.[1] Support to FCS has been identified as a high priority under the new strategic goals of inclusive growth and shared prosperity.

The *World Development Report 2011: Conflict, Security and Development* reported that 70 percent of fragile states have experienced conflict since 1989 (World Bank 2011). Recent research has identified the stark relationship between fragility and poverty (Collier 2007) and drawn attention to the repeated cycles of violence that pervade FCS (World Bank 2011). Chronic insecurity due to such violence is one of the biggest threats to development in the 21st century. Poverty rates in FCS average 54 percent. Although global poverty has declined sharply, this has occurred in states that are not fragile, and a new feature of the poverty landscape is the high share of poor living in fragile states (Kharas and Rogerson 2012: 7–8).

Addressing issues of recurring conflict and political violence and helping build legitimate and accountable institutions are central to the Bank Group's poverty reduction mission. Support for FCS has been a growing priority for more than a decade. It was one of the Bank Group's six strategic themes announced in 2008. In a 2008 speech, former President Zoellick highlighted the link between security and development in FCS and laid out a road map to break the conflict-poverty trap through a broader approach toward state-building and conflict prevention (Zoellick 2008). At the 2012 Annual Meetings, President Kim reiterated the critical importance of security, justice, and jobs in helping countries overcome conflict, and stressed the Bank Group will need to move forward with an ever greater sense of urgency in assisting fragile states.

This growing focus on FCS has given further impetus to the Bank Group's engagement in the dialogue among international partners on state- and peace-building. Fragility and conflict were featured as a special theme in the IDA Fifteenth Replenishment, or IDA15 (IDA 2009). The World Bank defines "fragile situations," under an agreement reached at the beginning of IDA15 with other multilateral development banks, as having either: (a) a harmonized average Country Policy and Institutional Assessment (World Bank/Asian Development Bank/African

Development Bank) rating of 3.2 or less; or (b) the presence of a United Nations and/or regional peacekeeping or peace-building mission (e.g., African Union, North Atlantic Treaty Organization), with the exclusion of border monitoring operations, during the past three years. Improving the effectiveness of development assistance to FCS is one the four special themes identified by IDA deputies for the IDA Sixteenth Replenishment (IDA16) and the IDA Seventeenth Replenishment (IDA17) periods FY12–14 and FY15–17 (IDA 2012, 2013).

The international community has also renewed its attention to fragility, leading to the establishment of the g7+ coalition among fragile states[2] in 2010 and agreement on a "New Deal for Engagement in Fragile States" at the Fourth High-Level Forum on Aid Effectiveness held in Busan, Republic of Korea, in 2011. The forum acknowledged that although 30 percent of official development assistance (ODA) has been spent on FCS, these countries are farthest from achieving the Millennium Development Goals (MDGs), and basic governance transformations may take 20 to 40 years. The New Deal envisions a new development architecture and new ways of working, better tailored to the situation and challenges of fragile contexts. The International Dialogue on Peacebuilding and Statebuilding, comprised of the g7+ group of 19 fragile and conflict-affected countries, development partners, and international organizations, adopted the principles of the New Deal, and in its statement:

- Recognized that transitioning out of fragility is a long political process that requires country leadership and ownership using Peacebuilding and Statebuilding Goals as an important foundation for development.

- Committed to focus on new ways of engaging, to support inclusive country-led and country-owned transitions out of fragility based on a country-led fragility assessment, a country-led vision and plan and inclusive and participatory political dialogue.

- Committed to build mutual trust by providing aid and managing resources more effectively and aligning these resources for results by enhancing transparency, risk management to use country systems; strengthening national capacities and timeliness of aid; and improving the speed and predictability of funding to achieve better results.

## Purpose, Coverage, and Evaluation Questions

This evaluation assesses the relevance and effectiveness of World Bank Group strategies and assistance programs to FCS among IDA-only countries. Countries not classified as FCS but affected by fragile and conflict-affected situations are not covered by this evaluation and will be reviewed by a separate Independent Evaluation Group (IEG) evaluation. This evaluation is motivated both by the renewed attention to conflict and fragility by the international community and the World Bank Group, and by the interest of the Bank Group's shareholders in the operationalization of the 2011-WDR and the ongoing discussions for IDA17. The evaluation is designed to inform internal and external stakeholders and Bank Group management of the extent to which the Bank Group's support is responsive to the specific development challenges, opportunities, and risks in FCS and to enhance the understanding

TABLE 1.1  Categorization of IDA-Only Countries

| Always FCS | | Partial FCS | Never FCS | |
|---|---|---|---|---|
| Afghanistan | Guinea | Cambodia | Bangladesh | Mauritania |
| Angola | Guinea-Bissau | Cameroon | Benin | Micronesia, Fed. Sts. |
| Burundi | Haiti | Djibouti | Bhutan | |
| Central African Republic | Kosovo | Gambia, The | Burkina Faso | Moldova |
| | Liberia | Kiribati | Ethiopia | Mongolia |
| Chad | Sierra Leone | Lao PDR | Ghana | Mozambique |
| Comoros | Solomon Islands | Nepal | Guyana | Nicaragua |
| Congo, Dem. Rep. | Somalia | São Tomé and Príncipe | Honduras | Niger |
| | Sudan | Tajikistan | Kenya | Rwanda |
| Congo, Rep. | Timor-Leste | Tonga | Kyrgyz Republic | Samoa |
| Côte d'Ivoire | Togo | Vanuatu | Lesotho | Senegal |
| Eritrea | | Yemen, Rep. | Madagascar | Sri Lanka |
| | | | Malawi | Tanzania |
| | | | Maldives | Tuvalu |
| | | | Mali | Uganda |
| | | | Marshall Islands | Zambia |

SOURCE: Annual World Bank FCS lists.
NOTE: The categorization covers IDA-only countries and is derived from the FCS lists for FY06–12. Partial FCS countries are those classified as FCS in at least two years during this period. Myanmar was left off the list of Always FCS as it received no IDA financing during FY01–12.

of how this assistance contributes to a broader peace- and state-building agenda. This is also highly relevant to the poverty objectives in the new World Bank Strategy for eliminating poverty by 2030. The key questions for this evaluation are:

- To what extent have Bank Group assistance programs in FCS been strategically relevant to the needs of and tailored to the risks in FCS contexts?

- How effective has implementation of the Bank Group's assistance programs and projects in FCS been in achieving results and strengthening institutional capacity?

- What drivers of success and failure in FCS were under the Bank Group's control, and how have they affected the results and performance of the Bank Group's assistance to FCS?

- What external drivers have been most critical, and what have been their effects on the results of Bank Group assistance to FCS?

As a corollary, the operationalization of the 2011 WDR in this short time frame is also reviewed to see how the framework and the intended focus on citizen security, justice, and jobs have been reflected in subsequent analytical work, country assistance strategies, and the lending program. In addition to assessing the effectiveness of Bank Group assistance—policy advice, institutional strengthening, financing, and knowledge and advisory services—the evaluation report also draws lessons from evaluative evidence to identify good practices and systemic challenges that can be replicated or addressed in FCS.

The evaluation focuses on IDA-only countries and evaluates Bank Group performance in 33 fragile and conflict-affected states against that of countries that were never classified as FCS, which is the benchmark for measuring performance. The 33 FCS countries included 21 always on the FCS list and 12 on the list for part of the review period (Table 1.1).

## Poverty and Growth in FCS

An estimated 370 million people reside in fragile and conflict-affected states among low-income countries, and worldwide about 1.25 billion live in countries affected by fragility, conflict, and violence. The population within the 33 FCS IDA-only countries alone is 370 million. Another 88 million live in FCS that are International Bank for Reconstruction and Development (IBRD) or blend countries, and at least 785 million live in countries that are not classified as FCS but have significant, persistent conflict, violence, or political instability, bringing the total number affected by violence, conflict, or fragility to an estimated 1.25 billion.

Fragile and conflict-affected states are much poorer, grow more slowly, and have higher population growth rates than non-FCS. Using the measure of $1.25 a day, poverty is 57 percent in the 21 Always FCS compared to 43 percent in Never FCS. It should be noted that in socioeconomic terms the 12 Partial FCS (i.e., IDA countries that have been on the FCS list for part of the evaluation period) are closer to the 31 countries that were never listed as FCS (Never FCS or non-FCS).[3] Even including the 12 Partial FCS, whose economies are somewhat stronger than the Always FCS group, poverty in all 33 FCS remains around 54 percent. The poverty challenge is compounded by the fact that annual population growth is 2.4 percent in FCS compared to 1.9 percent in Never FCS.

There is a substantial gap in average gross domestic product (GDP) per capita between FCS and countries that were Never FCS (see Figure 1.1), measured both in constant U.S. dollars and purchasing power parity (PPP). The gap between FCS and Never FCS in GDP per capita expanded over 2000–2011 due to lower growth in FCS (21.1 percent) compared to countries that were Never FCS (35.4 percent). On average, annual growth in FCS is 1.8 percent compared to 3.3 percent in IDA countries that are Never FCS.[4]

Among the FCS, per capita GDP tends to be highest in countries abundant in natural resources such as Angola (3,833 international $) and the Republic of Congo (3,403 International $), if the small island states are excluded. In spite of their natural resource wealth, they are still affected by poverty and regional inequality. The best performers among Never FCS, such as Bhutan (3,799 international $) and Sri Lanka (3,759 international $) have more diversified economies with relatively well developed trade and financial linkages with other countries and are less dependent on natural resources.

The poorest countries among the FCS and Never FCS are concentrated in Sub-Saharan Africa and have been affected by conflict or violence in the past decade. Among the FCS, the Democratic Republic of Congo (282 international $) and Liberia (412 international $) had the lowest per capita GDP measured in PPP. Even among the Never FCS, the countries with lowest GDP per capita in PPP, that is Ethiopia, Malawi, Mozambique, and Rwanda, were also from the Africa Region.

Private capital flows to FCS have increased significantly in the last decade, but remain well below public aid, are highly concentrated in a few countries, and have been shrinking relative to foreign direct investment (FDI) flows to Never FCS. FDI more than doubled between 2000–2005 and 2006–2011 to an annual average of $10.9 billion, but this level remains well below that of ODA to FCS. In addition, FDI flows are highly concentrated among a few resource-rich countries. The top five countries account for two-thirds of FDI inflows.

FIGURE 1.1 Average GDP per Capita in FCS and Never FCS IDA Countries

SIMPLE AVERAGE OF GDP PER CAPITA (CONSTANT 2000 US$)

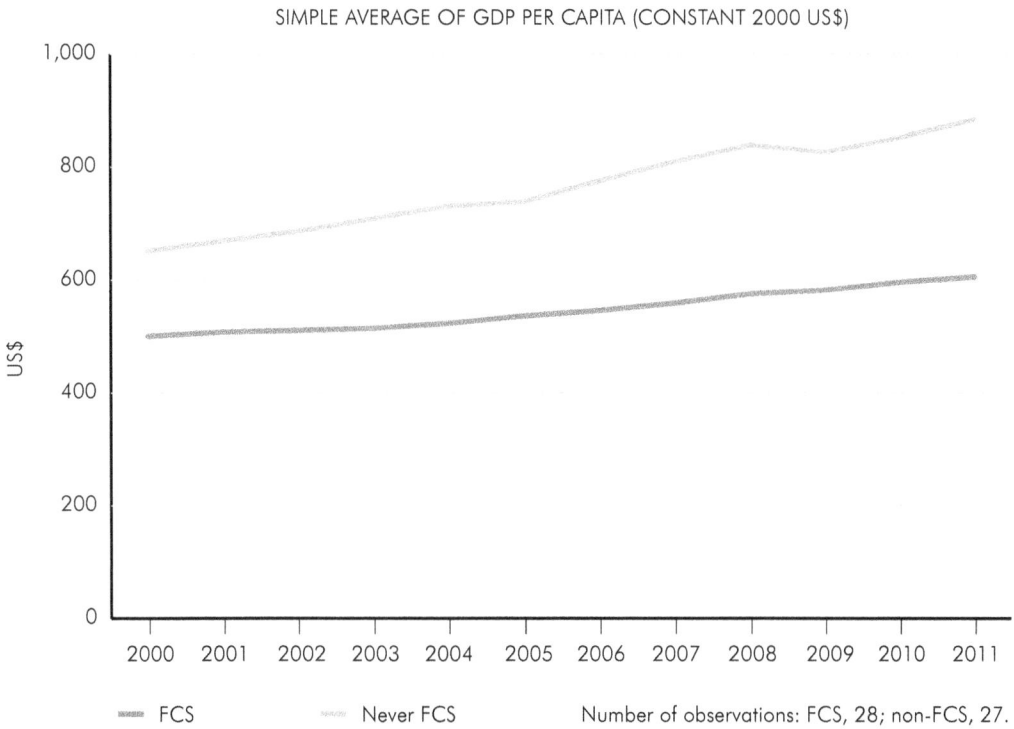

FCS      Never FCS      Number of observations: FCS, 28; non-FCS, 27.

SIMPLE GDP PER CAPITA, PPP (CONSTANT 2005 INTERNATIONAL PPP)

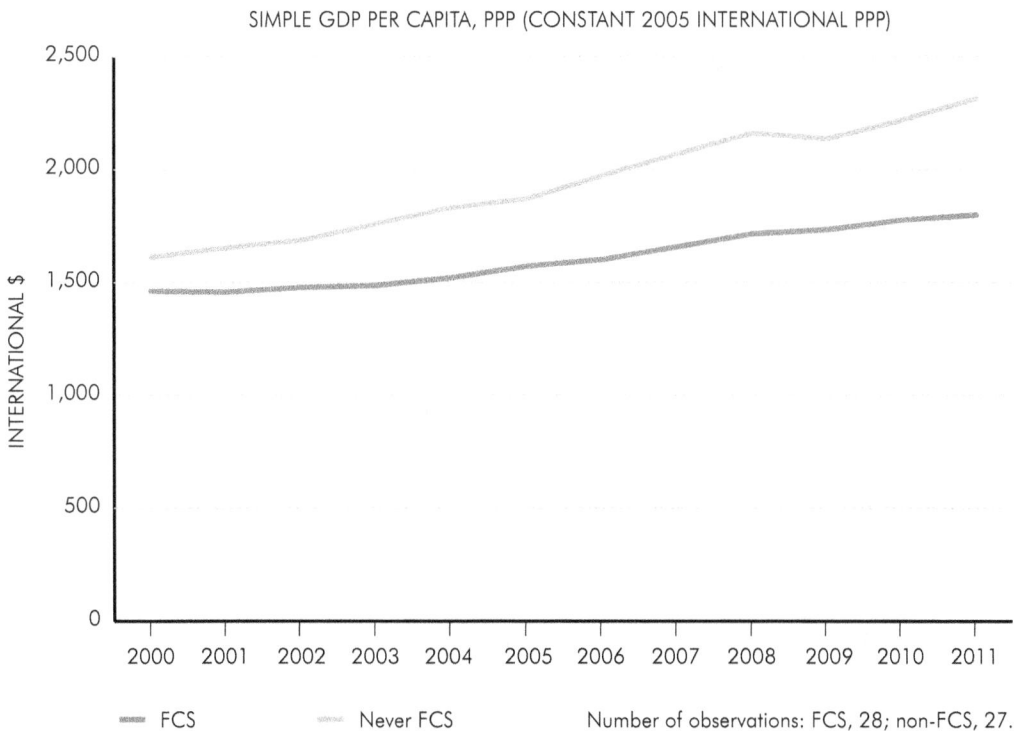

FCS      Never FCS      Number of observations: FCS, 28; non-FCS, 27.

SOURCE: World Development Indicators.

# Bank Group Actions to Enhance Support to FCS

The Bank's work in post-conflict environments initially arose as an extension of its work on emergency recovery in response to natural disasters. The Policy on Development Cooperation and Conflict (OP/BP 2.30) was issued in January 2001 and, aside from minor revisions in 2005 and 2009, still largely governs the Bank's work in conflict-affected countries.[5] While OP/BP 2.30 remains the overarching policy for engagement in FCS, the Bank's operational framework for FCS has been strengthened with a revised policy framework for responding to emergencies (World Bank 2007a), a revamped human resources approach that increases staff incentives to work in FCS (World Bank 2007b), the production of the 2011 WDR, and the establishment in FY12 of the Global Center on Conflict, Security and Development in the Operations Policy and Country Services Vice Presidency in Nairobi. The 2007 governance and anticorruption strategy also put the spotlight on governance in FCS (IEG 2011a).

FIGURE 1.2 Results Chain of World Bank Group Assistance to FCS

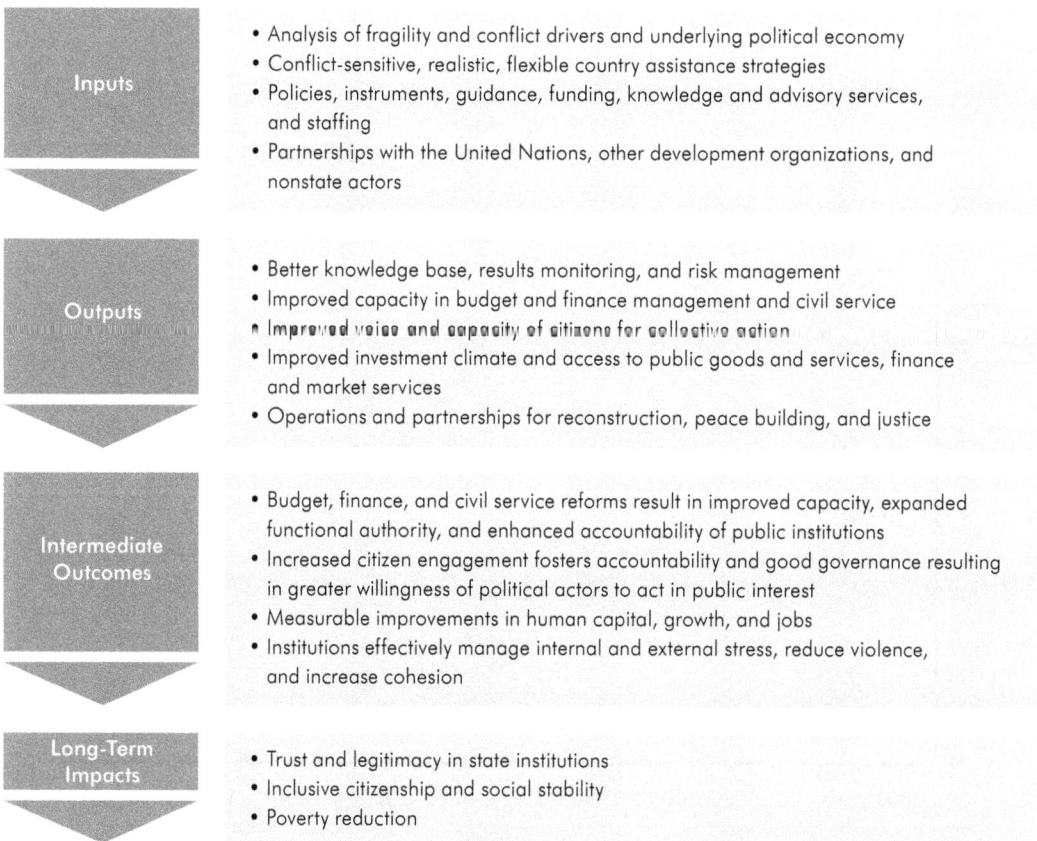

| Inputs | • Analysis of fragility and conflict drivers and underlying political economy<br>• Conflict-sensitive, realistic, flexible country assistance strategies<br>• Policies, instruments, guidance, funding, knowledge and advisory services, and staffing<br>• Partnerships with the United Nations, other development organizations, and nonstate actors |
|---|---|
| Outputs | • Better knowledge base, results monitoring, and risk management<br>• Improved capacity in budget and finance management and civil service<br>• Improved voice and capacity of citizens for collective action<br>• Improved investment climate and access to public goods and services, finance and market services<br>• Operations and partnerships for reconstruction, peace building, and justice |
| Intermediate Outcomes | • Budget, finance, and civil service reforms result in improved capacity, expanded functional authority, and enhanced accountability of public institutions<br>• Increased citizen engagement fosters accountability and good governance resulting in greater willingness of political actors to act in public interest<br>• Measurable improvements in human capital, growth, and jobs<br>• Institutions effectively manage internal and external stress, reduce violence, and increase cohesion |
| Long-Term Impacts | • Trust and legitimacy in state institutions<br>• Inclusive citizenship and social stability<br>• Poverty reduction |

The 2007 policy reform involved revisions to the Bank Group's operational policy and accompanying procedures to improve the flexibility, speed, and effectiveness of the Bank's emergency response and approach for disaster risk reduction and crisis prevention in high-risk countries. The new policy, OP 8.00 Rapid Response to Crises and Emergencies[6] also permitted the Bank to assist member country agencies and institutions involved in emergency recovery efforts and to develop partnership arrangements with other donors in line with their comparative advantage (World Bank 2007b: 37).

The 2007 human resources reforms in the Bank were designed to strengthen support to high-risk environments by increasing field presence on the frontline in fragile states. Incentives were increased to make postings in such high-risk environments attractive to staff, and a callable roster of staff and experts was established to provide operational support to teams in fragile states.

Support for private sector development in FCS by the World Bank's Financial and Private Sector Development Network has been complemented by investment and advisory services operations of the International Finance Corporation (IFC) and Multilateral Investment Guarantee Agency (MIGA) political risk insurance.

IFC's approach to FCS has also evolved and in FY10, IFC added support to FCS to its strategic priorities. IFC launched the Post-Conflict Countries Initiative in 2007 and has augmented funds for advisory services in FCS since 2008 through the Conflict Affected States in Africa (CASA) initiative.[7] IFC's Road Map FY09–11 identified IFC's approach to FCS as focusing on infrastructure, agribusiness, financial markets for women and small and medium enterprises, health, and education. In 2010, IFC added FCS to its first strategic pillar by including it in the definition of frontier markets (IFC 2009). In 2012, IFC created a small unit to coordinate FCS efforts within IFC, and with the World Bank, MIGA, and external parties. IFC's most recent strategy, for FY14–16, proposes to step up operations in FCS for both investments and advisory services by increasing investments by at least 50 percent above FY12 levels by FY16.[8]

Support to projects in FCS has been a strategic priority for MIGA since 2005, which has been reiterated in its FY12–14 strategy (MIGA 2011). MIGA has defined its additionality in supporting projects in FCS based on the perception of high risk that may preclude other providers from offering coverage in these countries. More recently, the agency has established a broader, multicountry trust fund, the Conflict-Affected and Fragile Economies Facility (CAFEF) with the objective of catalyzing private capital flows to FCS by expanding political risk insurance (MIGA 2013).The MIGA-administered facility, which was launched at the end of FY13, provides risk sharing between CAFEF and MIGA.[9]

## Conceptual Evolution of Bank Group Approach

At least since 2003, the Bank Group has acknowledged the intrinsic link between conflict and development. "The risk of civil war is much higher in low-income countries than in middle-income countries. Civil war thus reflects not just a problem for development but a failure of development" (World Bank 2003: ix). While country circumstances matter, the risks of civil war tend to be more acute in low-income countries, justifying an international response and development aid to help these countries break out of the conflict trap (World Bank 2003).

The 2011 World Development Report (WDR) calls for sequencing of interventions and highlights that transformation of FCS is a long-term agenda requiring measures for restoring confidence and transforming institutions. A key message of the WDR is "strengthening legitimate institutions and governance to provide citizen security, justice, and jobs is crucial to breaking the cycles of violence" (World Bank 2011: 2) in FCS; other reforms will need to be sequenced and paced over time (World Bank 2011: 13). Trust in government institutions is vital to ensure peace and prosperity (Braithwaite and Levi 1998; Fukuyama 1995), and the WDR recommends support for inclusive-enough coalitions and quick wins that help build trust in government institutions and state legitimacy.

The 2011 WDR's framework places citizens at the center of engagement in FCS both as active participants in reconstruction and development processes and as beneficiaries of assistance to FCS. Security is the highest priority of governments, citizens whose lives and property remain at risk from repeated cycles of violence, and external development partners. Support for building state capacity is essential to create the enabling conditions for the economy and society to function by providing security and delivering public goods and services. The 2011WDR recognizes that success in FCS depends heavily on partnerships with other donors, civil society organizations, and the private sector, each operating in their domains of comparative advantage. In FCS, even more than in countries with well-functioning markets, interventions for economic development need to ensure equal attention to growth and jobs to ensure inclusive growth.

The 2013 WDR highlights the centrality of jobs, relevant to the FCS evaluation. In FCS, many jobs are informal or based on agriculture or other family enterprises. Jobs can help manage social tensions by encouraging people to straddle ethnic lines, or in extreme cases a lack of job opportunities can contribute to violence or social unrest, especially among the youth (World Bank 2012: 132). Short-term jobs can also contribute to social cohesion by facilitating demobilization of soldiers and expanding opportunities for excluded groups. While not all jobs affect social cohesion, those that shape social identity, build networks, and increase fairness, particularly for excluded groups, can defuse tensions (World Bank 2012: 140–144).

Drawing on the concepts mapped out in the 2011 WDR, the evaluation examines the relevance and effectiveness of Bank Group support for building capacity of the state, building capacity of citizens (through human and social development), and promoting inclusive growth and jobs. In the FCS context this implies supporting clients to create an effective, responsive, and accountable state and an inclusive society and economy.

## Evaluation Framework

The results chain for the evaluation (Figure 1.2) combines attention to fragility and conflict with the Bank Group's core development mandate. It draws on the synergies arising from support for building state capacity, citizen engagement to enhance social cohesion and peace building, and economic development through inclusive growth to sustain state revenues while investing in jobs and sustainable livelihoods. The assessment of risks, design of risk-adjusted strategies and assistance programs, and their implementation arrangements are captured under inputs. Relevant results in the short- and medium-term are reflected under outputs and outcomes. This framework has been derived from the concepts and priorities articulated in recent WDRs, policy papers, and progress reports issued by management, based on past experience, to draw lessons from FCS.

Bank Group support is clustered and assessed under three major themes emerging from the 2011 WDR: building state capacity, building capacity of citizens, and promoting inclusive growth and jobs. The framework recognizes that transnational forces have a bearing on conflict and violence, particularly in fragile environments. Cross-border engagement can facilitate economic development as well as foster peace building and conflict prevention. Nonetheless, since the country model is the primary vehicle for delivery of the Bank Group's assistance program, the country level will remain an important unit of analysis along with the project and program levels.

The evaluation has examined Bank Group support to FCS through its country assistance strategies and operations as well as its engagement with international partners to enhance knowledge, operational experience, and donor coordination in FCS. A considerable body of this work builds on previous country program evaluations and operations, utilizing the criteria—relevance, effectiveness, and efficiency—against which achievement of objectives have been assessed.

## Evaluation Methodology

Evidence for this evaluation comes from a wide variety of documents and databases, supplemented by quantitative and qualitative data collected for the assessment. Results were triangulated and synthesized to answer the evaluation questions. The sources of data and evaluation methodology are summarized below, with more details provided in appendix A.

Data on the portfolio, administrative budget, and human resources were obtained from Bank Group databases and previous IEG evaluations. They were subjected to comparative analysis both over time and across country groups, comparing results from FCS with countries that were never on the FCS list among IDA-only countries. IBRD countries are not covered by this evaluation. Time series analysis of portfolio data covers the period FY01–12, which was subdivided into two equal periods for comparative analysis. The second period, FY07–12, witnessed internal reforms aimed at enhancing World Bank support to FCS, after IEG's 2006 evaluation of fragile states, which provides an opportunity to assess the effects of those reforms (IEG 2006).

The evaluation carried out six new country case studies in FCS selected through purposive sampling, including three Always FCS—the Democratic Republic of Congo, Sierra Leone, and Solomon Islands—with persistent fragility and three Partial FCS—Cameroon, Nepal, and Republic of Yemen. These case studies and three Country Program Evaluations on FCS—Afghanistan, Liberia, and Timor-Leste carried out in FY11–12 (IEG 2011b; 2012a,b)— provide the empirical evidence for an in-depth assessment of the Bank Group's strategies and assistance programs in these countries.

Drawing on the country case studies and review of relevant portfolio and analytical work, the evaluation also undertook more in-depth analyses of gender as a cross-cutting theme and of the contribution of private sector development, agriculture, and natural resources management to growth and jobs in FCS. Further analysis was undertaken on growth and aid in FCS and on the relationship between budget support to FCS and changes in the Country Policy and Institutional Assessment (CPIA) ratings. Econometric analysis was employed to examine this relationship and to test the results from the portfolio outcome analysis.

At the request of the Committee on Development Effectiveness, the evaluation also undertook a review of multi-donor trust funds in FCS, including six single-country multisector and two multicountry, multi-donor trust funds focusing on demobilization, disarmament, and reintegration. A field visit to Haiti was undertaken as part of the trust fund review. Perception surveys of World Bank staff, IFC and MIGA staff, and in-country stakeholders were also undertaken to obtain feedback on Bank Group engagement in FCS.

## Organization of the Report

The rest of the report is organized into eight chapters. Chapter 2 reviews country assistance strategies in the FCS; chapter 3 reviews the Bank Group's portfolio. This is followed by three chapters discussing Bank Group support for building state capacity, building capacity of citizens, and promoting inclusive growth and jobs. Chapter 7 discusses Bank Group support on gender. Chapter 8 analyzes internal inputs and processes, including the efficacy of enhanced support from the Bank Group in FCS. Chapter 9 discusses external drivers, especially donor partnerships and aid flows to FCS. The concluding chapter summarizes the key findings and provides recommendations for strengthening the Bank Group's engagement in FCS. Additional findings from the country studies and background papers are summarized in the form of appendixes to this report, which are available online.

### Endnotes

[1] The FCS list consists of (a) IDA-eligible countries with a harmonized average country rating under the Bank's CPIA of 3.2 or less (or no CPIA), or (b) the presence of a United Nations and/or regional peacekeeping or peace-building mission during the past three years. This list includes nonmember or inactive territories and countries. It excludes IBRD-only countries for which CPIA scores are not currently disclosed.

[2] The g7+ was established in April 2010 at the OECD International Dialogue on Peacebuilding and Statebuilding held in Dili, Timor-Leste. The group has grown from its original membership of 7 states to include 19 countries across Africa, Asia, and the Pacific.

[3] GDP per capita (in constant 2000 U.S. dollars) in Partial FCS is $487, $481 in Never FCS, and $389 in Always FCS. Due to the inclusion of oil-and mineral-exporting countries such as Cameroon, Djibouti, and The Gambia, poverty headcounts are lower in the Partial FCS.

[4] This excludes the contraction in average GDP per capita in Never FCS by 1.7 percent during 2009.

[5] This was supplemented by another policy on Dealings with de facto Governments (OP/BP 7.30) in July 2001 to make provisions for situations where a constitutional government does not exist.

[6] Most of the provisions of OP/BP 8.00 that deal with crises and emergencies have been integrated in the consolidated policy on investment lending (OP/BP 10.00) approved by the Board in 2012.

[7] A mid-term review of CASA, being undertaken for IFC in 2012, concluded that the program had been effective in expanding advisory services activities in the FCS countries covered by CASA, but had fallen short in adapting advisory product offerings to the FCS context.

[8] IFC proposed and the Board approved a budget increase of 3.5 percent in real terms for FY14 to support scaling up of its investment and advisory services activities in FCS (IFC 2013).

[9] CAFEF would provide up to $80 million in a first and second loss layer initially, with MIGA contributing up to $20 million for the first loss. MIGA (and its reinsurance partners) would cover any excess loss over and above the first and second loss.

# References

Braithwaite, Valerie, and Margaret Levi, eds. 1998. *Trust and Governance*. Stockholm: Almqvist & Wiksell International.

Collier, Paul. 2007. *The Bottom Billion: Why the Poorest Countries Are Failing and What Can Be Done About It.* New York: Oxford University Press.

Collier, Paul, and Anke Hoeffler. 1998. "On Economic Causes of Civil War." *Oxford Economic Papers* 50 (4): 563–73.

_____. 2004. "Greed and Grievance in Civil War." *Oxford Economic Papers* 56 (4): 563–95.

Collier, Paul, and Nicholas Sambanis, eds. 2005. *Understanding Civil War: Evidence and Analysis*. Washington, DC: World Bank.

DFID (U.K. Department for International Development). 2010. "The Politics of Poverty: Elites, Citizens, and States." Findings from ten years of DFID-funded research on Governance and Fragile States 2001–2010, a Synthesis Paper, DFID, London.

Fukuyama, Francis. 1995. *Trust: The Social Virtues and the Creation of Prosperity*. New York: Free Press.

_____. 2004. *State-Building: Governance and World Order in the 21st Century*. Ithaca, NY: Cornell University Press.

Ghani, Ashraf, and Clare Lockhart. 2008. *Fixing Failed States: A Framework for Rebuilding a Fractured World*. New York: Oxford University Press.

Hoff, Karla, and Joseph E. Stiglitz. 2008. "Exiting a Lawless State." *Economic Journal* 118 (531): 1474–97.

IDA (International Development Association). 2009. "IDA's Support to Fragile and Conflict-Affected Countries: Progress Report 2007–2009." IDA15 Mid-Term Review, Operations Policy and Country Services, November 2009, World Bank Group, Washington, DC.

_____. 2012. "Progress Report on IDA Support to Fragile and Conflict-Affected Countries." IDA16 Mid-Term Review, IDA Resource Mobilization Department Concessional Finance and Global Partnerships, October 2012, World Bank Group, Washington, DC.

_____. 2013. "Special Themes for IDA17." IDA Resource Mobilization Department Concessional Finance and Global Partnerships, June 2013, World Bank Group, Washington, DC.

IEG (Independent Evaluation Group). 2006. *Engaging with Fragile States: An IEG Review of World Bank Support to Low-Income Countries Under Stress*. Washington, DC: World Bank.

_____. 2011a. World Bank *Country-Level Engagement on Governance and Anticorruption: An Evaluation of the 2007 Strategy and Implementation Plan*. Washington, DC: World Bank.

_____. 2011b. *Timor-Leste Country Program Evaluation, 2002–2011*. Washington, DC: World Bank.

_____. 2012a. *Afghanistan Country Program Evaluation, 2002–11*. Washington, DC: World Bank.

_____. 2012b. *Liberia Country Program Evaluation, 2003–2011*. Washington, DC: World Bank.

IFC (International Finance Corporation). 2009. "IFC Road Map FY10–12: Creating Opportunity in Extraordinary Times." SecM2009–14, IFC, Washington, DC.

_____. 2013. "IFC Road Map FY14–16: Leveraging the Private Sector to Eradicate Extreme Poverty and Pursue Shared Prosperity." SecM2013–0039, IFC, Washington, DC.

Kharas, Homi, and Andrew Rogerson. 2012. *Horizon 2025: Creative Destruction in the Aid Industry.* London: Overseas Development Institute.

MIGA (Multilateral Investment Guarantee Agency). 2011. "MIGA FY12–14 Strategy: Achieving Value-Driven Volume." R2011–0027. Washington, DC: MIGA.

_____. 2013. "Proposed Conflict-Affected and Fragile Economies Facility (CAFEF) Established as a Trust Fund." R2013–0022. Washington, DC: MIGA.

Migdal, Joel S. 1998. *Strong Society and Weak States: State-Society Relations and State Capabilities in the Third World.* Princeton, NJ: Princeton University Press.

World Bank. 2003. *Breaking the Conflict Trap: Civil War and Development Policy.* A World Bank Policy Research Report. Washington, DC: World Bank and Oxford University Press.

_____. 2007a. "Toward a New Framework for Rapid Bank Response to Crises and Emergencies." Operations Policy and Country Services, January 12, 2007, World Bank, Washington, DC.

_____. 2007b. "Strengthening the World Bank's Rapid Response and Long-Term Engagement in Fragile States." Operations Policy and Country Services, March 30, 2007, World Bank, Washington, DC.

_____. 2011. *World Development Report 2011: Conflict, Security, and Development.* Washington, DC: World Bank.

_____. 2012. *World Development Report 2013: Jobs.* Washington, DC: World Bank.

Zoellick, Robert, B. 2008. "Fragile States: Securing Development." The International Institute for Strategic Studies, September 12, 2008.

conflict development
fragility
infrastructure
civil society
human capital
local economic
institutional

equitable social contract
reconstruction
reintegration
political settlement
reconciliation
statebuilding
gender equity
inclusive growth
rule of law

trust
transparency
transition
reconciliation
access 2 services
donor harmonization
new deal new rule

access 2 opportunities
donor harmonization
revenue mobilization
transition
political settlement
country ownership
transformation
citizen voice
accountability

jobs
justice
legitimacy
resilience
transformation
reintegration
peacebuilding
inclusion

security

# 2

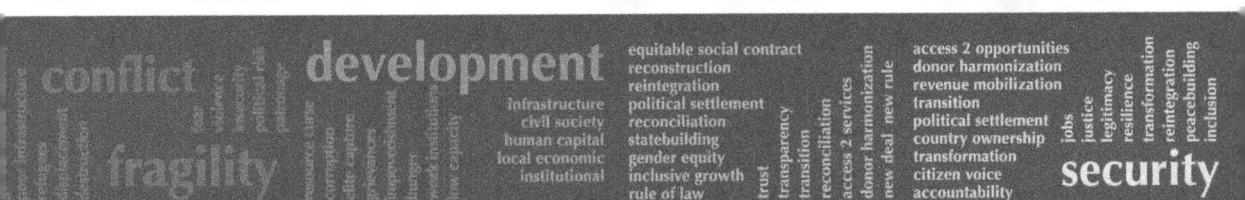

# World Bank Group Country Assistance Strategies in FCS

## CHAPTER HIGHLIGHTS

- The Bank is most responsive to fragile and conflict-affected states in the immediate aftermath of conflict.

- Relevance of the Bank's medium-term strategy as reflected in the country assistance strategies in FCS has been lower because of a lack of adequate strategic underpinning and focus.

- Until recently, country strategies were not well adapted to FCS conditions.

- In practice, the distinction between the Interim Strategy Note and the country assistance strategy has been blurred with prolonged use of Interim Strategy Notes over several strategy cycles and much longer duration than envisaged in the policy.

- Lack of realism and selectivity in most FCS country strategies evaluated has resulted in lower outcome ratings for Country Assistance Strategy Completion Reports.

- In most of the FCS there was inadequate attention to dividing up areas of focus among donors and harmonization in practice to reduce demands on the limited capacity of the government and allow donors to have a greater impact.

- There is a significant variation in total annual per capita ODA to the FCS: Conflict-affected countries like Nepal and Sierra Leone, where poverty remains high and with more progress on Millennium Development Goals and policy reforms, have received less support from IDA and much lower ODA than Afghanistan and Liberia.

- Development policy lending has been an important and useful instrument of Bank support in FCS.

The country model is the World Bank Group's primary means of engagement in client countries, and country assistance strategies (CASs) provide the framework for country engagement. The nature of CASs has been evolving in recent years (and is expected to evolve further into country partnership frameworks) with greater emphasis on joint CASs and partnerships both with the government and other development partners. The CAS identifies the key areas in which Bank Group support can best assist a country in achieving sustainable development and poverty reduction (BP 2.11 Country Assistance Strategies). The CAS in its various incarnations is the vehicle for signaling the Bank Group's priorities to the government and other in-country stakeholders, the Bank Group's shareholders, Bank Group staffs, and other development partners.

When the Bank resumes operations that had been previously interrupted in fragile and conflict-affected states (FCS), particularly in the immediate period following conflict, Bank policy (OP 2.30 Development Cooperation and Conflict) allows the use of an Interim Strategy Note (ISN) to develop a short- to medium-term plan of assistance in lieu of a CAS. The ISN can be prepared quickly to lay out some immediate and obvious areas that the Bank can support, while it prepares a longer-term strategic approach to its operations as the basis for normal operations. An ISN may be put in place for a period of up to 24 months and may be renewed for additional periods with the endorsement of the executive directors. A regular CAS is normally prepared when an International Development Association (IDA) country has developed its own poverty reduction strategy, and the Bank has conducted a conflict analysis to identify the drivers of conflict so Bank (and other donor) assistance can be targeted to dealing with the causes and consequences of conflict. ISNs are expected to have greater flexibility during implementation while CASs are more elaborate both in the analytical underpinnings and in the formulation of their results frameworks.

In practice the distinction between the ISN and CAS has been blurred with prolonged use of ISNs over several strategy cycles and much longer duration than envisaged in the policy. The Afghanistan program, for example, is still being governed by an ISN more than 10 years after the resumption of Bank operations. The post-conflict program in Sierra Leone was governed by three ISNs for a period of seven years. One consequence of this expedient approach has been that programs continued for a prolonged period without a formal assessment (since ISNs are exempt from this requirement), and the program continued to lack a more strategic approach to Bank operations. This has been a significant weakness of Bank programs in many FCS.

In the rest of this chapter, drawing heavily on the case study findings, the evaluation examines the relevance and effectiveness of the CAS or ISN to the needs of FCS and derives lessons to achieve more realistic country strategies and inferences for assessment of country-level performance by the Independent Evaluation Group (IEG). This will include a discussion of the relevant analytical underpinnings needed to tailor the CAS to the FCS context. The current instruments and criteria for determining FCS status are then reviewed to assess if further refinement is needed to encourage more systematic use of fragility and conflict assessments for countries at risk. The final section of this chapter examines the effectiveness of budget support, which is one of the core forms of assistance to build capacity of state institutions, and offers lessons for this mode of engagement in FCS.

As discussed in chapter 1, the Bank draws up the FCS list of countries based primarily on Country Policy and Institutional Assessment (CPIA) ratings unless a United Nations (UN) and/or regional peacekeeping or peace-building mission is present in the country. In practice, the CPIA index that was designed originally to capture institutional and policy weaknesses in the country has proved to be an unreliable means of predicting fragility. The discussion below deals with the relevance and effectiveness of strategies in countries formally classified as FCS. Here it leaves aside the question of whether there are other countries that are otherwise fragile where country strategies should have been designed with a fragility lens. FCS classification issues are discussed in chapter 8.

## Relevance of Country Assistance Strategies in FCS

The Bank has been most responsive to FCS in the immediate aftermath of conflict with high relevance of ISNs. Findings from Afghanistan, Liberia, Sierra Leone, and Timor-Leste indicate that the Bank has been at its best in conducting needs assessments, often done jointly with other development partners, and rapidly mobilizing and deploying financial and staff resources for reconstruction and rehabilitation. In many FCS, it also successfully launched programs for demobilization, disarmament, and reintegration (DDR) and short-term job creation through public works or community-driven development programs.

Relevance of the Bank's medium-term strategy as reflected in the ISNs and country assistance strategies in FCS has been lower because of a lack of adequate strategic underpinning and focus. The ISN period provides the opportunity to carry out a fragility analysis to identify the key drivers of fragility that should determine the focus and approach of the Bank. The ISN period is also expected to be used to carry out the necessary economic and sector work to underpin initial Bank operations in different sectors. In many cases, such work has not been done apace with the preparation of a CAS.

The Bank has increasingly carried out political economy or fragility analyses, but until recently this has not been adequately reflected in the design of CASs. In part, this is because of the politically sensitive nature of the fragility assessments which in various ways point to acute weaknesses in governance and political structures. The fact that political economy analysis is often kept confidential, and is often not available to all members of the country team, has led to insufficient awareness and attention to this important dimension of fragility during preparation of a CAS. The Bank needs to promote a more open discussion of these analyses, even if it may not always be politically expedient.

In several cases the program did not give sufficient priority to the drivers and consequences of conflict. In the Democratic Republic of Congo, Liberia, and Sierra Leone, where women were subjected to acute gender-based violence, these issues were not prioritized, and the Bank chose to rely primarily on gender mainstreaming within the human development sectors. In Cameroon and the Democratic Republic of Congo (until the 2013 CAS), societal fragility stemming from regional inequalities received insufficient attention. The Cameroon country team was surprised to learn that Cameroon had ever been classified as fragile, although IEG's evaluation found that Cameroon meets many of the criteria of fragility. Even the most recent CAS in the Democratic Republic of Congo (which is unlikely to meet any of the Millennium Development Goals (MDGs) and has the highest portfolio risk among the case study countries in Africa) has opted to support a ring-fenced project for conflict mitigation rather than applying a conflict lens across the portfolio.

Bank FCS strategies in practice implicitly or explicitly include activities that address the key action areas relevant for fragility—building state capacity, social inclusion, and growth and jobs—but their relevance is diminished by a lack of selectivity and strategic focus. In all case study countries, there appears to be a rush to move into projects in each and every sector, often without underpinning by relevant sectoral analysis, and insufficient consideration of limits of state capacity and the need for strategic sequencing. In Sierra Leone, for instance, despite a relatively small volume of annual Bank lending (about $30 million), Bank operations span virtually every sector and subsector. Complex operations were launched in power and agriculture without the benefit of sectoral and institutional analysis. There are one-off projects in many sectors that have not allowed sustained Bank involvement that is often needed to make an impact. Cameroon and the Democratic Republic of Congo programs exhibit similarly diffused efforts. In general, Bank strategies in FCS look no different than they do in countries that are not FCS.

The need for selectivity and strategic sequencing, while important for all countries, is particularly critical in FCS because of the severe limitations in state capacity. Immediate reconstruction operations are justified in the immediate post-conflict period, many utilizing emergency or nontraditional delivery mechanisms. But longer-term development requires the establishment of a functioning state. State-building is a multifaceted undertaking spanning many aspects of governance. As the 2011 World Development Report (WDR) points out, it is also an inherently long-term process that can be expected to span over several CAS cycles. Resumption of conventional lending for discrete projects should be synchronized with the development of institutions necessary for implementation. While individual country circumstances dictate the pace and sequence, in practice, there is little evidence of such strategic choices having been in made in the case study countries. In most cases, there was continued reliance on expedient methods to implement projects at the cost of delaying capacity building of relevant institutions. This issue is discussed further in chapter 4.

Donor coordination is given prominence in most CASs, but it is weak in practice on the ground. Donor coordination has largely emphasized information sharing and, to some extent, harmonized approaches in different sectors. But in most of the FCS there was inadequate attention to dividing up areas of focus among donors and harmonization in practice to reduce demands on the limited capacity of the government and to allow donors to have a greater impact in their respective focus areas. While the government attempted to limit donors to certain sectors or geographic areas, in practice it was unable to get the donors to follow the approach (except between the Bank and the Asian Development Bank in Afghanistan). In Sierra Leone, despite a joint CAS between the Bank and the African Development Bank, in practice the two have continued to pursue their own projects independently. In Afghanistan and the Democratic Republic of Congo, geographic distribution led to proliferation of multiple uncoordinated approaches. While the difficulty of coordinating donors with diverse interests and stakeholder pressures cannot be minimized, the Bank could have shown greater discipline by limiting its own involvement through sustained support to the most critical sectors. Bank staff cite pressures from the government and often from other donors for Bank presence in every sector. But discussions in the field indicate that some of the pressures also came from different sectoral constituencies within the Bank, each advocating for their sectors during CAS preparation.

Recent CASs in the FCS are more sensitive to fragility and conflict, but their relevance will depend on how these are implemented in practice. In view of the self-assessment of CAS and ISNs undertaken by the Center on Conflict, Security and Development (see Box 2.1). IEG did not undertake a comprehensive review of country assistance strategies. However, the CAS and ISNs in the case study countries provide evidence of greater use of political economy analysis and fragility or conflict assessments. The Bank has undertaken assessments of societal fragility in 12 FCS (including Mali and the Republic of Yemen) where the social situation deteriorated recently. In Timor-Leste the Bank assisted the g7+ in carrying out a fragility assessment, and in Sierra Leone and Timor-Leste it is drawing on fragility assessments by the g7+ to prepare the next CAS. In Solomon Islands, the 2013 ISN benefited from an external fragility assessment. The 2013 CAS for the Democratic Republic of Congo includes a thorough discussion of

The Center for Conflict, Security and Development undertook a self-assessment of CASs and ISNs that evaluated 53 strategies prepared during FY08–12. The study aimed to establish a baseline of evaluated CASs and ISNs and assess the degree to which they are "fragility sensitive" and help to customize Bank Group support to the needs of countries facing fragility, conflict, and violence (FCV). The self-assessment covered 33 CASs and 20 ISNs. Of the evaluated strategies, 16 were developed in the post-WDR 2011 period, which allowed comparison of the strategies pre- and post-WDR.

Overall, less than half of the strategies specified appropriate FCS frameworks. There was a marginal positive improvement in the fragility sensitiveness among post-WDR strategies. Some of the best strategies were found in countries that experienced recent episodes of conflict, low-income countries, and countries with larger portfolios. ISNs performed better than CASs in nearly all evaluated dimensions, except for result frameworks. The latter are not mandatory for ISNs.

A majority of the strategies included FCV analyses that were well or moderately aligned to the 2011 WDR framework. But less than half of CASs and ISNs contained solid analysis of the drivers of fragility and adequately translated FCV issues into interventions. Most strategies recognized implementation challenges in FCS environments. However, only a small minority of strategies formulated relevant risks frameworks and delineated appropriate responses, and more than half formulated weak results frameworks. While many strategies considered partnerships from a strategic perspective, partnerships were often understood in the context of generic aid effectiveness agendas. Few strategies included an in-depth understanding of the connections between gender issues and social cohesion and, generally, FCV frameworks.

fragility and conflict drivers, albeit with limited impact on the design of the CAS. The ISNs prepared for Afghanistan in FY12 and Nepal in FY13 were also preceded by political economy analyses.

Finally, there is little evidence yet of the 2011 WDR's impact on Bank Group operations. The 2011 WDR had recommended increased attention to security, justice, and jobs. On security and justice, there is no observable increase in Bank operations in FCS. In the past two years only one judicial reform project (in Afghanistan) has been added to the portfolio; even its status is unsatisfactory. Other than support for demobilization and reintegration of ex-combatants from trust funds and demand for specialized services such as public expenditure reviews of the security sector conducted in partnership with UN agencies, IEG found little demand for Bank work in the security and justice sectors from clients or country departments. In contrast, there is significant, unmet demand for Bank Group support for job creation in FCS, which will be discussed in chapter 6.

CASs are not the key determinants of IFC and MIGA engagement in IDA FCS. Although IFC and MIGA have increasingly contributed to formulating CASs and ISNs in the FCS, their engagement has been driven by the existence of capable project sponsors willing to invest in FCS and alignment with corporate strategies rather than the CAS or ISN. The few instances of collaboration across Bank Group institutions in the case study countries—such as telecommunications in Afghanistan and oil, gas, and power in Cameroon—suggest that these synergies can benefit strategic investments in other sectors. The piloting of Bank Group joint business plans for several FCS appears to be a useful mechanism to foster more collaborative approaches.

## Effectiveness of Bank Group Strategies

IEG has utilized two different approaches to assess the effectiveness of Bank Group strategies. At the aggregate level, results from existing IEG reviews of CAS Completion Reports (CASCR) have been tabulated to compare country-level ratings of FCS with other country groups; the findings are discussed below. For a more in-depth treatment of effectiveness, the portfolio in FCS has been classified under the three themes derived from the 2011 WDR—building state capacity; building capacity of citizens; and promoting inclusive growth and jobs. These are discussed in three separate chapters (4-6) following analysis of the aggregate portfolio in chapter 3.

Lack of realism and selectivity in most FCS country strategies evaluated has resulted in lower outcome ratings for CASCRs. During the period FY07–13, a total of 118 CASCR reviews were undertaken of which 50 were in IDA-only countries, while 68 were for International Bank for Reconstruction and Development (IBRD) or blend countries. Within the IDA-only countries, only 12 were FCS. The data show that CASCR outcome ratings are significantly lower in IDA-only countries than in blend and IBRD countries, and that these ratings are even lower in FCS, including countries that are Always FCS and Partial FCS (Figure 2.1). The ratings for Bank performance in FCS were better but also lagged behind the ratings for Never FCS and the blend and IBRD countries. The CASCR reviews for FCS identified lack of realism and strategic selectivity as the primary deficiencies in most country strategies. However, strategies in FCS currently do not include contingencies based on political economy and conflict risks, with built-in mechanisms to adjust objectives and results if the risks materialize.

FIGURE 2.1 Country Assistance Strategy Completion Report Review Ratings (FY07–13)

A. OUTCOME RATINGS

IDA

PERCENT MODERATELY SATISFACTORY OR BETTER

| | Always | Partial | Always + Partial FCS | Never FCS | Other (Blend and IBRD) |
|---|---|---|---|---|---|
| | 40 | 29 | 33 | 53 | 69 |

B. BANK PERFORMANCE RATINGS

IDA

PERCENT MODERATELY SATISFACTORY OR BETTER

| | Always | Partial | Always + Partial FCS | Never FCS | Other (Blend and IBRD) |
|---|---|---|---|---|---|
| | 60 | 43 | 50 | 87 | 76 |

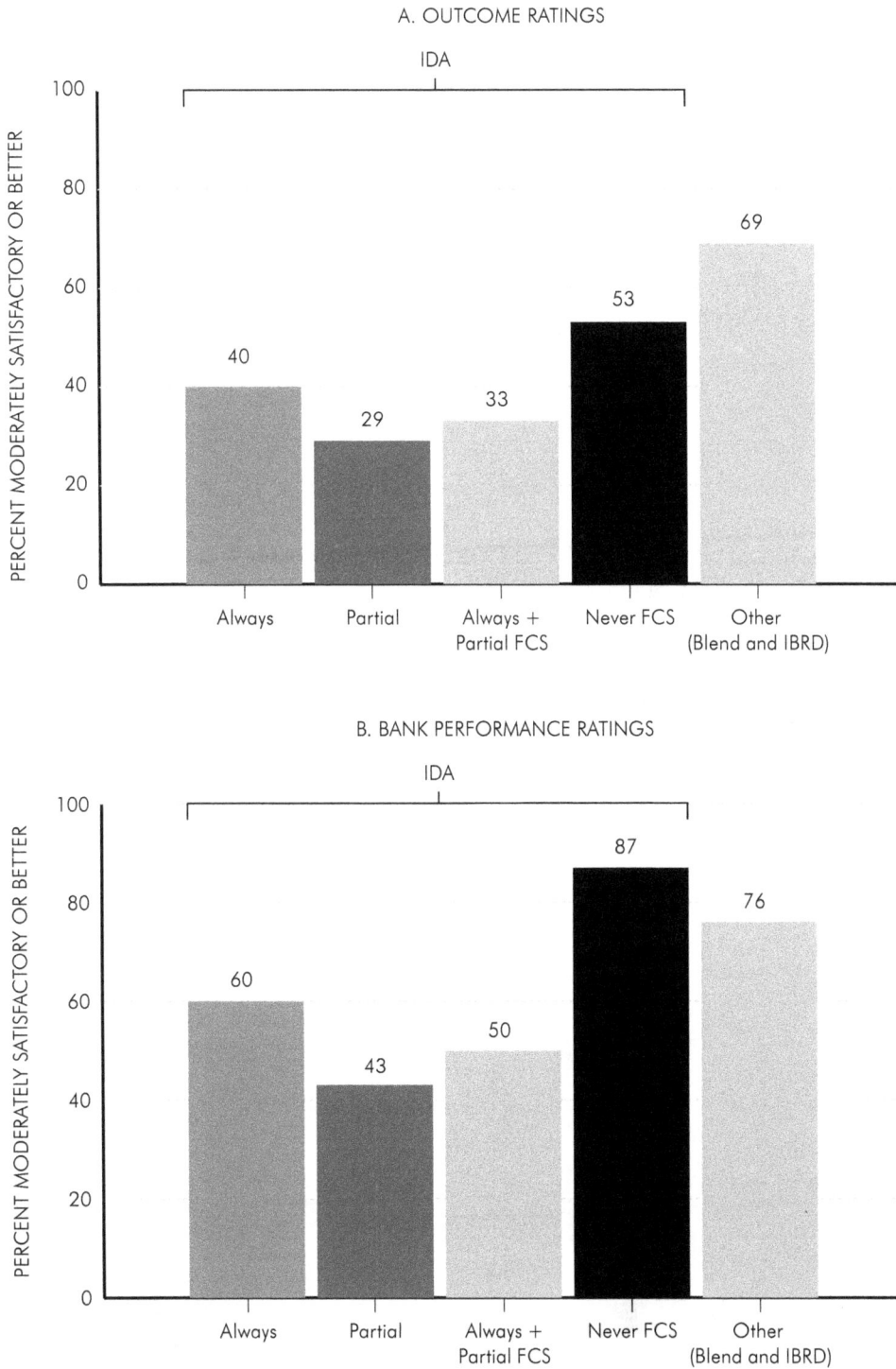

SOURCE: IEG CAS Completion Report review database.

CASCR review outcome ratings are affected by the undercounting of FCS, due to the lack of evaluations for several FCS, including for some of the better performing countries like Afghanistan. The primary reason for the small number of FCS in the universe is that management does not prepare a CASCR for the FCS where Bank Group assistance is governed by ISNs. This in turn prevents IEG from undertaking CASCR reviews for those countries. CASCR reviews are only prepared for countries when a full CAS is under preparation. In practice, this means that countries like Afghanistan, which continue to function with a series of ISNs, have not undertaken a systematic self-assessment of strengths and weaknesses in the country assistance strategy for the past 12 years. In IEG's view, this is a missed opportunity to identify and address strategic gaps.

TABLE 2.1 Average Annual per Capita IDA and Overall ODA Allocation for FCS Case Study Countries

| Country | FY07–12 | 2006–2011 |
|---|---|---|
| | IDA and Trust Fund Commitments Per Capita (US$) | ODA (2011 Constant US$, millions) |
| Afghanistan | 25 | 171 |
| Cameroon | 5 | 59 |
| Congo, Dem. Rep. | 6 | 46 |
| Liberia | 42 | 229 |
| Nepal | 9 | 27 |
| Sierra Leone | 10 | 83 |
| Solomon Islands | 19 | 641 |
| Timor-Leste | 14 | 273 |
| Yemen, Rep. | 6 | 20 |

SOURCE: Organisation for Economic Co-operation and Development and World Bank databases.

# IDA Financing for FCS

There is a significant variation in total annual per capita official development assistance (ODA) to the FCS, and IDA and grant allocations by the World Bank largely mirror the distribution of overall ODA. The highest aid recipients from other donors—Afghanistan and Liberia—were also the largest beneficiaries from IDA and Bank-administered trust funds. IDA allocations are derived from its performance-based allocation policy, which links IDA allocations to CPIA ratings. This is topped up by exceptional financing for countries just emerging from conflict or which are reengaging with the Bank after a prolonged discontinuity. IDA allocations, however, do not take into account the availability of other concessional financing to the country that varies considerably among the FCS countries driven in large part from geopolitical interests (Table 2.1). Countries like Nepal and Sierra Leone, where poverty remains high and where the conflict had severe domestic effects, received lower allocations from IDA and much lower ODA from the broader donor community than countries like Afghanistan and Liberia,

FIGURE 2.2  Development Policy Lending as a Share of Total IDA Commitments
(3-year moving average)

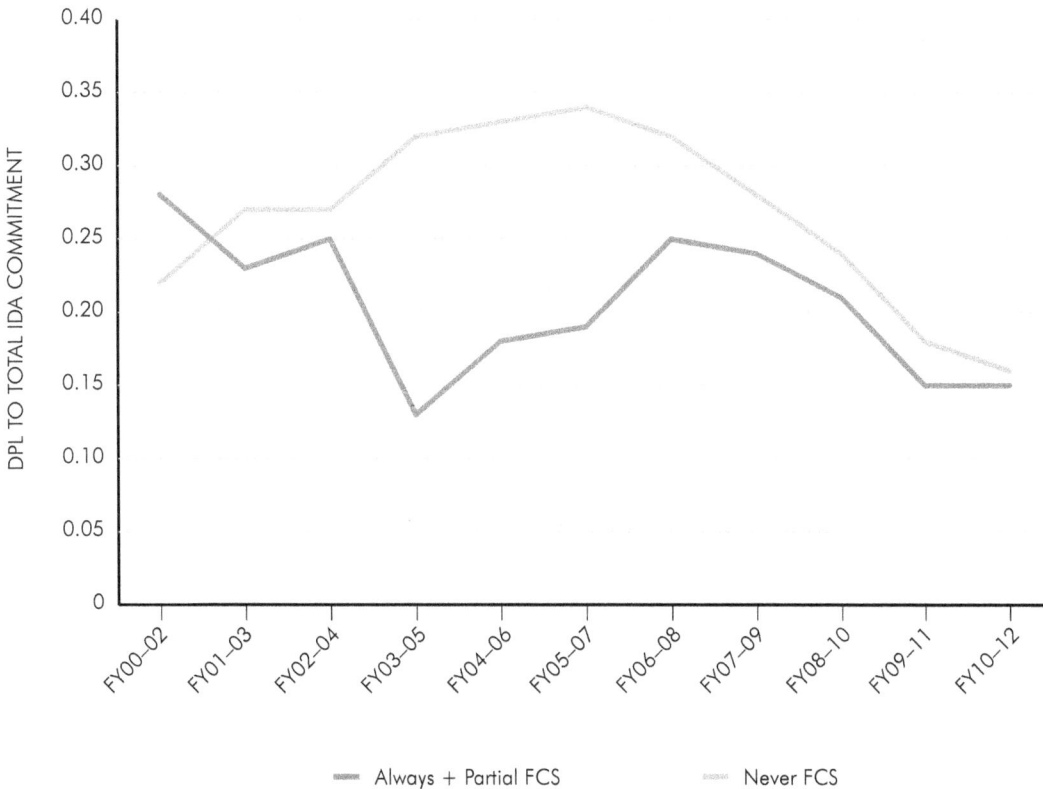

SOURCE: World Bank databases.

FIGURE 2.3 Change in CPIA Ratings by Number of Years with DPLs

A. COUNTRY POLICY AND INSTITUTIONAL ASSESSMENT (CPIA) CHANGE IN FCS

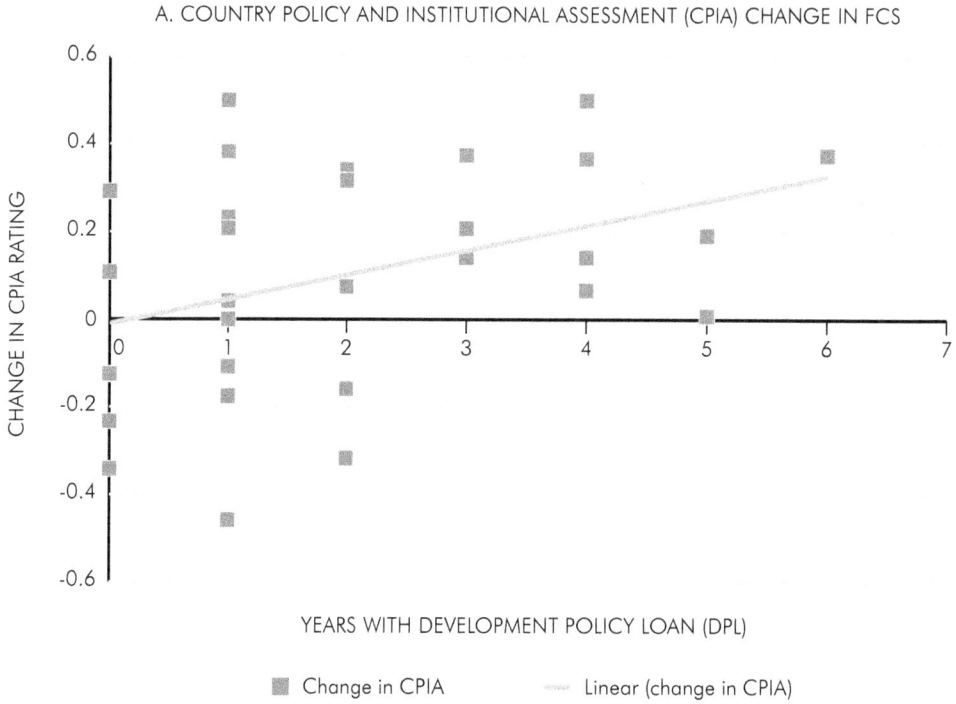

YEARS WITH DEVELOPMENT POLICY LOAN (DPL)

■ Change in CPIA            Linear (change in CPIA)

B. YEARS WITH DEVELOPMENT POLICY LOAN (DPL)

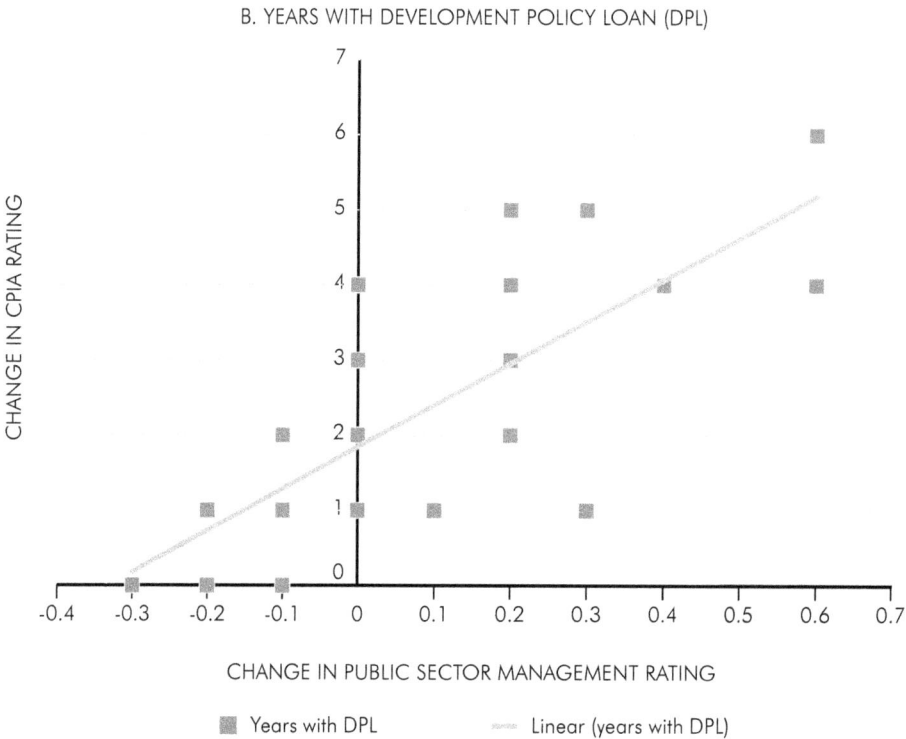

CHANGE IN PUBLIC SECTOR MANAGEMENT RATING

■ Years with DPL            Linear (years with DPL)

SOURCE: World Bank databases.

although Nepal is achieving better results on the MDGs, and Sierra Leone is demonstrating more rapid improvement in CPIA ratings.

Development policy lending (DPL) has been a significant part of support to FCS countries, averaging 15–25 percent of total IDA commitments. While the proportion of DPL financing as a share of IDA commitments was lower in FCS than in the Never FCS in the first half of the review period, it has been at par in recent years (Figure 2.2). This reflects the progress that has been made in institutional and policy reforms in FCS. While in the early years after the conflict, DPLs provided financing for clearing arrears, it has subsequently been a critical source of much needed budget support.

DPLs have also been useful in promoting institutional and policy reforms in FCS. The IEG analysis shows a positive and statistically significant correlation between improvements in CPIA ratings with the number of DPLs received by the FCS. The relationship is stronger with the number of years with at least one DPL (Figure 2.3a). Interestingly, the relationship is stronger in FCS countries than in other IDA countries. These relationships do not indicate causality, but at a minimum they indicate that DPLs have been provided in FCS countries that have been reforming. This is consistent with the idea of a virtuous circle between regularity of budget support and policy and institutional reforms which are reflected in higher CPIA ratings. Among the four dimensions measured in the CPIA, improvement in public sector management has a stronger relationship than other dimensions with the regularity and number of DPLs (Figure 2.3b).

## Conclusions

While Bank strategies in FCS have been relevant in the early stages of post-conflict reconstruction, they have generally not been designed appropriately for medium- and long-term development. They either continued the rehabilitation initiated under an emergency mode longer than was necessary or moved directly into longer-term development without an adequate transition. For most of the period reviewed, CASs and ISNs have not been supported by adequate analysis of fragility and conflict drivers, and they have often not been designed to address the key drivers of fragility as the first priority. They have often lacked strategic focus and realism. Many have lacked an underpinning by strategic sector analysis carried out in advance of a serious engagement in a particular sector. There has been a rush to move toward financing projects in every possible sector, driven partly by pressures from the countries and sometime other partners, but also from internal pressures from different sector groupings in the Bank.

Recent CASs show much more sensitivity to fragility and conflict drivers and appear more in line with the 2011 WDR. But much will depend on how these strategies affect the design of assistance programs and operations, and how they are actually implemented in practice. This should be an area of continued management attention.

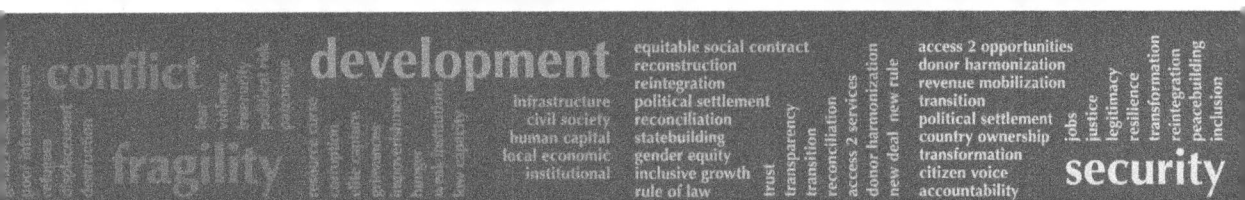

conflict
development
fragility

equitable social contract
reconstruction
reintegration
infrastructure        political settlement
civil society         reconciliation
human capital         statebuilding
local economic        gender equity
institutional         inclusive growth
                      rule of law

access 2 opportunities
donor harmonization
revenue mobilization
transition
political settlement
country ownership
transformation
citizen voice
accountability

security

# 3

# Bank Group Portfolio and Performance

## CHAPTER HIGHLIGHTS

- Since FY09, the World Bank's portfolio in fragile and conflict-affected states has had better outcome ratings than other IDA countries.

- FCS ratings in IDA-only countries are now comparable with Bankwide ratings.

- Outcome ratings lagged in the Africa Region, but by FY10 they had caught up with other FCS.

- IFC investments in FCS are poorer performing than those in IDA-only countries that are Never FCS.

- IFC's Advisory Services in Always FCS perform at par with IDA-only countries that were not fragile.

- The FCS portfolio is riskier, but this risk has to be taken on and managed if improvements are to be sustained, since it is also central to delivering the Bank Group's strategic goals on poverty.

## Bank Operations in FCS

In commitment amounts, International Development Association (IDA) financing from the World Bank's portfolio to fragile and conflict-affected states (FCS) more than doubled immediately after FY01, but commitments to IDA-only countries that were not FCS have also risen, especially since FY09 (Figure 3.1). The largest increase occurred in FY03, followed by another spike in FY09, when IDA financing to FCS rose to 40 percent of total IDA commitments but returned rapidly to under 30 percent. A large part of the surge during the peak years was due to large commitments in Afghanistan and Liberia as well as the Democratic Republic of Congo. Both countries also received significant trust funds resources to supplement IDA financing. During the period FY07–12, annual IDA commitments for all of the 33 FCS together averaged $1.9 billion annually, of which $1.32 billion was in the 21 countries that were Always FCS, compared with the average of $5 billion in annual commitments in the 31 IDA-only countries that were Never FCS.

In new commitments to the 33 countries that were classified as FCS, the World Bank provided a total of $19.7 billion in FY01–12, of which $11.5 billion was in FY07–12 (Table N.2). These commitments include IDA credits and grants, but it excludes a small amount of financing from the International Bank for Reconstruction and Development (IBRD) as well as funds from the Heavily Indebted Poor Countries (HIPC) Initiative[1] and grants from the Institutional Development Fund. During the same period, the World Bank provided $8.5 billion from trust funds administered by the World Bank to all 33 FCS, of which $4.4 billion was in FY07–12. Using the same definition, new commitments to the 21 IDA-only countries that were Always FCS amounted to $13.8 billion from IDA (plus $7.4 billion from trust funds) in FY01–12, of which $7.9 billion from IDA (plus $3.5 billion from trust funds) was in FY07–12. As a benchmark, new commitments in the 31 Never FCS amounted to $54 billion from IDA (plus $6.4 billion from trust funds) in FY01–12, of which $32.9 billion from IDA (plus $5.2 billion from trust funds) was in FY07–12.

The sector composition of new commitments from IDA and trust funds in FCS during FY07–12 shows the dominance of infrastructure sectors ($5 billion), followed by the human development sectors ($3.8 billion). Among individual sectors, agriculture and rural development ($2.9 billion) made the largest volume of new commitments primarily for budget support, followed by economic policy ($2.5 billion). The latter included very large investments in community-driven development (CDD) projects for rural development, which as a whole were larger than the investments in agriculture. Among the infrastructure sectors, transport ($2 billion) was the largest, followed by urban ($1.2 billion) and energy and mining ($1.1 billion). Among the human development sectors, education dominated ($1.9 billion), followed by $1.1 billion for the health sector (Table N.4).

FIGURE 3.1 IDA Commitments in FCS and Non-FCS IDA-Only Countries

IDA COMMITMENT AMOUNT

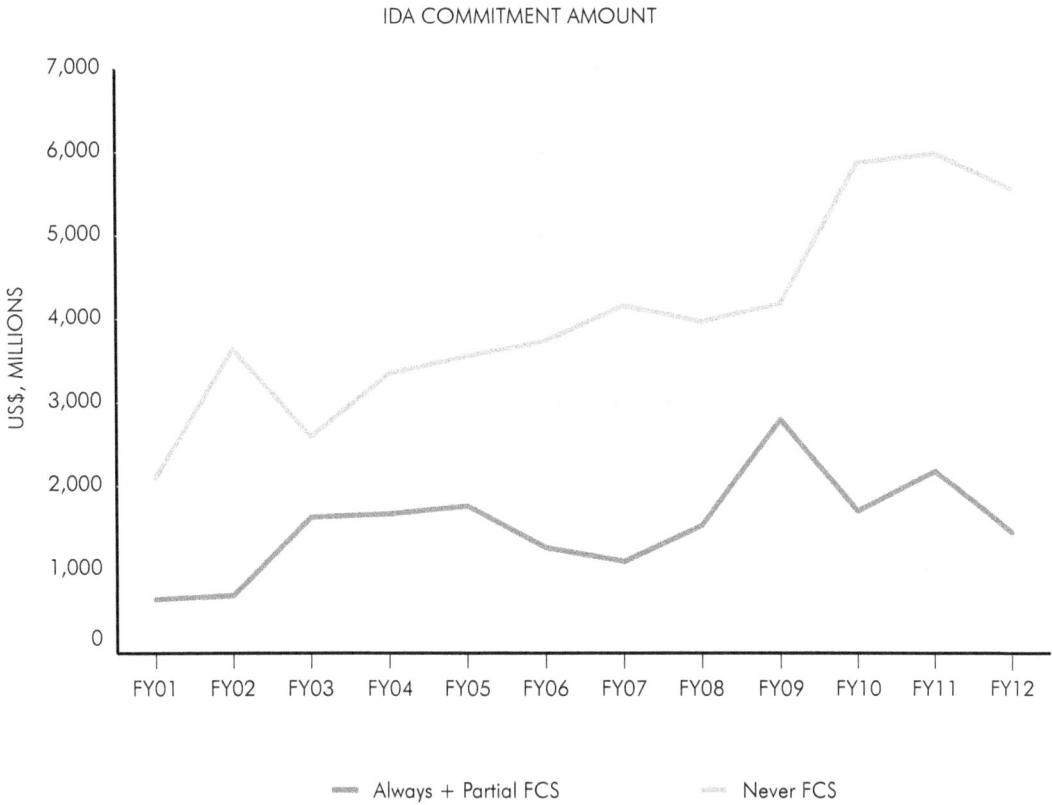

— Always + Partial FCS          ···· Never FCS

SOURCE: World Bank databases.

The pattern in FY07–12 was slightly different in the Never FCS. In this group of countries when IDA and trust funds are combined, the social protection sector ($5 billion) was the largest, followed by the transport sector ($4.7 billion); the energy and mining as well as agriculture and rural development sectors ($4.3 billion each) dominated, followed by the economic policy sector ($3.6 billion).

## PERFORMANCE OF BANK OPERATIONS IN FCS

Since FY09, the portfolio in FCS has had better outcome ratings than other IDA countries. The Independent Evaluation Group (IEG) outcome ratings for all projects exiting the portfolio between FY01 and FY12 were compared to examine trends. Historically, outcome ratings in IDA countries lagged behind IBRD countries, and the aggregate outcome ratings for FCS lagged even further, but this trend appears to have changed in recent years. Figure 3.2

FIGURE 3.2 Percentage of Projects and Commitment Volume Rated Moderately Satisfactory
or Higher at Exit (3-year moving average)

## A. BY NUMBER OF PROJECTS

Legend: Always + Partial FCS    Never FCS    Bankwide

## B. BY COMMITMENT VOLUME

Legend: Always + Partial FCS    Never FCS    Bankwide

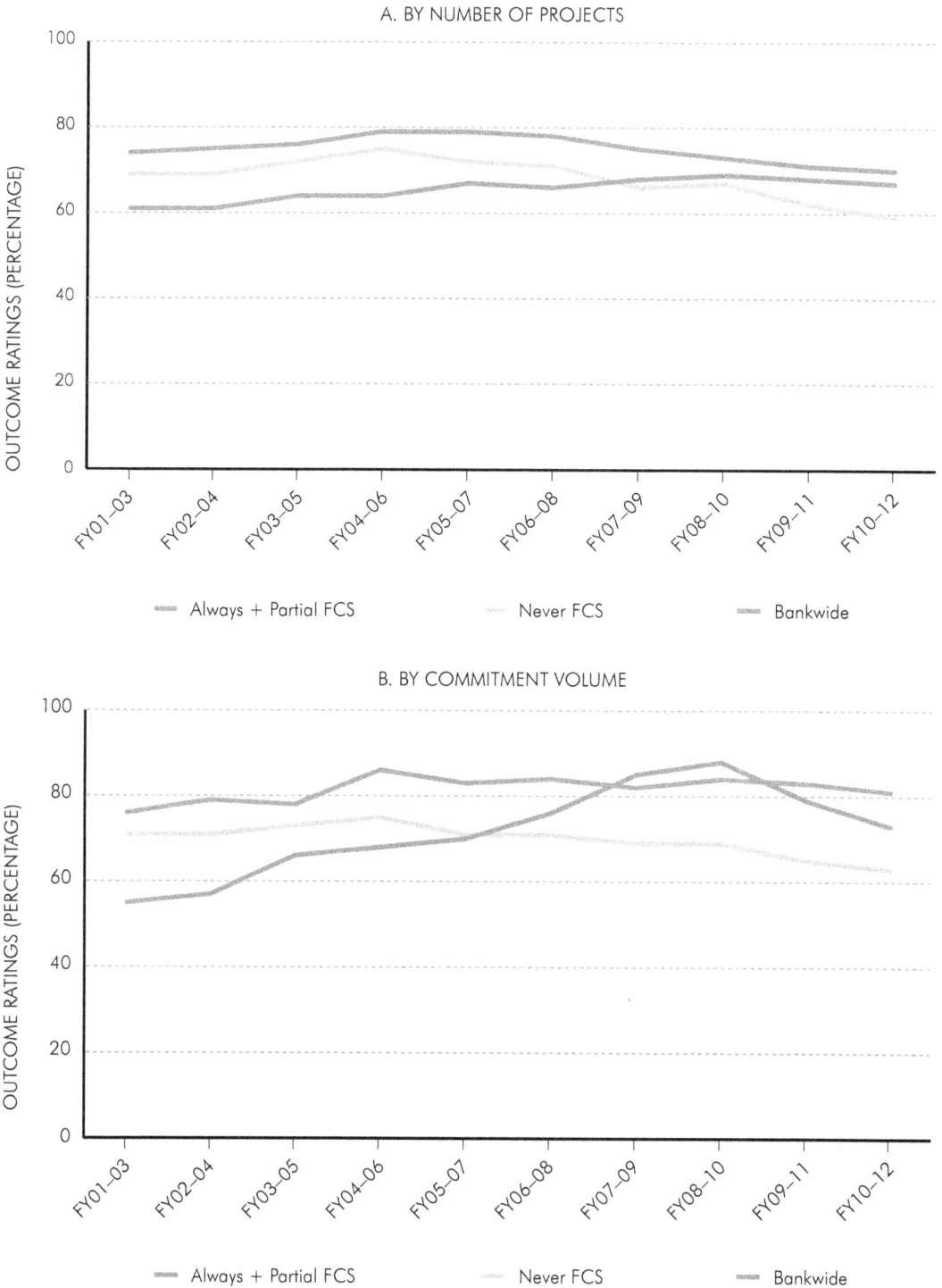

SOURCE: Business Warehouse.

FIGURE 3.3 Percentage of Commitment Volume Rated Moderately Satisfactory
or Higher at Exit (3-year moving average)

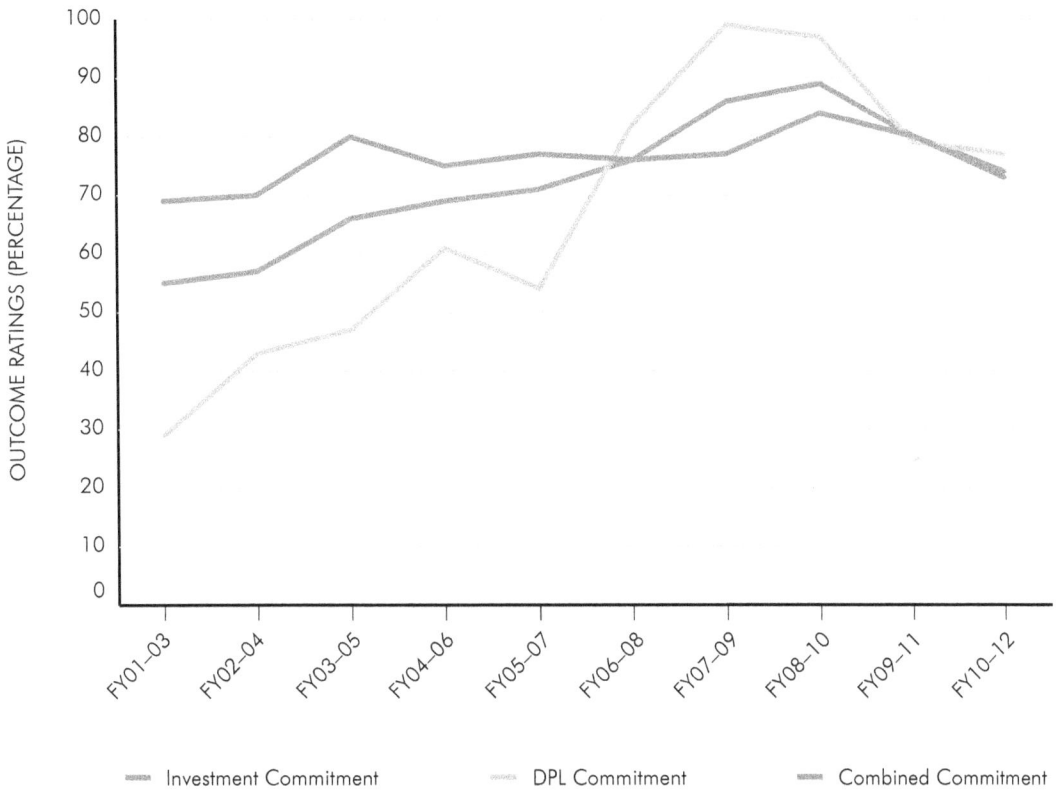

SOURCE: IEG Implementation Completion Report (ICR) review data.

depicts the three-year moving average of outcome ratings for all lending operations and
shows that by FY09, FCS was outperforming IDA-only countries that are not FCS. The change
is both due to the improvement in outcome ratings for FCS and because of the decline
in outcome ratings for Never FCS. The relative improvement in outcome ratings for FCS
compared to Never FCS holds true both as a percent of projects and, even more strikingly,
by commitment volume. FCS ratings in IDA-only countries are now comparable with
Bankwide ratings, which include the ratings for all IBRD operations.

Portfolio performance in FCS indicates that larger projects perform better. The improvement
is greater by commitment volume than by number of projects both in outcome ratings
(Figure 3.4) but also in Bank and Borrower performance (Table N.11). The implication
is that selectivity and focus on priority areas could yield even better results.

Recognizing the historical lag in FCS performance, the World Bank Group's corporate scorecard differentiates targets for IEG outcome ratings at project completion (i.e., exit) by country groups. The scorecard provides a target of 80 percent moderately satisfactory or better for outcome ratings of lending operations in IBRD countries, 75 percent for IDA countries, and 70 percent for FCS.[2] Projects in FCS countries are much closer to meeting their target than projects from Never FCS or IBRD countries, both of which have suffered deterioration.

There is statistical evidence that among IDA-only countries, FCS has performed better than countries that were Never FCS over the period FY01–12. Outcome ratings by exit year in Never FCS have declined. Since FY09, FCS performed as well or better than Never FCS. Several regressions were run to test the statistical significance of the changes in outcome ratings. The observed relative improvement in performance of FCS compared to non-FCS is statistically more robust when the trend is analyzed using the full six-point scale for outcome ratings.[3]

Several factors appear to explain the improvement in outcome ratings of Bank operations in FCS. Increased support from the World Bank both in terms of administrative budgets (see appendix M) and international staff deployed in FCS country offices (chapter 8) have contributed to this trend. The increase, however, is also due to the effect of development policy lending which has increased in quantity but perhaps more important, in quality over the review period (Figure 3.3), which accounts for a significant but not exclusive share of the improvement. Another factor is the increased lending in FY07–12 in transport and economic policy operations with high performance, and improvement in some others (Table N.13)

Outcome ratings lagged among FCS in the Africa Region, but by FY10 average outcome ratings for FCS among IDA-only countries in Sub-Saharan Africa had caught up with the rest of FCS. Outcome ratings at exit from FY01–12 reveal that portfolio outcomes in Africa fell in the last decade but, on aggregate, appear to have recovered, although there are significant risks among some of the larger FCS, including Cameroon and the Democratic Republic of Congo. Data for FY12 are partial and could change since results for half of the exited operations are still awaited (Figure 3.4).

The FCS portfolio is riskier, but this risk has to be taken on and managed if improvements are to be sustained, since it is also central to delivering the World Bank Group's strategic goals on poverty. Portfolio status data (Table N.14) reveal that among the World Bank's FY12 portfolio, 19 percent of the projects are at risk globally while 14.1 percent of the commitments are at risk. The numbers for the Africa Region as a whole being very similar (20 percent projects at risk; 16.1 percent commitments at risk). Among the FCS group, projects at risk represent

**FIGURE 3.4** Investment Project Outcome Ratings at Exit in Always FCS in the Africa Region versus FCS in Other Regions (percent of projects rated moderately satisfactory or better, 3-year moving average)

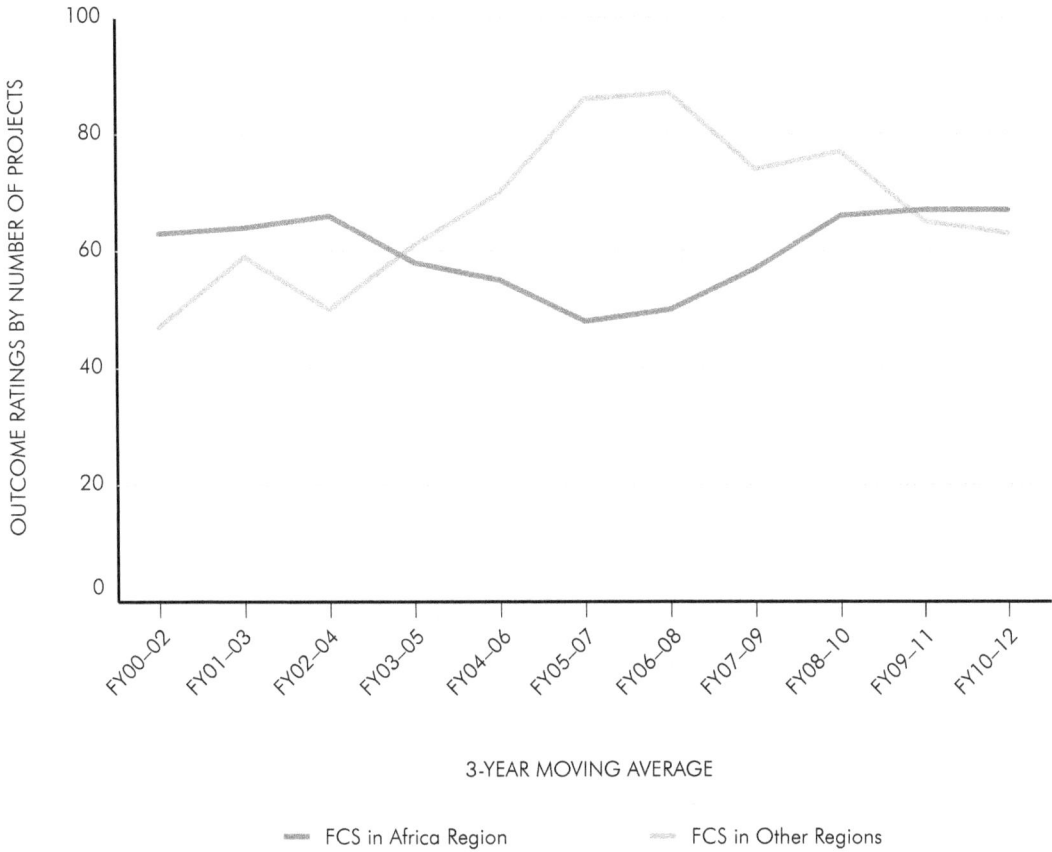

SOURCE: IEG ICR review data.

37 percent and commitments at risk, 40.6 percent. Among the case study countries, riskiness measured by commitments at risk was highest in the Republic of Yemen (76 percent), followed by the Democratic Republic of Congo (75 percent), Solomon Islands (75 percent), Liberia (56 percent), and Cameroon (54 percent). While mid-cycle riskiness can be corrected by project completion, these data do reveal the fragility in FCS, particularly within Africa. The portfolio will therefore need to be managed intensively to meet the target of 70 percent satisfactory and to deliver on the Bank Group's strategic goals on poverty.

## World Bank Support for Analytical and Advisory Activities

Bank support for analytical and advisory activities (AAA) has increased more substantially, with huge increases in spending on technical assistance to build institutional capacity within FCS. As a whole, AAA spending in FCS was 130 percent greater during FY07–12 than in FY01–06; comparing the same periods, there was a 70 percent increase in AAA spending in Never FCS. While the number of AAA did not expand much, expenditures on economic and sector work (ESW) in FCS increased by about 50 percent, but technical assistance expenditures shot up five-fold in FCS and six-fold within the 21 Always FCS. As a result, total spending during FY07–12 on technical assistance in FCS ($86 million, of which $57 million was for Always FCS) outstripped spending on ESW ($77 million, of which $48 million was for Always FCS). In Never FCS, expenditure on technical assistance was less than two-thirds of that on ESW (appendix M). The increased share of technical assistance in response to the weak institutional capacities in the FCS may also have contributed to the improvements in project outcomes.

## Bank Group Support for Private Sector Development

The World Bank Group has supported private sector development (PSD) in FCS through lending and analytical and knowledge products to governments by the World Bank, largely through the Financial and Private Sector Development Network (FPD); investment and advisory services operations by the IFC, the latter targeted to both governments and firms; and political risk insurance by MIGA.

Direct financial support for PSD has remained modest over the period FY01–12. Lending and grants from FPD to FCS totaled $1.1 billion during FY01–12, 4.5 percent of total World Bank lending and grants to FCS. Bank support to other sectors, including infrastructure and mining projects, undertaken by the Sustainable Development Network (SDN), which are also relevant to private sector development, have been more substantial. SDN projects, some of which were undertaken by private sector agencies, in energy and mining accounted for 4 percent while transport was 14 percent of Bank lending in Always FCS. The share of Bank lending for energy and mining (including power) projects in Always FCS is below that in Never FCS while the shares are about equal for transport. IFC's investments in private companies in FCS were $1.7 billion during FY01–12, or 2 percent of total IFC commitments, and MIGA issued $1.3 billion in new guarantees, 7 percent of total guarantee volume.

IFC's portfolio in FCS, while small, increased over time in parallel with the expansion of IFC's exposure in IDA countries. IFC approved 53 investment projects for a total of $437 million between FY01 and FY06, and $1.3 billion for 97 projects between FY07 and FY12 in FCS. By volume, IFC committed three times more in FCS in the second half of the decade than it did in the earlier period. The increase in lending to FCS mirrors the trend in IFC's overall lending and does not represent a significant shift in IFC's overall portfolio toward FCS, but rather to frontier markets more generally. The share of IFC's commitments in FCS has remained constant at roughly 2 percent of new commitments (5 percent of projects) over the entire period while the share of lending to Never FCS has fluctuated, averaging 6 percent of IFC's commitments (14 percent of projects) between FY01 and FY12.

Investments in FCS are on average smaller and riskier than investments in other IDA countries. The average investment in FCS was about $12 million whereas the average investment in Never FCS was roughly $14 million. Investments in FCS have multiple or layered risks. Nearly one-third of projects in Always FCS had three high-risk factors present, which is a risk intensity present in only 15 percent in Never FCS. Projects in FCS are also associated with higher-risk sponsors (i.e., less experienced and with lower capacity, commitment, and reputation), and are more likely to be greenfield projects (i.e., startups), especially in Always FCS countries. Using the Institutional Investor's Country Credit Rating, which measures the ability of the country to service its financial obligations or the likelihood of default and weighing it by IFC's commitment in each country, IFC's portfolio in FCS is significantly riskier than in Never FCS. However, market risk of projects in FCS is only slightly higher than in countries that are Never FCS although they are much higher than in non-IDA countries.

IFC's long-term investment projects in FCS are highly concentrated, with 78 percent of commitments (60 percent of projects) in Always FCS made in three sectors: telecommunications, transportation, and oil, gas, and mining. Conversely, the FCS portfolio in FY01–12 is less focused on financial markets than in countries that are not FCS. IFC's short-term finance, including the Global Trade Finance Program (GTFP), considered an instrument for early engagement in high-risk environments. GTFP have been deployed to a lesser extent in FCS than in non-FCS, despite its relevance and potential. IEG (2013) reported that most of the volume of the GTFP is in low-risk countries, although the volume in high-risk countries has increased over time.[4] IEG's evaluation of trade finance noted the high additionality of IFC's GTFP in the Democratic Republic of Congo, Côte d'Ivoire, and Liberia.

Foreign direct investment is low in FCS, but the private sector can (and does) engage early in post-conflict situations in certain types of investment, such as in telecommunications, which is more resilient to the operating environment; and in extractive industries, which while high risk, can be highly profitable. Partial FCS are also receiving investments in long-term infrastructure like power.

Consistent with IFC's strategic intentions and approach, its Advisory Services (AS) are relatively more focused on FCS than investments with 14 percent of AS expenditures in fragile states versus 2 percent of IFC's project investments in FCS. Between FY05 and FY12, roughly

FIGURE 3.5 Share of IFC Advisory Services Expenditures in Fragile and Conflict-Affected States

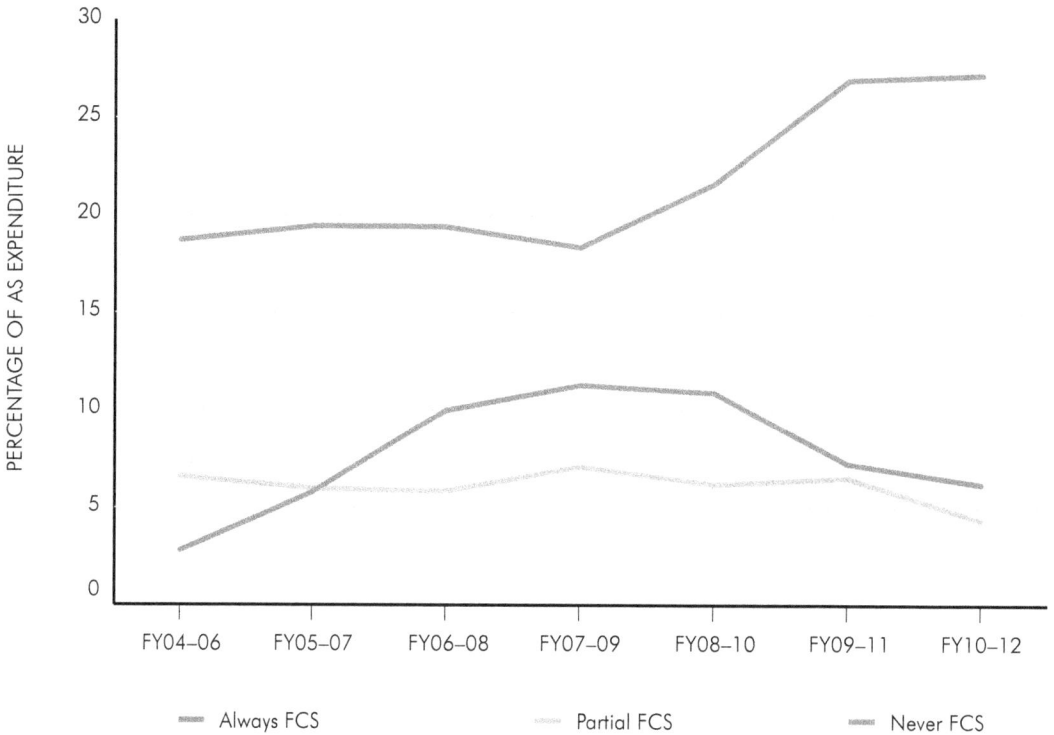

SOURCE: IEG database.

$137 million has been spent on AS in the FCS, of which $81 million is in Always FCS.[5] Since 2009, the share of AS expenditures in FCS has fallen compared to Never FCS (Figure 3.5). IFC and others emphasize investment climate reforms, such as business regulation, trade, competition, and public-private dialogue, as first-stage interventions for state-building, which can then catalyze economic growth and foster long-term growth.

MIGA's guarantee volume in FCS increased significantly since FY11 (Figure 3.6). MIGA had identified support to FCS as a strategic priority since 2005. MIGA's portfolio of 35 projects in FY01–12 totaling $1.3 billion in guarantees is characterized by a mix of large projects and Small Investment Program (SIP) projects, which includes guarantees up to $10 million. About 30 percent of SIP projects have been in FCS.[6] SIP guarantees account for half of MIGA projects in FCS (17 of 35) but only 3 percent of guarantee exposure. MIGA guarantee exposure in FCS is more highly concentrated in infrastructure (74 percent) than in Never

FIGURE 3.6 MIGA Portfolio (3-year moving average)

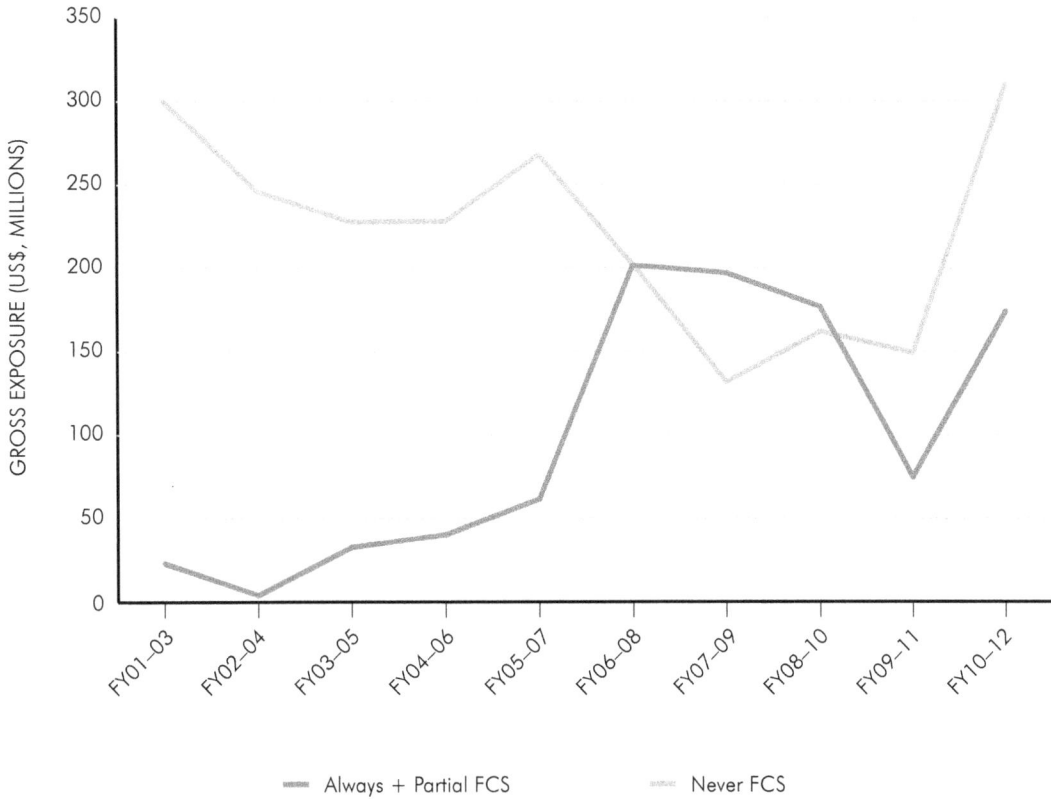

SOURCE: IEG database.

FCS (58 percent), driven by large size guarantees in telecommunications, a port facility, transportation, and power (10 projects). As a result, the share of MIGA exposure in FCS has reached 10 percent in the FY07–12 period. Similar to patterns observed for IFC, MIGA exposure in financial sector projects in FCS is small (5 percent); however, a sizeable share of MIGA's portfolio is in the agribusiness, manufacturing, and services sectors (21 percent of exposure in FCS). Overall, these portfolio patterns are similar to those for IDA countries as a whole.

Among providers of political risk insurance (PRI) in FCS, MIGA played a more modest role. Berne Union data suggest that MIGA's share of PRI coverage provided in FCS was around 6 percent between 2005 and 2012, versus a MIGA share in Never FCS of 10 percent. MIGA's exposure within FCS is relatively concentrated in 15 countries. In some of these, it has provided the majority of outstanding PRI: Afghanistan, Djibouti, and Liberia, driven by support for large projects in these countries. MIGA's share is lower in countries where other PRI providers, including public sector export credit agencies, have been active such as Angola, Cambodia, the Lao People's Democratic Republic, and Sierra Leone (such as an Asian export credit agency, which issued $12 billion in investment insurance in FCS in 2005–2012 compared to MIGA's $1.7 billion).

Even though FCS have higher country risk profiles than Never FCS, in practice, MIGA's portfolio in FCS has not proved more risky than its overall portfolio. This suggests that the perception of high risk was not borne out by actual portfolio risk. The agency suffered only two claims related to war and civil disturbance coverage in FCS, one of which was small, in Afghanistan and Nepal.[7] This is consistent with the experience of other PRI providers, indicating that the ratio of claims to outstanding PRI liabilities does not differ significantly between FCS and Never FCS. Among the elements of MIGA's project level risk management is its ability to resolve investments disputes (pre-claims) related to insured risks (except for events under war and civil disturbance coverage noted above). The mediation function distinguishes MIGA from other insurers and key aspect of its value added. In FCS countries, MIGA was involved in seven pre-claims situations, similar to the frequency in Never-FCS (13 pre-claims).

## Portfolio Effectiveness

Although other Bank Networks also engage with the private sector, the FPD portfolio provides a window to understand the impact of Bank support to the private sector in FCS. Against a backdrop of a challenging environment in FCS countries and weak capacity to implement reforms, Bank FPD projects have had poor performance. One-third of the 23 FPD projects in FCS that exited the portfolio between FY01 and FY12 were rated moderately satisfactory or better compared to 67 percent of projects in Never FCS. Among projects reviewed by IEG for the country case studies, project components related to reform and privatization of state-owned enterprises supported by the Bank have been complex and progressed slowly due to the need to address worker retrenchment issues, social liabilities, and resistance to reform. In other cases, conflict-related events or political developments weakened the government's commitment to privatization even after successful restructuring of state-owned banks.

IFC investments in FCS have low outcome ratings. Based on 26 ex-post evaluations of projects in FCS completed in 2001–2011, the development outcome ratings in FCS were modest (54 percent, or 14 out of 26 with mostly successful and better ratings), and somewhat lower than those in Never FCS (59 percent mostly successful). In both groups, project business performance was low, with less than half of evaluated projects reaching satisfactory financial benchmarks, driving lower development outcome ratings. IFC projects in FCS must meet a higher cost of capital benchmarks due to higher risk profiles of FCS. Ratings for environmental and social effects and PSD effects (which measure firm-level effects beyond the project itself) were equally high in both country groups.

IEG conducted additional analysis using IFC Development Outcome Tracking System (DOTS) ratings, a self-monitoring system, to test the findings from ex post evaluations (i.e., Expanded Project Supervision Reports) for the population of more recent investments in FCS. The review concluded that projects in FCS tend to perform less well than in Never FCS and have low project business success ratings, but the differences among the country groups are not statistically significant.[8]

IFC's Advisory Services in Always FCS perform at par with those in Never FCS. In Partial FCS, IFC has been more successful; 12 out of 19 projects, or 63 percent, were rated moderately satisfactory or higher. The performance of these projects was comparable to that of IFC's non-IDA Advisory Services. They also outperformed Never FCS projects, where 53 percent were rated moderately satisfactory or higher.

Too few MIGA guarantees have been evaluated to draw conclusions. Available results from four out of five projects indicate that MIGA-supported projects in telecommunications and mining had satisfactory development outcomes. Project reviews undertaken as part of the country case studies for this evaluation indicate that projects underwritten by the SIP, mainly in manufacturing, services, and agribusiness, have been relevant in targeting smaller size investments in FCS. However, the projects have struggled financially and operationally.

## Endnotes

[1] The HIPC Initiative provides special grant financing to write off previous debts in order to reduce the debt servicing burden for heavily indebted poor countries. Countries seeking HIPC debt relief have to meet special policy and reform conditions to reach the HIPC completion point before debt relief is awarded.

[2] Although the Corporate Scorecard reports the targets for percent IEG ratings satisfactory, in fact these ratings include all projects rated moderately satisfactory, satisfactory, or highly satisfactory on the six-point scale from highly unsatisfactory to highly satisfactory.

[3] Using a six-point scale, results are statistically significant at the 0.1 level (Prob > F = 0.0834), while running the same test with a binary scale for moderately satisfactory and higher or not, yields results that are significant at the 0.2 level (Prob > chi2 = 0.1533).

[4] During FY06–13, short-term finance accounted for 29 percent of IFC commitments in FCS compared with 44 percent in Never FCS. The portfolio analysis for IFC reflects long-term finance only.

[5] The time period reported for advisory services starts in FY05 because this product was rolled out at the corporate level in FY05. This analysis includes the Conflict Affected States in Africa Initiative but excludes other global and regional advisory projects, a few of which cover FCS.

[6] Of the 50 projects supported during FY06–12 under the Small Investment Program, 17 were in FCS.

[7] In all, MIGA paid claims under its war and civil disturbance coverage (including in FCS and non-FCSs) in four cases out of six claims paid since the inception of the agency in 1988.

[8] The DOTS analysis covered 107 projects committed between FY00 and FY09.

## Reference

IEG (Independent Evaluation Group). 2013. *Fragile States 2013: Resource Flows and Trends in a Shifting World.* Washington, DC: World Bank.

conflict    development    equitable social contract    access 2 opportunities    security
                           reconstruction               donor harmonization
                           reintegration                revenue mobilization
             infrastructure political settlement        transition
             civil society  reconciliation              political settlement    jobs
             human capital  statebuilding               country ownership
             local economic gender equity               transformation
fragility    institutional  inclusive growth            citizen voice
                            rule of law                  accountability

# 4 Bank Support for Building State Capacity

## CHAPTER HIGHLIGHTS

- There has been relatively good progress on public financial management in fragile and conflict-affected states.

- Efficiency of revenue mobilization has improved in FCS.

- The World Bank has made considerable effort, but there has been lack of traction on civil service reform.

- On decentralization, while some effort and results were recorded in the African Region, in other regions the Bank has had less success because of political obstacles to decentralization and its own reticence to engage with decentralization.

- While the Bank has supported different elements of state-building, it has not placed these efforts in a strategic long-term framework with appropriate and customized sequencing of its different elements.

- Public financial management should be seen as a starting point for a long-term, multipronged agenda of institution building.

Building state capacity in fragile and conflict-affected states (FCS) requires a particularly strong understanding of the contextual drivers of conflict and fragility. Understanding the criteria through which an effective, responsive, and accountable state can be supported must be the primary entry point for successful World Bank engagement in FCS. While there has been relatively good progress on public financial management (PFM) in FCS in the last 10 years, finding the right approach to the lack of capacity, weak infrastructure and services, and social tensions has been difficult. There are few examples where World Bank country strategies have successfully responded to these issues, effectively prioritized actions, and sequenced interventions to ensure the development of a sustainable state structure.

The challenge in building state capacity in FCS is large, and it needs to be sequenced and paced realistically. Priorities need to be based on the needs of governments, the needs of donors, the expectations of citizens, and the major political economy risks in the country. These demands encompass the range of ways the Bank supports institution building through PFM including public expenditure, procurement, revenue collection and management, civil service reform, and decentralization. These aspects are generally handled in the Bank by different units in an uncoordinated manner which has reduced the effectiveness of state-building. Making the right strategic choices and trade-offs where Bank efforts are to be directed requires a thorough understanding of the country's political economy and insight on the drivers of fragility.

## Investing in Building State Capacity

In all, 16 percent of Bank financing in FCS has been committed to building state capacity, PFM reforms for state-building being the actions of choice to reengage with FCS.[1] A review of the Bank's portfolio in FCS during FY01–12 reveals that the majority of projects had a component dealing with public expenditure management. Procurement, civil service reform, and revenue collection reforms and activities were found in 40 to 58 percent of operations approved in FCS, while very few addressed decentralization (Table 4.1).

The volume of Bank support to core public sector reforms in FCS has varied over time, budget support through development policy lending (DPLs) being the preferred instrument. While lending for FCS has been growing, the mix and sequencing of DPL and investment projects to support core public sector reforms have not been optimal. Bank financing in FCS came equally from DPLs and investment projects. In FCS, DPLs were primarily used to clear arrears to the International Bank for Reconstruction and Development or the International Development Association (IDA), and to provide budget support to the government after reengagement. But initial support during the reengagement period tapered off in some countries, and was not accompanied by timely technical support for weak governments.

TABLE 4.1 Presence of Reform Categories in Projects for Core Public Sector Activities (percentage of operations)

| Country Status | Expenditure Management | Revenue Mobilization | Procurement | Civil Service Reform | Decentralization |
|---|---|---|---|---|---|
| Always FCS | 98 | 42 | 53 | 51 | 11 |
| Partial FCS | 88 | 37 | 63 | 49 | 2 |
| Unweighted Average | 93 | 40 | 58 | 50 | 7 |

SOURCE: World Bank internal data.

For example, in the Democratic Republic of Congo, early reengagement consisted of supporting core public sector reforms through a series of DPLs (FY02–06) as well as reforms undertaken as part of the enhanced Heavily Indebted Poor Countries (HIPC) Initiative. However, a lack of accompanying technical assistance undermined progress toward reform. Subsequently, between 2008 and 2012, the PFM portfolio consisted of investment lending spread too widely across a mix of central and subnational programs that lacked the impetus provided by earlier budget support.

Expenditures on analytical and advisory activities (AAA), including technical assistance for building state capacity, were higher in FCS than in Never FCS, and there was a greater share of financing from trust funds and a larger volume of technical assistance provided in FCS. In the Always FCS group of countries, trust funds financed 38 percent of AAA.

## Public Expenditure Management

World Bank support to public expenditure management in FCS has been good, but progress has been uneven across countries and reform areas. Out of the nine countries examined in detail by the Independent Evaluation Group (IEG), two rounds of Public Expenditure and Accountability (PEFA) indicators were available for six of them. The ratings for these six countries increased from an unweighted average of 1.9 during the first PEFA round to 2.1 during the second round, on a four-point scale. Afghanistan,[2] the Democratic Republic of Congo, and the Solomon Islands showed the most improvement overall but from a lower base in the last two countries (Table 4.2). PEFA ratings for four or more indicators improved in these countries.

Among the case study countries, most improvement was in the accounting, recording, and reporting of the budget, followed by the comprehensiveness and transparency of budget execution. In the Solomon Islands, direct Bank support through targeted technical assistance and advice ensured the transparent reporting of budgets over the last three years. Likewise, in the case of Afghanistan, progress in public expenditure management was associated with strong support from the donor community through the recurrent cost window of the Afghanistan Reconstruction Trust Fund, which supported PFM reforms, among other things. While reporting and transparency have improved, the ratings for donor practices, the credibility of the budget, and external scrutiny have worsened over time. Without adequately responding to the unique expenditure management problems of the various FCS and balancing the range of budgetary needs, progress in this area remains incomplete.

Despite some progress on budget management, PFM needs to go beyond the initial emphasis on cash management, payroll, and record keeping if it is to adequately build a sustainable medium-term expenditure program and ensure independent external oversight and scrutiny. In Liberia, sensible transition planning and effective capacity building has illustrated how this can occur. From a situation of total breakdown of the government's fiduciary systems in 2006, the budget is now prepared on time and published annually. Recent budgets have been cast in a medium-term context, and public spending has grown from 11 percent of gross domestic product (GDP) to 30 percent in three years, with improved controls. But these reforms have taken time. PFM is a long-term agenda that requires sustained support of central and subnational reforms that support inclusive and equitable budget management and effective service delivery. In FCS countries, the Bank's support has been largely confined to supporting public financial management reform within ministries of finance with little support for line ministries and subnational entities. Thus, while Bank support has seen an improvement in the central budgets of FCS, this has not always resulted in the provision of citizen services. PFM, which is generally initially focused on the core ministries dealing with budget and finance, should be seen as a starting point for a long-term, multipronged agenda of institution building which includes strengthening the ministries responsible for service delivery, civil service reform, and decentralization. While the Bank has addressed each of these to some extent in many FCS, there has been a lack of coordination among the different units supporting these components, thus reducing its effectiveness.

The Bank has increased its attention to the security sector in Public Expenditure Reviews and PFM analyses. In Afghanistan the work on the Economics of Transition was an important input into donor conferences in 2012 and informed the government-donor discussions on the sustainability of security sectors and development investments after 2014 when responsibility for security will be handed over by the international coalition to the Afghan government. Public

TABLE 4.2 Public Expenditure and Financial Accountability Ratings for Country Case Studies

| Public Financial Management Performance Indicator | Overall Rating | | | | | | | | | | | |
|---|---|---|---|---|---|---|---|---|---|---|---|---|
| | Afghanistan | | Congo, Dem. Rep. | | Liberia | | Sierra Leone | | Solomon Islands | | Timor-Leste | |
| | 2005 | 2008 | 2008 | 2012 | 2007 | 2012 | 2007 | 2010 | 2008 | 2012 | 2007 | 2010 |
| Credibility of the budget | 2.5 | 1.9 | 1.8 | 1.8 | 2.4 | 1.6 | 2.7 | 2.1 | 2.0 | 2.2 | 2.0 | 2.1 |
| Comprehensiveness and Transparency | 1.8 | 2.3 | 1.8 | 2.6 | 1.7 | 1.9 | 2.8 | 3.1 | 1.8 | 2.7 | 2.8 | 2.5 |
| Policy-based Budgeting | 1.8 | 3.0 | 1.3 | 2.3 | 2.3 | 2.8 | 2.0 | 1.8 | 1.5 | 2.5 | 3.3 | 2.0 |
| Predictability and Control in Budget Execution | 1.9 | 2.5 | 1.3 | 2.3 | 1.9 | 2.2 | 2.1 | 2.3 | 1.4 | 2.1 | 2.0 | 1.9 |
| Accounting, Recording, and Reporting | 1.9 | 2.5 | 2.0 | 2.8 | 1.3 | 1.5 | 2.5 | 3.3 | 1.6 | 2.3 | 1.8 | 2.3 |
| External Scrutiny and Audit | 1.3 | 2.7 | 1.5 | 1.7 | 1.8 | 1.7 | 1.8 | 2.0 | 2.2 | 1.3 | 1.8 | 2.2 |
| Donor Practices | 2.2 | 1.0 | 1.3 | 1.0 | 1.0 | 1.2 | 1.7 | 1.2 | 1.3 | 1.5 | 1.2 | 1.3 |
| Unweighted Average | 1.9 | 2.3 | 1.6 | 2.1 | 1.8 | 1.8 | 2.2 | 2.3 | 1.7 | 2.1 | 2.1 | 2.0 |

SOURCE: World Bank data.

expenditure analysis of the security sector has also been carried out in the Central African Republic in 2009, Liberia in 2012, and Mali and Niger in FY13. Development partners view this contribution to the work on the security sector, often carried out in partnership with United Nations (UN) agencies, as valuable, drawing on the comparative advantage of skills more prevalent in the Bank than elsewhere.

## Procurement

Procurement issues in Bank operations within FCS continue to face challenges (Box 4.1), despite attempts to provide technical capacity in this area.[3] There are at least two facets to procurement in FCS. First, there are issues with how the donors get things done. Second, there is the approach to strengthening recipient government systems and building internal capacity in the longer term. The Bank's solution to the first of these issues was to establish Program Implementation Units (PIUs) and to use long-term advisers (Afghanistan, Liberia, Sierra Leone, and Timor-Leste) to bolster government systems and ensure the efficient utilization of project funds. While this was helpful in the short term in getting things done, it worked as a disincentive for the second issue regarding the reform of government procurement systems. In Afghanistan and Timor-Leste, the result of this approach was growing resentment among government officials about wage disparities. Similarly, in Sierra Leone there are currently 295 ongoing donor-funded projects using PIUs for implementation that hire qualified personnel away from the civil service, thereby causing significant constraints in the provision of government services. Bank interventions have not focused sufficiently on strengthening the procurement systems of governments and using them for the delivery of IDA investments.

The lack of procurement capacity, integrity, and transparency remains a key concern in FCS. Where these issues are addressed with long-term programs, countries develop strategies to deal with the transition from a fragile state to a functioning one. This is illustrated in the progress made recently in the Democratic Republic of Congo where the 2012 PEFA found major improvements in procurement between 2008 and 2012. The improvement came from sustained Bank support to the legal and regulatory system promoting competition and transparency, the creation of an independent institution to handle procurement complaints, the use of a transparent bidding methods, and easy public access to information related to procurement. There are still serious issues with procurement controls in the Democratic Republic of Congo, but the investment in government systems has seen greater confidence in line ministries and their ability to deliver projects through their budgets. In Afghanistan a central procurement policy unit was created and is functioning, and a public procurement law and the public financial and expenditure management law were approved to deal with the transition of projects into government budgets. While there are still serious weaknesses in ministry spending of funds and in the limited ability of the market to furnish bids, the process allows most ministries to prepare procurement plans and to illustrate budgetary responsibility. This support to working through and supporting government systems is necessary if FCS countries are to transition out of their fragile status.

The overall message from a forthcoming IEG evaluation of procurement in Bank operations is that the greatest constraint in FCS is not Bank procurement policies, which include provisions for flexibility, but rather capacity constraints in their implementation. The evaluation found that:

- Two-thirds of the 25 CASs reviewed in FCS identified procurement problems that limit development effectiveness; half of the CASs identified lack of procurement capacity; and 40 percent identified weak public administration systems and problems with integrity and transparency in procurement.

- A survey of procurement issues administered to 15 procurement specialists and hub coordinators also identified country procurement capacity as the most limiting factor in FCS. Other issues included low private sector capacity, lack of technical expertise, and difficulty in attracting procurement specialists to relocate to FCS. Risk aversion is reported to be more prevalent among junior staff who lack incentives and hesitate to make difficult judgments.

However, the majority of Bank staff surveyed for the FCS evaluation felt that procurement procedures were not well adapted to FCS (see appendix H). Only one-third of Bank staff working on FCS felt that procurement procedures are adapted to a large or moderate extent to the low-capacity and high-risk environments prevalent in FCS.

SOURCE: World Bank 2014; IEG FCS staff survey, 2013.

## Revenue Collection and Management

Overall, the performance on the efficiency of revenue mobilizationin FCS has been good. Tax revenues in FCS countries have increased during the review period.

During the period FY00–12, tax revenue as a percentage of GDP improved in seven of the nine case study countries (Table 4.3). On average, about 35 percent of World Bank supported PFM operations had activities related to revenue collection.

In the Democratic Republic of Congo, revenue mobilization increased dramatically from 7.7 percent in FY03 to 20.3 percent of GDP in FY08 mainly due to the significant growth in revenues coming from the mining sector. Likewise, in Liberia and Timor-Leste, there has been significant growth fueled by returns on extractives and supported by better revenue management due partly to Bank programs. However, in the Democratic Republic of Congo

TABLE 4.3 Tax Revenue as Percentage of GDP

| FCS Case Study Country | 2002 | 2005 | 2008 | 2011 |
|---|---|---|---|---|
| Afghanistan | 3 | 7 | 8 | 11 |
| Cameroon | — | 17 | 18 | 18 |
| Congo, Dem. Rep. | 8 | 15 | 19 | 27 |
| Liberia | 13 | 15 | 21 | 24 |
| Nepal | 11 | 12 | 12 | 15 |
| Sierra Leone | 9 | 9 | 9 | 12 |
| Solomon Islands | — | 21 | 28 | 33 |
| Timor-Leste[a] | 14 | 69 | 81 | 78 |
| Yemen, Rep.[b] | 34 | 35 | 37 | 26 |

SOURCE: World Bank data.
NOTE: — = not available. a. Includes grants. b. Includes oil revenues.

the level of government revenue is far from reaching the country's potential, as revenue leakages remain high due to governance and corruption issues. The amount of total taxes, fees, and royalties collected from the 500 extractive companies holding exploration or production licenses in the Democratic Republic of Congo is reported to be $876 million, representing 5 percent of GDP, or just $13 per capita (EITI 2013a). The Bank has estimated that the government collects less than 20 percent of the mining royalties to which it is entitled (World Bank 2008a). The story is similar in the Solomon Islands where revenue gains have been impressive, but significant taxes (around 30 percent of total logging revenues) continue to be lost in the commercial timber sector due to corruption (World Bank 2008b). Thus, the Bank needs to balance its support with a strong understanding of the political economy of revenue streams. Knowing how the politics of resource rents operates is central to finding the most effective way of equitably collecting revenues and sharing returns among citizens.

Revenue from high value natural resources accounts for a significant share of total public revenues in IDA FCS, ranging from 98.2 percent in Timor-Leste to 68 percent in Republic of Yemen and 57 percent in Cameroon. This includes revenues from oil, gas and mining as well as high-value timber.

Overall, the World Bank has been effective in strengthening the regulatory framework in natural resource sectors but less effective in assisting its clients in FCS to accurately value and negotiate resource contracts. Recognizing that mismanagement of mineral resources had contributed to conflict in several FCS countries, the Bank Group focused its support on reforming the regulatory framework in the mining sector. The Bank provided assistance to FCS countries in reviewing and reformulating mining and forest codes and laws, and helped to put in place regulations that have attracted critically needed foreign investment in the mining, minerals, and commercial timber sectors. But to date, this assistance has had little effect in assisting FCS to accurately value, negotiate, and award resource contracts (Table 4.4). In Sierra Leone, for example, while Bank support for a new Mining Policy (2003) helped to restart its large-scale mining operations, its profitability has been undermined by the government awarding different fiscal terms to individual mining companies (NACE 2009). In the Democratic Republic of Congo, despite good practice standards set by the mining law supported by the Bank, exploration and extraction rights are commonly allocated on a discretionary basis without a bidding process (Barma et al. 2012, Chevallier and Kaiser 2010). The result has been notable gains in legislative reform not supported by behavioral change in the sector.

Revenue management of extractive industries is difficult, and progress is slow. While the sector has the potential to contribute positively to development if revenues are soundly managed and invested toward inclusive growth they also increase the risk of conflict and fragility. The Bank has provided technical assistance and analytical advice for better revenue management and benefit sharing with varying results across FCS. Of the 33 countries on the FCS list, only two—Angola and Timor-Leste—have set up a sovereign wealth fund to manage their resources. The Bank's support for Timor-Leste's Sovereign Wealth Fund offers lessons on the challenge of balancing saving with spending when poverty remains endemic.

Monitoring and transparent reporting can support more robust revenue valuation, collection, and management of extractives, however, FCS countries fare worse on average than non-FCS with regard to compliance with the standards set by the Extractive Industries Transparency Initiative (EITI [2013b]). The Bank has helped to harness donor resources to develop and broaden the EITI process through the multi-donor trust fund (MDTF) for EITI, and partly as a result, contract and revenue transparency increased in FCS. Sixteen of the 37 countries registered with EITI are FCS. However, only two of these are compliant with EITI

TABLE 4.4 Effectiveness of World Bank Support for FCS Countries along the NRM Value Chain

| High-Value NRM Dependent FCS | Sector Organization/Contract Awards | Regulation and Monitoring of Operations | Collection of Taxes and Royalties | Revenue Management and Distribution | Sound and Sustainable Policies | Natural Resource Sectors Supported by World Bank |
|---|---|---|---|---|---|---|
| Afghanistan | High | Substantial | Substantial | Modest | Substantial | Mining |
| Cameroon | High | Substantial | Substantial | Modest | Negligible | Forests |
| Congo, Dem. Rep. | Modest | Negligible | Negligible | Negligible | Negligible | Mining, forests |
| Liberia | Substantial | Substantial | Modest | Negligible | Modest | Forests |
| Sierra Leone | Substantial | Modest | Modest | Modest | Modest | Mining |
| Solomon Islands | Modest | Negligible | Negligible | Modest | Negligible | Forests, more recently mining |
| Timor-Leste | High | High | High | Substantial | Modest | Oil |
| Yemen, Rep. | Substantial | Modest | Substantial | Modest | Negligible | Oil, gas |

SOURCE: IEG 2013a.
NOTE: Performance is assessed against a score of high, substantial, modest, and negligible. NRM = natural resource management.

standards (Timor-Leste and Liberia) out of the 21 compliant countries. In addition, four of the six countries that have been suspended from EITI are FCS (Central African Republic, the Democratic Republic of Congo, Sierra Leone, and Yemen). This suggests that governance standards are only one aspect of an effective management system, and greater Bank focus on the other elements of the revenue chain is required if the FCS are to improve their management of extractive resources. To date, the Bank has managed to establish useful benchmarks for the sector, but has not fully internalized and addressed the political economy interests of the sector to ensure effective management of shared resources in the FCS.

In countries where conflict was fueled by a failure to share the benefits of resource revenues, the attitude and perceptions of mining-affected communities are critical to achieving sustained peace and stability. In Sierra Leone, the mining law stipulates that community development agreements should be signed between companies and communities prior to operations, and that these should be financed with no less than 0.1 percent of gross revenues. A field mission to the mining areas in Tonkolili District, Sierra Leone, revealed that the government has little capacity to effectively oversee the engagement between mining companies and communities, and that communities face an asymmetry of information when it comes to negotiations over land, resettlement, and their rights provided under the mining law. Given the significance of these issues, the Bank would benefit from more actively engaging with the nature of resource deals and the facilitation of more equitable allocation of benefits.

## Civil Service Reform

The World Bank has made considerable effort but there has been a lack of traction on civil service reform (Table 4.5). These reforms are not easy; political economy interests and bureaucratic inertia tend to weaken client ownership. Autocratic governments may be unwilling to share power or reluctant to accept accountability mechanisms. In many cases, the Bank (and other donors) filled the capacity gap by hiring long-term externally-funded advisers, often at very high cost, to perform basic functions of the civil service. While this approach was necessary in the short-run, continued reliance on such advisers for prolonged periods has actually hampered the development of the civil service. What has been missing in the Bank's work on civil service reform is an understanding of the most critical gaps and a strategy and long-term approach to addressing them. With no outline for change, it is hard to see how technical solutions to these difficult reforms can succeed.

In Afghanistan, finding the right balance to reform has been a challenge. PIUs managed projects in the Ministry of Finance and in line ministries in recent years in an effort to restart the systems of government. While this structure helped with disbursements, it also crowded out the development of internal capacity. Civil service reforms were developed to address the transition process. These included recommendations on the basic size and structure for the civil service and the numbers of staff needed across ministries and agencies; the determination of an affordable pay scale for civil servants, including pensions and the launch of a rules-based civil service charter. A database is now maintained for 669,000 registered government employees, which is the basis for setting up payroll applications in 70 locations in Kabul and nine provinces. Payroll management has improved through direct deposits of salary payments to the bank accounts of 450,000 government employees through the verified payment program as of December 2011, and there are plans to increase this to 520,000 by 2014. However, most of these gains have relied on a "second civil service" of professionals paid on a significantly higher scale to manage these complex arrangements (IEG 2012a).

TABLE 4.5 Civil Service Reforms in FCS Countries (FY01–12)

| FCS Case Study Countries | Civil Service Substitution | | Managing the Size and Structure of the Public Workforce | Performance Management of Public Employees Through Pay and Recruitment Reform | World Bank Contribution |
|---|---|---|---|---|---|
| | Reliance on Long-Term Advisers | Reliance on Project Implementation Units | | | |
| Afghanistan | High | High | Substantial | Substantial | Substantial |
| Cameroon | Negligible | Modest | Negligible | Negligible | Negligible |
| Congo, Dem. Rep. | Negligible | High | Modest | Negligible | Modest |
| Liberia | High | High | Substantial | Substantial | Substantial |
| Nepal | Negligible | Modest | Negligible | Negligible | Negligible |
| Sierra Leone | High | High | Substantial | Substantial | Substantial |
| Solomon Islands | Substantial | Negligible | Modest | Substantial | Negligible |
| Timor-Leste | High | High | Modest | Modest | Negligible |
| Yemen, Rep. | Negligible | High | Negligible | Negligible | Negligible |

NOTE: The countries listed include the six FCS case study countries and the three FCS with country program evaluations undertaken in FY11–12. Negligible = reforms were insignificant; modest = few reforms; substantial = some reforms; high = advanced reforms.

The gains are important to establishing a workable civil service, but there is some debate as to whether the reforms are the right ones in Afghanistan at this stage of its development. The 2012 Afghanistan Country Program Evaluation recommended the development of a transition plan toward a more sustainable civil service.

In Liberia, the civil service reform strategy has been more successful. There the Bank has worked with the government to complete and implement a restructuring program in nine ministries and in the Civil Service Agency. This has reduced the number of employees and ghost workers from 45,000 to 34,000 in four years, and the linking of biometric identification to the human resource information system is ongoing to further systematize a sustainable approach (IEG 2012b). These long-term commitments and innovative approaches are necessary if the fragility constraints of FCS are to be overcome with effective mechanisms.

In contrast, the reliance on long-term advisers in the civil service has limited sustainability. In Sierra Leone, the civil service reform program did little to curb the high level of remuneration of most long-term advisers (estimated at around 200, of which about 60 are in the Ministry of Finance). Besides the financial burden of their high salaries (reported to be $5,000–$10,000 per month plus significant benefits), their presence is a continuing source of friction with other civil servants. Although the government recently decided to fund these advisers from its budget—something it can currently afford to do because of the windfall from mineral revenues—this is not a sustainable approach in the long-term. It also does not ameliorate the inevitable friction with the regular civil servants. For projects, the Bank (and other donors) continues to rely on PIUs that are outside the normal civil service, and while reform programs are put in place, they do little to address the capacity constraints that drive the need for additional or alternative human resources.

Institutional development in line ministries could have been more effective with budget support rather than through launching multiple discreet project efforts relying on PIUs. For example, while the initial plan for public sector management in Sierra Leone was conceptualized well around the three-pronged approach of PFM, civil service reform, and decentralization, the Bank has inexplicably moved the funding of decentralization to the Decentralized Service Delivery Program under social protection. This weakened the attention to important aspects of local government capacity building, PFM for local governments, and longer-term policies for the fiscal relationship between the center and local governments. Understanding how these components relate is an essential part of finding a reform model that will last, and Bank country strategies need to be better at identifying these links.

In the Democratic Republic of Congo, the Bank has also struggled to overcome the challenge of undertaking civil service reform while using PIUs for Bank projects. The PIUs have attracted the best civil servants, undermining public sector capacity. With the exception of some progress in implementing mandatory retirement of average workers in two pilot public organizations, there has been little progress. Even relatively basic reforms, such as a civil service census, have not been completed. Key challenges have been the inability for the country to mobilize the resources needed to retire overage civil servants and to find appropriate new recruitments. Political commitment to the retirement program remains unclear, and while the Bank remains engaged in civil service reform through further lending and AAA, there is little optimism as to where gains are likely to be made. In these environments, the Bank needs to be much clearer in tracking what works, what doesn't, and where to expend its efforts.

A clear message for all FCS countries is that the short-term expedient approaches to "buy capacity" must be taken with a coordinated and clear exit strategy, which does not exist so far in any FCS country.

## Decentralization

Decentralization is widely recognized as an important means to improve service delivery and enhance citizen accountability, but the Bank's strategy toward decentralization in FCS remains ambiguous. In FCS, where government responsiveness to citizens has been relatively weak, finding the right modality for reaching people with services is vital to avoiding further fragility and conflict. Decentralization is an important element to this approach. While some effort and

TABLE 4.6 Decentralization Reforms in FCS Countries (FY01–12)

| FCS Country Case Studies | Administrative Decentralization | Fiscal Decentralization | Decentralization of Services Delivery | Bank's Contribution |
|---|---|---|---|---|
| Afghanistan | Modest | Negligible | Substantial | Substantial |
| Cameroon | Modest | Negligible | Substantial | Modest |
| Congo, Dem. Rep. | Modest | Modest | Negligible | Modest |
| Liberia | Modest | Modest | Negligible | Negligible |
| Nepal | Negligible | Substantial | Substantial | Modest |
| Sierra Leone | High | High | High | Substantial |
| Solomon Islands | Negligible | Negligible | Modest | Negligible |
| Timor-Leste | Modest | Negligible | Modest | Negligible |
| Yemen, Rep. | Negligible | Negligible | Negligible | Negligible |

NOTE: The countries listed include the six FCS case study countries and the three FCS with country program evaluations undertaken in FY11–12. Negligible = reforms were insignificant; modest = few reforms; substantial = some reforms; high = advanced reforms.

results were recorded in the African Region, in other regions the Bank has had less success because of political obstacles to decentralization (Table 4.6).

Sierra Leone has made more progress on decentralization than other FCS with an innovative approach to legitimizing local government. Elected local councils were restored with the passage of the Local Government Act in 2004. The Act set out a schedule for the phased devolution of key services between 2004 and 2008. To date, eight ministries have decentralized their functions to the local level, with a corresponding transfer of budgets, and local councils are charged with the responsibility of planning and implementing these budgets (World Bank 2012). Bank support to local government has been provided through technical assistance for training and capacity building for local governments, fiscal transfers to local governments, and funding of local governments directly that emphasize a community-based participatory approach. However, after a promising start that envisaged decentralization as a part of the broader state-building agenda, largely due to internal Bank organizational issues, the Bank shifted its focus as additional objectives such as participatory planning and social protection were added to local governance and decentralized service delivery, thereby increasing design and coordination complexities.

The Sierra Leone experience offers several lessons: the importance of fiscal decentralization as the driving force of decentralization; the importance of sequencing interventions to generate early results and to continuously expand the constituency for reform; the power of transparency, participation, and internal checks and balance; the limitations of technical interventions if political will is lacking; and the need for a multipronged approach coordinated across the Bank's different organizational units.

In Cameroon, outreach to subnational entities was effective although fiscal decentralization and budget transfers to local government levels have lagged behind. While fiscal decentralization continues to be a legal priority for the government, Cameroon lacks an effective strategy and an operational plan for decentralization. Even with improvements in the country's legal and regulatory framework for decentralization, including the 2009 promulgation of law on local taxes and financial regime of municipalities and regions, implementation has been slow. Some line ministries appear to regard decentralization as a threat to their control over resources and influence. Bank support for local government was made through decentralized community development plans and service delivery. The participatory development program improved access to education, health facilities, domestic water supplies, and road access to markets and social services, but the integration of the various components has not led to an established system.

In the Democratic Republic of Congo, decentralization has become a political imperative to safeguard national unity and address the insurgency. The 2006 Constitution transferred competencies and responsibilities previously assumed by the central government to governors in provinces and new officials in the Decentralized Territorial Entities. The intention to reorganize the current 11 provinces into 26 administrative territorial entities by 2010 has been put on hold because of the lack of adequate infrastructure in the new administrative centers. To enable the functioning of provinces and Decentralized Territorial Entities, the Constitution provides that 40 percent of the revenue generated by the provinces will be allocated to them, and 10 percent of that revenue will be allocated to the Equalization Fund for funding national investments. In turn, the provinces are required to transfer to Decentralized Territorial Entities 40 percent of the resources allocated to them by the central government. Implementation of this framework is proceeding despite difficulties and transitory arrangements, but results are still limited. Bank support has been in the form of two investment lending operations and AAA, which have madesome progress in increasing the share of national revenue transferred from the central government from 11 to 31.5 percent for four provinces during 2008–2011.

In Afghanistan and Nepal, the Bank does not yet have a clear approach to decentralization. Provincial councils in Afghanistan were elected in 2005 and 2009, but with limited and unclear functions. They are still seeking effective roles in securing provincial development, while district and village councils have not yet been established. Bank support has focused on subnational public administration where payroll systems have improved, but other PFM standards for deconcentrated units at the subnational level are very weak and bottom-up accountability is happening too slowly. Some bilateral donors are assisting the provinces where they are working to strengthen local government facilities, but these efforts are not consistent and only cover a handful of provinces (IEG 2012a). In Nepal, despite professed intentions to support the local government dialogue, the Bank opted not to participate with eight bilateral donors and several UN agencies in a collaborative effort by development partners to support the country's Local Governance and Community Development Program because of what the Bank considered to be inadequate political consensus on decentralization and concerns about capacity of interim local government arrangements in the absence of elected local government. In the absence of a stable political system, the civil service is managing budgets and services both at the central and local government levels and are the main interlocutors of the Bank and other development partners in most sectors, except in administering local government funds. Other development partners have made a deliberate choice to invest in building local government capacity while the Bank has chosen to abstain from this partnership. In both Afghanistan and Nepal, the structure of decentralization is under discussion within the government, and the Bank appears to be more reticent than other development partners to engage more systematically in this domain.

Decentralization, like PFM, civil service reform, and capacity building of service delivery ministries, should be seen as just one part of the overall effort of state-building. None of the elements in themselves is the solution. What the Bank needs is, consistent with the 2011 WDR recommendation, a longer-term strategy spanning over many years with careful sequencing of individual elements over time, and with cross-sectoral coordination. The relative priorities and sequencing of individual components needs to be customized based on country circumstances and opportunities. This is line with one of the main recommendations of the IEG review of low-income countries under stress (IEG 2006).

## Conclusions

State-building requires the design of a strategic and comprehensive approach to establish an effective, responsive, and accountable state. In order to accelerate the state-building agenda, greater emphasis is needed on understanding the contextual realities and fragility drivers of FCS. These countries generally suffer from a lack of capacity, weak infrastructure and services, and social tensions that prevent public sector reforms from taking root. In order to progress, the Bank needs to utilize multiple instruments—including analytical work to understand the FCS context and sector needs and a mix of sustained budget support and investment projects with complementary technical assistance—to better support state-building. State capacity building requires careful sequencing, better use of political economy analysis, and careful prioritizing of long-term reforms. The case studies found evidence of relevant Bank programs in some areas in some countries, but there are few examples where a measured and informed country strategy has built a sustained state-building model over time which meets the expectations of their citizens.

---

### Endnotes

[1] The remaining funds were divided among the other two themes, with 38 percent for building capacity of citizens and 46 percent for promoting inclusive growth and jobs.

[2] Performance in Afghanistan was reflected by the following achievements: 18 PEFA process indicators improved from 2005 to 2007; the Open Budget Index Score improved from 8 percent to 21 percent from 2008 to 2010; the Afghanistan Financial Management Information System now connects to all 54 line ministries and agencies and all 34 provinces; central government financial statements are published each month within 25 days of month's end; and audited annual appropriations statements are submitted to Parliament within six months of fiscal year end.

[3] Some of the findings on procurement are from a parallel IEG evaluation of the Bank's procurement work in client countries.

# References

Barma, Naazneen, Kai Kaiser, Tuan Minh Le, and Lorena Vinuela. 2012. *Rents to Riches? The Political Economy of Natural Resource-Led Development.* Washington, DC: World Bank.

Chevallier, Jérôme, and Kai Kaiser. 2010. "The Political Economy of Mining in the Democratic Republic of Congo (DRC)." Unpublished manuscript, World Bank, Washington, DC.

EITI (Extractive Industries Transparency Initiative). 2013a. *République Démocratique du Congo Report 2010.* Kinshasa: Democratic Republic of Congo. http://eiti.org/report/democratic-republic-congo/2010

____. 2013b. *Progress Report 2013: Beyond Transparency.* Oslo: EITI International Secretariat.

IEG (Independent Evaluation Group). 2006. *Engaging with Fragile States: An IEG Review of World Bank Support to Low-Income Countries Under Stress.* Washington, DC: World Bank.

____. 2012a. *Afghanistan Country Program Evaluation, 2002–11.* Washington, DC: World Bank.

____. 2012b. *Liberia Country Program Evaluation, 2003–2011.* Washington, DC: World Bank.

____. 2013. *Fragile States 2013: Resource Flows and Trends in a Shifting World.* Washington, DC: World Bank.

NACE (National Advocacy Coalition on Extractives). 2009. *Sierra Leone at the Crossroads: Seizing the Chance to Benefit from Mining.* Freetown, Sierra Leone: NACE.

World Bank. 2008a. *Democratic Republic of Congo: Growth with Governance in the Mining Sector.* Washington, DC: World Bank.

____. 2008b. *Solomon Islands Sources of Growth.* Washington, DC: World Bank.

____. 2012. *Public Financial Management Reforms in Post-Conflict Countries: Synthesis Report.* Washington, DC: World Bank.

____. 2014. *The World Bank and Public Procurement: An Independent Evaluation.* 2 vols. Washington, DC: World Bank.

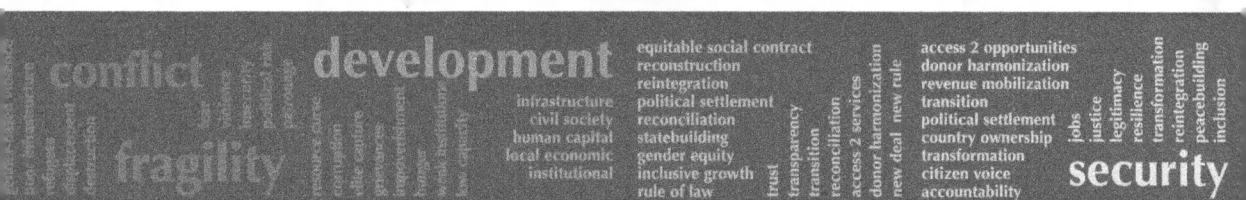

conflict development equitable social contract reconstruction reintegration infrastructure political settlement civil society reconciliation human capital statebuilding local economic gender equity institutional inclusive growth rule of law

trust transparency transition reconciliation access 2 services donor harmonization new deal new rule

access 2 opportunities donor harmonization revenue mobilization transition political settlement country ownership transformation citizen voice accountability

jobs justice legitimacy resilience transformation reintegration peacebuilding inclusion

fragility security

# 5 Bank Support for Building Capacity of Citizens

## CHAPTER HIGHLIGHTS

- The 2011 World Development Report had expressed concern that none of the fragile and conflict-affected states were likely to achieve any of the Millennium Development Goals. Progress improved by 2013, and the average Always FCS is likely to achieve more than one MDG target, although the FCS group continues to lag behind other IDA countries.

- During FY07–12, World Bank support for the education and health sector increased more rapidly than in non-FCS countries.

- While the governments in FCS countries, with considerable donor support, have clearly played an important role in service delivery, in some countries their capacity has been supplemented by service providers from the private and nonprofit sector.

- Health projects were more likely than education projects to use innovative implementation arrangements through hiring nongovernmental organizations as well as performance-based contracting.

- Community-driven development programs have grown much faster in FCS than in non-FCS and have been effective in providing essential short-term development assistance to local communities to finance public goods and services.

- Community-driven development programs have not evolved over time and lack plans for institutional sustainability.

- The Bank has little to show in FCS on the 2011 World Development Report's priority of enhancing work on justice.

Poverty reduction and shared prosperity among citizens are the strategic goals of the World Bank Group and the raison d'etre of its engagement in reconstruction and development. Countries that are fragile and conflict-affected typically suffer from some or all of the following traits: absence of political settlement, regional inequality, social exclusion, weak administrative capacity, risk of corruption and elite capture, absence of the rule of law, and lack of accountability of citizens. Each of these traits affects citizens adversely trapping them in vicious cycles of fragility, conflict, and violence and undermining their capabilities to demonstrate resilience in response to these crises. For that reason, assistance for human and social development is an absolutely critical dimension of Bank Group support to fragile and conflict-affected states (FCS).

This chapter focuses on Bank efforts to support human and social development and address security and justice in the FCS. In the human development sectors, the evaluation focused primarily on the health, nutrition and population (henceforth called "health") and education sectors, which are essential to the Millennium Development Goals (MDGs). IFC's role in supporting health and education among the FCS has been small and is subsumed within the discussion on private sector development in the next chapter. Within the FCS, a substantial portion of the social protection portfolio consists of social funds public works programs. These are subsumed under the broad umbrella of community-driven development (CDD) which constitutes the second domain of Bank engagement discussed in this chapter. The final portion of this chapter discusses Bank support for justice activities.

Two questions of particular interest are: How relevant and responsive were the interventions to the particular challenges and conditions of FCS, and what results have been achieved?

## Bank Support for Human Capital Development

In the FCS, security considerations are paramount but thereafter education and health services are high among the priority demands of citizens, even though gains from human capital investments materialize more slowly than returns from jobs. In countries with weak capacity, weak resource mobilization, and weak infrastructure, delivering health and education services is a major challenge. In that context, it is noteworthy that most FCS are likely to achieve at least one MDG target, with progress on the health and education indicators being somewhat better than on meeting the poverty target within the FCS.

During FY07–12, World Bank support for the education and health sector increased more rapidly than in non-FCS countries, both by number of projects and commitment value. Bank lending commitments to the education sector doubled to $1.4 billion in FY07–12 compared to the previous six-year interval, while commitments to the health sector were maintained at $0.9 billion during the same period. Between the two time intervals, the combined commitment volume for health and education grew by 50 percent in FCS compared to 30 percent in the Never FCS.

The performance of the FY01–12 portfolio for the health and education sectors was reviewed and found on average to be better in the second half of this time period. IEG outcome ratings (moderately satisfactory or better) for the combined health and education portfolios were compared with outcome ratings for projects from all sectors that exited the portfolio during the periods FY01–06 and FY07–12 in the FCS relative to countries that were Never FCS. Projects from all sectors in the Never FCS performed better than those in FCS during the first time period, both by number and commitment value. During FY07–12, the outcome ratings for all sectors is similar between the FCS and Never FCS groups by number of projects, but by commitment volume the FCS perform better than Never FCS. Similarly, the combined health and education portfolio performs better by commitment volume during FY07–12 in FCS than in the Never FCS (Figure 5.1). As a percentage of projects the FCS lag behind the Never FCS group during FY07–12 because of the inconsistency in ratings by number of projects and commitment volume in the Partial FCS country group.

At the sector level, performance trends in FY07–12 have changed compared to the previous six years. Among the FCS, outcome ratings for the education sector decreased from 74 percent moderately satisfactory or better to 61 percent in FY07–12, while outcome ratings for health increased from 55 percent to 69 percent in FY07–12. While there is insufficient detailed evidence to explain the difference in outcomes between the two time periods, evidence from the case study countries, supplemented by a desk review of health and education projects,[1] points to two factors identified in the later time period that contribute to the variance in performance of these two sectors. Health projects in Always FCS were more likely to use innovative implementation arrangements and also tended to have better monitoring and evaluation of outcomes. Interestingly, the desk review found that project documents for the education sector discussed fragility and conflict drivers more than health sector documents did, and conflict analysis was far more prevalent among projects in the Always FCS than in the Partial FCS, even in countries where the evaluation found significant societal fragility.

A more extensive desk review of project documentation was undertaken for the 45 projects in FCS on the health and education sectors which were approved in FY06 or later and which had already closed. Project documentation included project appraisal documents,

FIGURE 5.1 Performance of Health and Education Portfolios for Always and Partial FCS, Never FCS, and All IDA Countries by Exit Fiscal Year

A. PERCENTAGE OF PROJECTS RATED MS+ BY IEG: ALL SECTORS

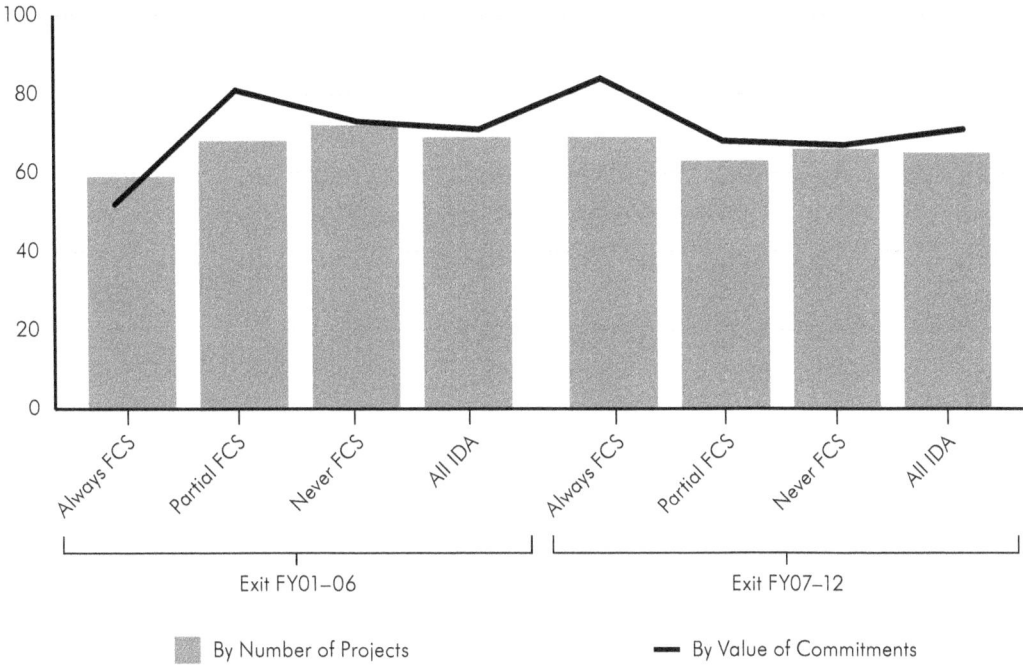

By Number of Projects          By Value of Commitments

B. PERCENTAGE OF PROJECTS RATED MS+ BY IEG: HEALTH AND EDUCATION

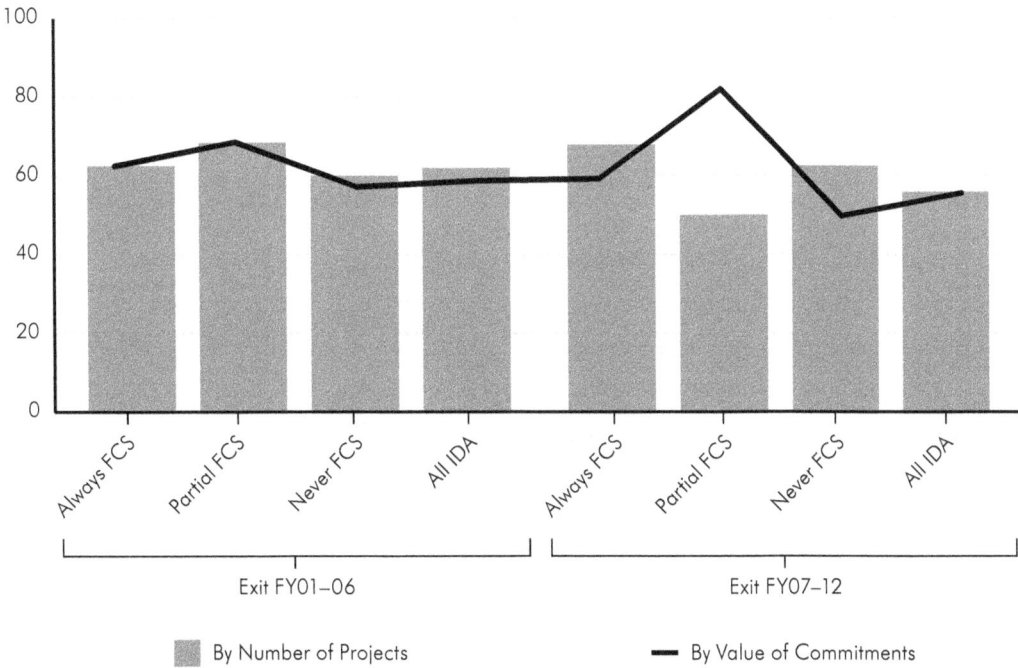

By Number of Projects          By Value of Commitments

NOTE: All = all projects in IDA countries; FCS = Always + Partial FCS IDA countries; ICRR = Implementation Completion and Results Report; IEG = Independent Evaluation Group; MS+ = moderately satisfactory or better; Never = non-FCS IDA countries.

project papers, technical annexes (for some grants), implementation completion reports, IEG implementation completion report reviews, and implementation status reviews. The analysis was limited by availability of project documentation. Of the projects reviewed, 12 were trust-funded projects for which usually less documentation is available. More specific findings from the review are:

- **Partnerships.** More than half of the projects reflected work being done by development partners and one-third either had extensive linkages between Bank work and that of other development partners or were cofinanced by other partners.

- **Adjustments for low capacity.** Nearly one-fourth made adjustments in design, such as simplification of project design, to accommodate for low capacity, and two-thirds included capacity building as a project component, but very few had included mechanisms to obtain user feedback.

- **Drivers of fragility.** Projects in Always FCS were more likely than those in Partial FCS to include a discussion of drivers of fragility. Health projects were more likely to report drivers of fragility and conflict as compounding factors which contributed to the need for intervention. For example, three projects that addressed HIV/AIDS indicated that war or complex emergency states were likely to lead to increased prevalence of the disease. On the other hand, education projects were more likely to cite the project as addressing a driver or drivers of fragility or conflict on the presumption that building human capital would lead to economic growth and poverty reduction, thereby mitigating social risk.

- **Mitigating conflict and fragility risks.** A few projects in Côte d'Ivoire, Haiti, and Nepal included measures to mitigate conflict risks, such as by ensuring a balanced distribution of beneficiaries.

- **Implementation arrangements to overcome low capacity.** Alternative service delivery methods were used by health projects in several countries to overcome low capacity in the public sector for project implementation in Always FCS. These innovations included using nongovernmental organizations for multiple components of a project and putting a financing for results model in place. In Rwanda, the government is implementing a results-based financing scheme with nongovernmental organizations for primary health care. There are some projects in Partial FCS and in education projects that also included innovations for one component of project implementation.

- **Monitoring of results.** Health projects were four times as likely as education projects to have better monitoring and evaluation of outcomes, including use of third-party monitoring, but even in the health sector this was not always the case. There is clearly room for improvement in monitoring and evaluation frameworks of projects in FCS.

The country case studies revealed that some of the FCS are likely to meet some of the MDGs. The 2011 World Development Report (WDR) had expressed concern that none of the FCS were likely to achieve any of the MDGs. Progress improved by 2013; the average Always FCS IDA country is likely to achieve more than one MDG target, provision of access to safe drinking water showing the best performance in FCS IDA countries (Box 5.1). These results are somewhat better than had been expected two years ago although the FCS group continues to lag behind other IDA countries.

While the governments in FCS countries, with considerable donor support, have clearly played an important role in service delivery, in some countries their capacity has been supplemented by service providers from the private and nonprofit sector. For example, despite 10 years of conflict and continued political instability, Nepal is projected to do well on several MDGs due to a relatively functional civil service and multiple service providers at the local level (IEG 2010). The resilience of Nepali society manifests itself in robust community participation which the Bank and other donors have recognized and strengthened. In Afghanistan, the absence of health sector workers enabled the government to opt for an outsourcing model for public health provisioning, which is yielding rapid results. Liberia too has opted for a health program outsourcing service provision. The lesson appears to suggest a need to rethink the role of the government as an enabler of effective services rather than a direct provider of all services.

Respondents from a perception survey conducted for the evaluation reported mixed results about the improvements in service delivery in FCS. The majority of respondents (72 percent) reported the most improvement in education services compared to health, water, and electricity, while 11 percent said health services improved the most. But education also received the largest share of votes for least improvement (11 percent), compared to 1 percent reporting the least improvement in health services.

**BOX 5.1** Progress toward MDG Targets

The 2011 WDR indicated that conflict and violence would prevent the FCS countries from achieving any of the MDGs. However, a report released in the same year by the Center for Global Development drawing on World Development Indicators (WDI) data found that some FCS countries were progressing at an adequate pace to achieve several of the MDG targets. Based on this country-level index, IEG estimates that FCS countries as a group (both Always and Partial) were on track to achieve an average of three out of the eight targets analyzed. Always FCS countries were projected to achieve the fewest MDGs compared to the Partial and Never FCS groups (see figure below).

The average Always FCS IDA country is expected to achieve more than one MDG target. FCS IDA countries are most likely to meet the environmental sustainability goal of halving the proportion of people without sustainable access to safe drinking water. Always FCS IDA countries have made less progress in poverty reduction and prevention of HIV/AIDS. Guinea is the only Always FCS IDA country likely to meet the poverty reduction goal. Seven FCS countries are not projected to meet any of the goals, but four of these will make at least 50 percent progress toward one or more goals.

A substantial gap exists between the FCS and Never FCS IDA countries in the areas of maternal and child health. In 2010, the latest year of available data in the WDI, infant mortality stood at 71 per 1,000 live births in FCS IDA countries while the rate was only 53 in Never FCS countries. The maternal mortality rate in FCS countries is also much higher, 534 deaths per 100,000 live births in FCS IDA countries versus 350 in Never FCS IDA. In terms of women's empowerment, girls face more limited access to education in FCS, with a 10 percent gap between male and female youth literacy in FCS countries compared to only a 2 percent gap in the Never FCS group.

The Never FCS IDA group is expected to meet four of the targets on average. Unlike the FCS IDA countries, Never FCS countries are most likely to meet the health-related goals: 80 percent are expected to reduce child mortality by two-thirds and maternal mortality by three-quarters, double the proportion of FCS IDA countries which will do so. In the Never FCS group, African countries stand out as the low performers: Kenya, Madagascar, and Tanzania will likely achieve only two out of eight goals studied. Small islands like Marshall Islands and Micronesia also do less well than the rest of Never FCS, but small island states perform better among the Partial FCS group. Overall, FCS IDA countries lag behind other IDA countries but there is substantial variation within each region.

*continued on next page*

FIGURE 5.2 Progress toward MDG Targets by FCS Classification

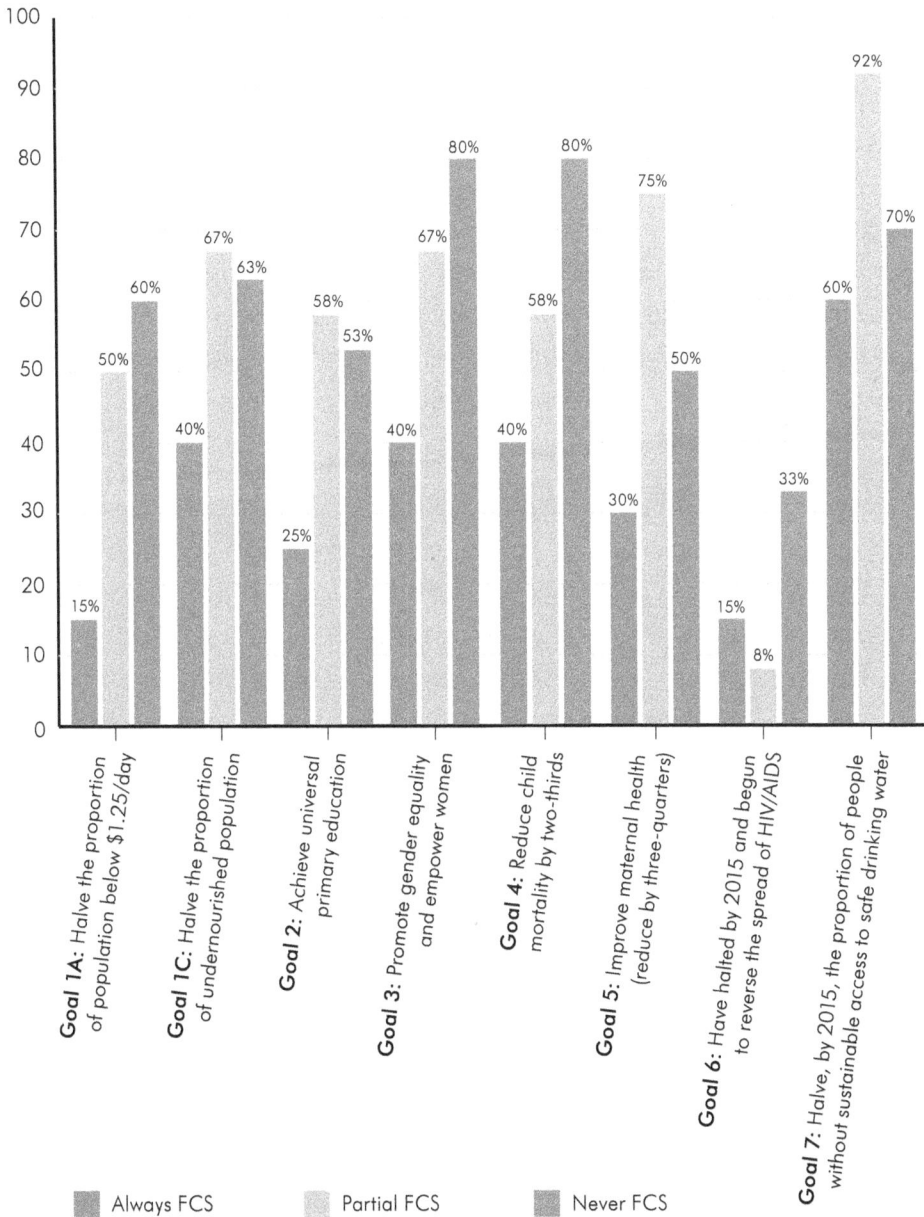

SOURCE: IEG calculations are based on the Center for Global Development's MDG Progress Index of 2011.
NOTE: Percentages show the share of countries in the group expected to make at least 50 percent progress toward the goal by 2015.

# Community-Driven Development in FCS

Community-driven development (CDD) projects supported by the World Bank have evolved over time from the initial aim of providing a safety net toward multiple objectives relevant to the FCS context. CDD projects emerged initially in the form of social funds during the 1990s as a safety net to offset the adverse impacts of structural adjustment loans. When the social development, agriculture and rural development, water, and urban sectors adopted CDD modalities, their scope expanded considerably. Within the FCS they have had three different objectives involving various forms and degrees of collective action, the emphasis varying across different projects: providing public goods and services to local communities; building local institutions; and enhancing downward accountability to citizens. In FCS, when implemented well, they have proved to be efficient vehicles for expanding the reach of the state and building state legitimacy. Several country directors have argued that CDD projects are quick-disbursing projects that are crucial to maintaining a good disbursement ration and, for that reason, have been reluctant to allow their design to evolve over time.

CDD projects have grown by number and commitment volume much faster in FCS than in IDA countries that were not FCS. CDD projects to FCS more than doubled in FY07–12 compared to the previous six years by number of projects and by commitment volume (Table 5.1). CDD projects have played an important role in financing public goods and services to local communities. More important, in several conflict-affected states, these projects have been the principal means of state engagement with distant communities. They have served to establish the presence of the state, and besides their short-term contribution to local economies, they have contributed to state legitimacy.

CDD programs have been a major feature of Bank assistance to FCS and have been effective in providing essential short-term development assistance to local communities to finance public goods and services. CDD covers a considerable range of demand-driven projects across many sectors. Most of them finance local infrastructure subprojects or service delivery subprojects, although some of them, like the Nepal Poverty Alleviation Fund (PAF) include a mix of subproject financing and microlending to local communities. Three common features are that typically they are demand driven; involve some form of community organization and community participation; and are administered by a special entity established by the government outside the structure of line ministries. Beyond that there is considerable variation in organizational structure, project objectives, and implementation modalities.

Afghanistan, Nepal, and Republic of Yemen have well-established, large-scale CDD programs functioning efficiently for more than a decade and reaching out to distant rural communities. Haiti too has relied on CDD to provide services to urban slum dwellers. These programs

TABLE 5.1  Number and Size of CDD and DDR Projects in IDA Countries

| Type of Project | Fiscal Year | Always FCS | | Partial FCS | | Never FCS | | Always + Partial FCS | |
|---|---|---|---|---|---|---|---|---|---|
| | | No | Commitment (US$, millions) | No | Commitment (US$, millions) | No | Commitment (US$, millions) | No | Commitment (US$, millions) |
| Community-Driven Development | 01–06 | 10 | 513 | 4 | 118 | 22 | 1,262 | 14 | 630 |
| | 07–12 | 24 | 1,326 | 11 | 179 | 28 | 2,699 | 35 | 1,506 |
| | **TOTAL** | **34** | **1,839** | **15** | **297** | **50** | **3,961** | **49** | **2,136** |
| Demobilization, Disarmament, and Reintegration | 01–06 | 12 | 648 | 1 | 21 | 2 | 210 | 13 | 669 |
| | 07–12 | 13 | 423 | 1 | 50 | 4 | 22 | 14 | 473 |
| | **TOTAL** | **25** | **1,071** | **2** | **71** | **6** | **232** | **27** | **1,142** |

were designed to fill the deficit in government services, and IEG evaluations have found them to be relatively well targeted and highly valued by their intended beneficiaries for achieving the first objective of CDD—provision of public goods and services. One noteworthy feature has been their outreach to women and ability to involve women in decision making, as evidenced by impact evaluations from all three countries. However, the reliance on project financing remains the Achilles heel of CDD programs, and without institutional evolution the second and third objectives of building sustainable local institutions and promoting downward accountability may not be achieved.

Despite its wide use, CDD projects remain controversial. One aspect of controversy is whether CDD projects undermine local government by creating parallel structures. The other aspect is the extent to which these projects lend themselves to elite capture. A recent policy research report concludes, "Only when projects explicitly link community-based organizations with markets, or provide skills training, do they tend to improve group cohesiveness and collective action beyond the life of the project" (Mansuri and Rao 2012). The report finds that community participation programs are most effective when they are systematically linked to state institutions: "Most successful programs tend to be those implemented by local governments that have some discretion and are downwardly accountable.... Local participation appears to increase, rather than diminish, the need for functional and strong institutions at the center." Mansuri and Rao conclude that local participation does not work when it is merely the ad hoc creation of a project. It works when it has teeth, when it builds on organic movements, when it is facilitated by a responsive center, when it is adequately and sustainably funded, and when interventions are conditioned by a culture of learning by doing. Given the scale and nature of CDD operations in the FCS, the evaluation focuses in particular on the institutional sustainability of these projects.

CDD programs involve institution building at two levels—the community level and the program level. The FCS case studies show that it is relatively easy to form ad hoc, informal community organizations when they are the conduit for receiving development grants. Their sustainability depends on the sustainability of the program and continuity in the stream of benefits. As in the case of microfinance, the support structure at the program level needs to be sustainable in order to sustain community involvement. Alternatively, the program can be linked to local government structures with regular fiscal transfers from the annual budget, as is the case in Bangladesh and Indonesia. Such a link between CDD programs and decentralized local government structures has not been established in any of the FCS. On the contrary, they appear to compete for the local governance space. Nor has any alternate institutional structure been established for these programs in FCS, even though viable apex organizations—microfinance in Afghanistan and Bangladesh and the PAF in Pakistan—have been established in fragile situations.

CDD programs are still projectized and function outside the sectoral structure of governments. While this is true for all IDA countries, the significance of this parallel structure is perhaps greater in the FCS where governments are often still in the process of reaching a political settlement with their own citizens or establishing their legitimacy. Subnational governments, particularly local governments at the district and subdistrict levels, need to play a critical role as the Bank and its development partners seek to promote local accountability and increase efficiency in service delivery. However, development of local governments is sometimes seen as contrary to the objective of building a strong and effective state. In some countries there is as yet no agreement on the structure of local government, which provides an easy justification to avoid engaging in the decentralization debate and to postpone the inevitable restructuring of CDD programs.

The consequence is that CDD programs are not joined up with local government, nor do they have any alternative system of ensuring institutional sustainability; as a result, they remain completely donor dependent. The National Solidarity Program in Afghanistan is the largest CDD program in FCS. It has been very successful in sponsoring the Community Development

Councils across the entire country, financing local subprojects, promoting local governance, empowering women, and in turn enhancing the writ and legitimacy of the Afghan state. Its financing model, however, is unsustainable and depends on large injections of donor financing for one-off grants to local communities. In FY14, more than a decade after its inception, the program is reported to be undertaking a set of studies to develop a more sustainable model, but with the 2014 transition fast approaching there is very little time left to test out and institutionalize an alternate model. Programs should start planning for institutional sustainability much earlier.

The 2013 impact evaluation reports positively about the program's role in improving access of villagers to basic utilities, education, health, and empowerment of women, but there is no impact on objective measures of economic activity. The program's biggest success midway—the promotion of local governance—declined by the end of the evaluation cycle with negative impact on local governance quality (Beath et al. 2012). The design of this flagship program has not evolved since it was first conceived in 2003, and the sporadic nature of external financing appears to have undermined the institutional gains which were at the heart of the program design.

The experience of Afghanistan's CDD program is similar to that in many other FCS. The programs play an important role in addressing fragility through short-term, intermittent measures to support local communities, when they are originally designed. But their very success as a safety net becomes an impediment to their evolution and institutional sustainability. It would be useful to take stock of this genre of projects to help to adapt and institutionalize them within country systems and country budgets over time. The Bank has not instituted alternate mechanisms to ensure their viability beyond the life of the projects supporting them. As a result, their institutional sustainability is questionable.

## Bank Support for Security Sector

In the FCS countries covered by this evaluation, security sector work has been largely aimed at demobilization, disarmament, and reintegration (DDR), with some more recent work in public expenditure reviews of the security sector and on forced displacement. Bank management estimates that its expenditure on studies, technical assistance, and lending interventions that target security outcomes and interact with the security sector amounted to a total of $2.6 billion from 1996 to 2013. This includes the work on DDR, internally displaced persons, crime and violence prevention in Latin America and the Caribbean Region, and public expenditure reviews.

Bank assistance for DDR projects has remained modest but significant. These projects have provided over $1.1 billion in finance to post-conflict countries, primarily from multi-donor trust funds, such as the Multicountry Demobilization and Reintegration Program for Africa's Great Lakes region. They remain the Bank Group's primary direct contribution to the security sector and are an important contribution to peace building. This evaluation was not able to detect an increase in DDR operations in the last few years (Table 5.1). Many of the DDR projects for community reintegration are carried out in a manner similar to the CDD programs. However, unlike CDD projects, they are designed to encourage armed combatants to take up some form of long-term civilian livelihoods, involving either a return to farming or through establishment of an urban enterprise. Another $650 million in Bank assistance is estimated to support internally displaced persons.

Discussions with client governments and other partners indicate that, given the Bank's mandate which constrains its ability to engage in overtly political or security issues, demand for Bank support is limited largely to analytical work. Public expenditure reviews are an example where, even though only a few have been undertaken, the Bank's expertise is valued. Defining a clear but limited niche where the Bank can complement the work done by United Nations and bilateral partners would be prudent and welcomed by other partners. It would give the Bank a seat at the table without encroaching on areas that other agencies feel are their mandate.

## Bank Support for Justice Activities in the FCS

The 2011 WDR identified justice as a core component of working effectively in FCS. It said that fragility and violence stem from the combination of exposure to economic, political, or security stresses and weak institutional capability for coping with these stresses. It committed to changing the way the Bank approached the justice sector and to incorporating justice issues into Bank operations. This evaluation reviewed the extent to which these priorities have been reflected in the country assistance strategies and programs in case study countries.

A recent strategy document prepared by the Legal Vice Presidency of the World Bank—*New Directions in Justice Reform*—argues that a functioning justice system is necessary for a capable and functioning state and that justice is a dimension of poverty; therefore the Bank's work will focus on "justice systems." It identifies five priorities for working in the sector: applying a problem-solving approach; identifying flagship justice reform initiatives as sites of innovation; integrating justice reform into Bank operations; developing a focus on justice reform in FCS; and developing organizational structures that strengthen the Bank's ability to realize this vision (World Bank 2012).

This assessment draws on six case studies (Cameroon, the Democratic Republic of Congo, Nepal, Sierra Leone, Solomon Islands, and Yemen) and three recent country program evaluations (Afghanistan, Liberia, and Timor-Leste) to determine what progress, if any, the Bank has made in meeting the ambitions of the 2011 WDR and the priorities outlined in the *New Directions in Justice Reform*. It does not include the broader justice components for programs in other sectors[2] nor does it include legal or justice reform work in relation to regulatory reform or the business environment; this is covered in the analysis of the private sector and was not central to the conclusions of the 2011 WDR.

## STATUS OF JUSTICE IN THE WORLD BANK PORTFOLIO IN FCS

In terms of core justice operations,[3] the Bank has little to show in FCS on justice. There were only three justice programs identified in FCS between 2001 and 2012, of which the only large-scale one is the Afghanistan Justice Reform Program in Afghanistan, whose second phase started in FY12, and a small project of less than $1 million in Liberia and the Justice for the Poor Program.

The Afghanistan 2nd Judicial Reform Project, an $85 million follow up to an earlier pilot, started in 2012. The judicial reform program under the new project seeks to strengthen the centralized state justice system in Afghanistan and increase access to justice for the Afghan people. The design envisages working with various state and nonstate actors to broaden access to justice services beyond existing structures and beyond Kabul. While changes in the project's second phase are in line with the recent Bank strategy to focus on justice in fragile contexts, it has not yet had much impact. The project was rated moderately unsatisfactory in the supervision report at the end of FY13. The Afghanistan project is the largest in the FCS justice portfolio, and yet there is no evidence of additional monitoring and evaluation, and performance tracking is limited. The activity completion report for phase one has limited information on program impact beyond the designated outputs, and there is no evidence of baseline work, planned for FY13, having being done yet for phase two.

The small Liberia Capacity Building for Judicial Services Project was developed in response to a request from the Chief Justice for training judicial officers. It funded training for court officers, the provision of books and documents, and vehicles for public prosecutors. The Liberia project finished in 2011, following which the Bank did not commit to further work on judicial reform. The project did not reflect the specific priorities outlined in the justice-reform strategy and had little to no impact on justice services in Liberia.

Justice for the Poor is a World Bank program sponsored by the Legal Vice Presidency. It has been funded almost entirely by trust funds: in the East Asian region (EAP) largely by the Australian Agency for International Development at least since FY07, with additional funding in Liberia and Sierra Leone from other trust funds and a small amount of Bank cross-support. In many ways, it provides a model of what has been more recently outlined in the New Directions in Justice Reform strategy. It takes a problem-solving approach to its work, seeks to influence other Bank operations through its analysis and advice, works predominantly in FCS, and invests in expertise in-country to support its approach. It has been active in Sierra Leone, Solomon Islands, and Timor-Leste and more recently in Liberia, and engages with justice reform as a cross-cutting issue but has had limited success in integrating justice reform into Bank operations in the case study countries, with the exception of Solomon Islands. The research program has received about $15 million in trust funds. The Bank has provided very little financing for Justice for the Poor from its own resources, which indicates that the ownership of the program by country departments is questionable.

Expanding the reach and influence of the approach has been difficult. To date, it has focused primarily on the preparation of analytical materials and the provision of advice to address issues of grievance and contestation in fragile and conflict-affected environments. The program has had limited results in establishing itself in core operations and in integrating justice reform into Bank operations. Only recently has it begun design work on operations in the Solomon Islands and Vanuatu.[4] In those countries the program has influenced key program choices and is represented in the country assistance strategy (CAS) documentation.

In other countries such as Sierra Leone and Timor-Leste, the impact is even more limited. In Sierra Leone, the FCS evaluation team found that the program had been confined to working on analytical studies. It was seen by Management and staff as somewhat removed from the core business of the Bank and was not captured in country strategy documents. In Timor-Leste, in the early period the program struggled to find interventions that could influence government and Bank operations. Its analytical work was of mixed quality, and it did not have much influence.

The evaluation team did not find any evidence in the case study countries of specific demand for a more proactive role by the Bank in the justice sector, nor did stakeholders feel the Bank had a comparative advantage in the justice sector. Partnership arrangements with other agencies were noted in conversations with in-country teams, but have not been reflected in most CASs, Interim Strategy Notes, and other instruments as was intended in the 2011 WDR. Although Justice for the Poor started in FY07, justice sector work is still nascent and it is too early to evaluate the outcomes of these programs at the project level or to be able to assess their broader impact. The Bank cannot address justice issues meaningfully without a serious commitment of its own resources to the sector and thoughtful selectivity to identify its niche and comparative advantage compared to those of partner organizations, such as the United Nations Development Programme, which sees this as part of its core business in FCS. In the absence of strategic priorities, the scope of its justice sector work remains unclear to operational staff and in-country stakeholders.

## Endnotes

[1] The desk review examined all 45 health and education projects approved after FY06 for which IEG reviews of Implementation Completion Reports were available.

[2] Management claims of justice sector support to a large number of projects in many sectors is impossible to verify as this is not recorded in Bank operational databases or reported or acknowledged in project documents. Where country programs identified or pointed to work on justice as a component of other work, it was investigated.

[3] This includes projects identified in the FCS operational review where the project title was linked to justice or where projects were identified as potentially having a primary justice objective. Where this was evident, the evaluation examined project descriptions. Field teams also collected any additional information on identified justice projects during missions.

[4] In addition, Justice for the Poor is also contributing to work for the Kecamatan Development Project in Indonesia.

## References

Beath, Andrew, Fotini Christia, and Ruben Enikolopov. 2012. "Randomized Impact Evaluation of Afghanistan's National Solidarity Programme: Final Report." MIT, Harvard, New Economic School, February 14, 2012. http://e-gap.org/wp /wp-content/uploads/20120220-BCE-NSP-IE-2FU-PAP.pdf.

IEG (Independent Evaluation Group). 2010. The World Bank in Nepal 2003–2008: Country Program Evaluation. Washington, DC: World Bank.

Mansuri, Ghazala, and Vijayendra Rao. 2012. Localizing Development: Does Participation Work? Washington, DC: World Bank.

World Bank. 2012. The World Bank: New Directions in Justice Reform. A Companion Piece to the Updated Strategy and Implementation Plan on Strengthening Governance, Tackling Corruption. Washington, DC: World Bank.

conflict development fragility security

equitable social contract
reconstruction
reintegration
infrastructure    political settlement
civil society     reconciliation
human capital     statebuilding
local economic    gender equity
institutional     inclusive growth
                  rule of law

trust
transparency
transition
reconciliation
access 2 services
donor harmonization
new deal  new rule

access 2 opportunities
donor harmonization
revenue mobilization
transition
political settlement
country ownership
transformation
citizen voice
accountability

jobs
justice
legitimacy
resilience
transformation
reintegration
peacebuilding
inclusion

# 6

# Promoting Inclusive Growth and Jobs

## CHAPTER HIGHLIGHTS

- Growth and job creation, important elements in a strategy to address conflict and fragility, have been slow and face challenges in fragile and conflict-affected states.

- World Bank Group support for private sector development has been focused on investment climate reform. Other constraints to private sector development—power, transport, and land rights—have not been adequately addressed.

- Bank Group support for agriculture has not been commensurate with its effects on food security and employment in FCS.

- Bank Group support for natural resources management has paid less attention to the distribution of benefits and local economic development and has not sufficiently addressed related fragility risks.

- The Bank Group lacks a strategic and effective framework for job creation in FCS: Short-term jobs and small skills development programs lack synergies with education and the private sector.

The World Bank Group has highlighted growth with jobs as a vital element of addressing fragility. The private sector can create jobs and drive economic growth, but it is constrained by lack of infrastructure, a business friendly environment, bankable projects, and skills. This chapter focuses on the Bank Group's contribution to inclusive growth and jobs. This agenda encompasses a large of the Bank Group's work. It includes infrastructure, private sector development (PSD), natural resources management, agriculture, as well as interventions for short-term employment and skills development, and comprises support to both the private and public sectors.

The overall conclusion is that the Bank Group's focus on private sector development as the primary vehicle for job creation has not borne results in the short run. The priority given to investment climate is necessary, but it is not a sufficient condition for the growth of the private sector and of jobs in the high-risk environment prevalent in the fragile and conflict-affected states (FCS) among International Development Association (IDA) countries.

## Context and Framework for Assessment

In the FCS context, a focus on inclusive growth and employment is a highly relevant strategy to address drivers of fragility, with important linkages to state- and peace-building activities. Vulnerability caused by low per capita income and high unemployment is a major driver of conflict (World Bank 2011). Unemployment or underemployment especially of the young remains rampant in FCS. Additionally, rent-seeking behavior and inequitable distribution of economic benefits, such as from extractive industries, can fuel conflict.

The sectors driving economic growth in FCS are not necessarily labor intensive, and in many cases growth has not been inclusive. Although economies recovered across all sectors, industry (dominated by extractives) and services have been the most dynamic sectors in Always FCS, performing better than agriculture, which employs more than 40 to 70 percent of the workforce in most of these countries. In the absence of deliberate attention, the job creation impact of extractives has been limited.

Informality plays a large role in employment and FCS economies. This evaluation adopts the definition of "jobs" introduced by the 2013 World Development Report, which includes both formal and informal, wage and nonwage employment. Forms of informal employment—considered particularly vulnerable, including subsistence farming or self-employment in agriculture or micro and small enterprises in FCS—account for the majority of firms in most FCS.

International migration is another important livelihood strategy in many IDA countries, especially in the short term when the local economy cannot provide a sufficient number of jobs. Migration and remittances are important drivers of economies in IDA countries both in FCS and Never FCS groups. Emigrants represent more than 5 percent of the population in 34 out of 62 countries,[1] and remittances have become an important source of capital flows to FCS. In 10 FCS, remittances were greater than official development assistance or foreign direct investment (FDI). However, the Bank Group has not paid much attention to the development of interventions targeted at migrants or migrant households, or to diaspora communities for private sector development.

Promoting inclusive growth and jobs needs sequencing and prioritization customized to FCS contexts. Violence and conflict have led to deterioration in trust and linkages between firms as well as in the infrastructure needed to access markets. In the FCS context, jobs not only provide livelihoods to people but also reconstruct the social fabric of society (World Bank 2012). Therefore, jobs are at the core of restoring confidence and transforming institutions to break the cycles of violence, but interventions need to be tailored to country conditions. Recovery may focus initially on emergency employment for high-risk and needy groups; a shift to income-generating activities, private sector development, and microfinance; and finally the creation of an enabling environment. These approaches can be pursued in parallel, but the emphasis and pace can evolve according to the conditions and needs in the country (DeVries and Specker 2009).

The private sector can create jobs and drive economic growth, while government plays an important role in providing the enabling environment (Commission on Growth and Development 2008). The private sector, comprising both local enterprises and foreign investment, can be remarkably resilient during conflict. It may even thrive in the absence of an effective government, and can be an important player in economic development and a focal point for development efforts (Porter Peschka 2011; Leo et al. 2012). However, the private sector may downscale or become more informal as a result of conflict and the collapse of government services.

Yet the private sector in FCS faces specific challenges which constrain it from effectively achieving growth and employment creation. According to World Bank enterprise surveys, political instability, corruption, access to electricity, access to finance, and access to land are all perceived as major or severe constraints by firms in FCS.[2] Based on enterprise surveys and the Independent Evaluation Group's (IEG's) analysis for the six country case studies, the following leading constraints and needs of the private sector in FCS were identified:

- Instability and political risk

- Access to electricity and transport infrastructure

- Weak capacity in the public and private sector (including weak governance and a skills deficit among potential workers)

- Poor investment climate (including business regulations and land rights)

- Access to finance

## Relevance and Effectiveness of Support to Inclusive Growth and Jobs

The evaluation finds that for the country programs reviewed by IEG, the World Bank Group did not adequately address major constraints and did not have a holistic approach to private sector development in FCS. The International Finance Corporation's (IFC's) investments in FCS have grown (Figure 6.1), but poor infrastructure is a main obstacle for private sector growth in FCS, and a large funding gap remains for infrastructure improvements especially in power, transport, and water (Foster and Briceño-Garmendia 2010).

### INFRASTRUCTURE

The World Bank prioritized transport, urban, and energy and mining sectors while IFC invested more in telecommunications in infrastructure. Access to electricity and transportation services are leading constraints for private sector development in FCS. Bank infrastructure lending to IDA countries has multiplied several-fold between FY01 and FY12, growing from $3.1 billion in FY01–06 to $5 billion in FY07–12 (Figure 6.2). During the period FY07–12, the Bank's infrastructure portfolio invested more in transport (36 projects worth $2 billion), urban (40 projects worth $1.2 billion), and energy and mining (78 projects worth $1.1 billion), with a much smaller share in water (18 projects worth $0.7 billion). IFC's support to infrastructure during FY01–12 was focused on telecommunications (20 projects worth $452 million) and to a lesser extent on power (13 projects worth $272 million). The telecommunications portfolio dominated IFC's investments in Always FCS (39 percent of investments), whereas investments in power were concentrated in Partial FCS countries. In terms of its guarantee volume, the Multilateral Investment Guarantee Agency's (MIGA's) support to FCS in FY01–12 was focused on infrastructure, especially transport ($572 million) and telecommunications ($289 million).

FIGURE 6.1 IFC Investments in IDA Countries by Fiscal Year (3-year moving average)

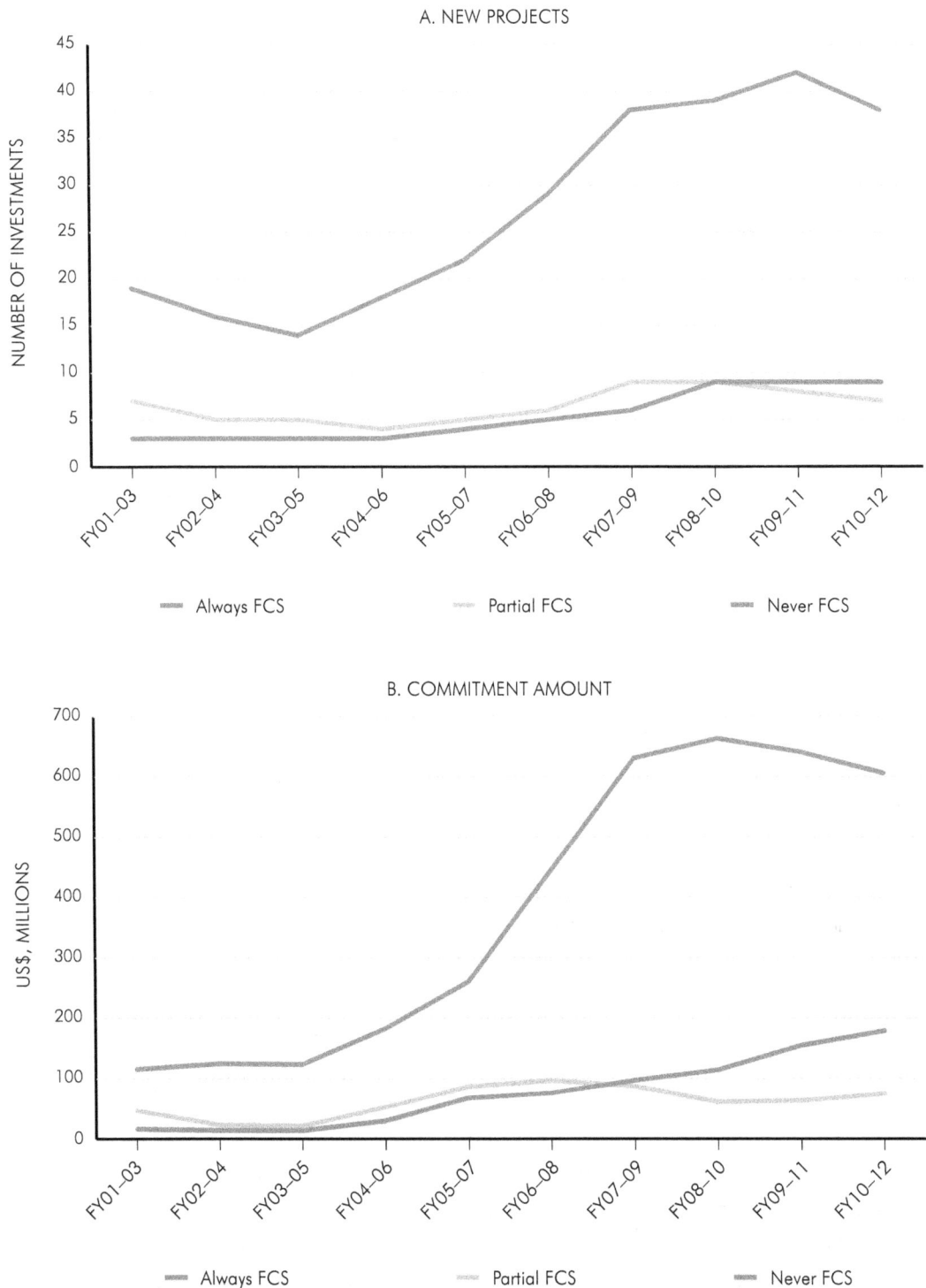

A. NEW PROJECTS

B. COMMITMENT AMOUNT

SOURCE: IEG database.

The Bank transport sector had a stellar performance during FY07–12 in FCS, and achieved 100 percent satisfactory outcome ratings at project completion. During the same period, two-thirds of the completed projects in energy and mining achieved their development objectives but only one-third of the water sector did so.

FCS countries have some of the lowest access rates to electricity. Despite considerable Bank Group support to the sector, it has been too small to have a significant impact. For instance, in the Democratic Republic of Congo, despite very significant Bank investments (over $1 billion during FY00–12) in power generation, transmission, and distribution, domestic access to power is below 10 percent. In Cameroon, the World Bank and IFC collaborated closely in the power sector, providing loans, guarantees, and investments to private power projects and capacity building to the relevant ministry. Access to power in Cameroon is 50 percent, compared with an average of 33 percent for Sub-Saharan Africa. To manage project-level risks in Cameroon, IFC invested alongside other international finance institutions. Nepal has enormous hydropower potential for growth and economic development, yet it suffers from a severe power crisis with rolling blackouts of up to 16 hours a day, and there has been little Bank Group investment despite its transformational potential. More recently, the Bank Group has initiated collaborative approaches in the power sector in FCS. For example in Nepal, hydropower has been identified as a transformational sector in a Joint Business Plan, and in Côte d'Ivoire the Bank Group is supporting work to both address main constraints and manage risks and challenges in the sector (Box 6.1).

The telecommunications sector has attracted private sector investments early even in conflict-affected countries and is considered "transformational" due to its potential to spur growth, entrepreneurship, and service delivery (IEG 2011). IFC-and MIGA-supported investments helped expand coverage and mobile penetration to areas outside major cities (see Box 6.2). Financially, several projects underperformed relative to IFC's expectations due to increasing competition from other networks and changes in the regulatory framework that negatively affected several projects. In Afghanistan, World Bank support to policy and regulatory reform, IFC investment, and MIGA guarantees collaborated effectively and complemented each other well, contributing to enhanced access and competition. These investments demonstrated the viability of private infrastructure investments in mobile phone projects even in a post-conflict environment.

Given the huge demand for infrastructure services, and the perception that the lack of infrastructure, especially in power and transport, remains a leading constraint to PSD and for growth, it is fair to conclude that the considerable Bank Group engagement in infrastructure as a whole has had limited impact. IFC has developed InfraVentures, a specialized instrument

FIGURE 6.2 Infrastructure Projects by Number and Commitment Volume

A. NEW PROJECTS APPROVED

Non-FCS IDA          FCS IDA

B. NEW COMMITMENTS APPROVED

Non-FCS IDA          FCS IDA

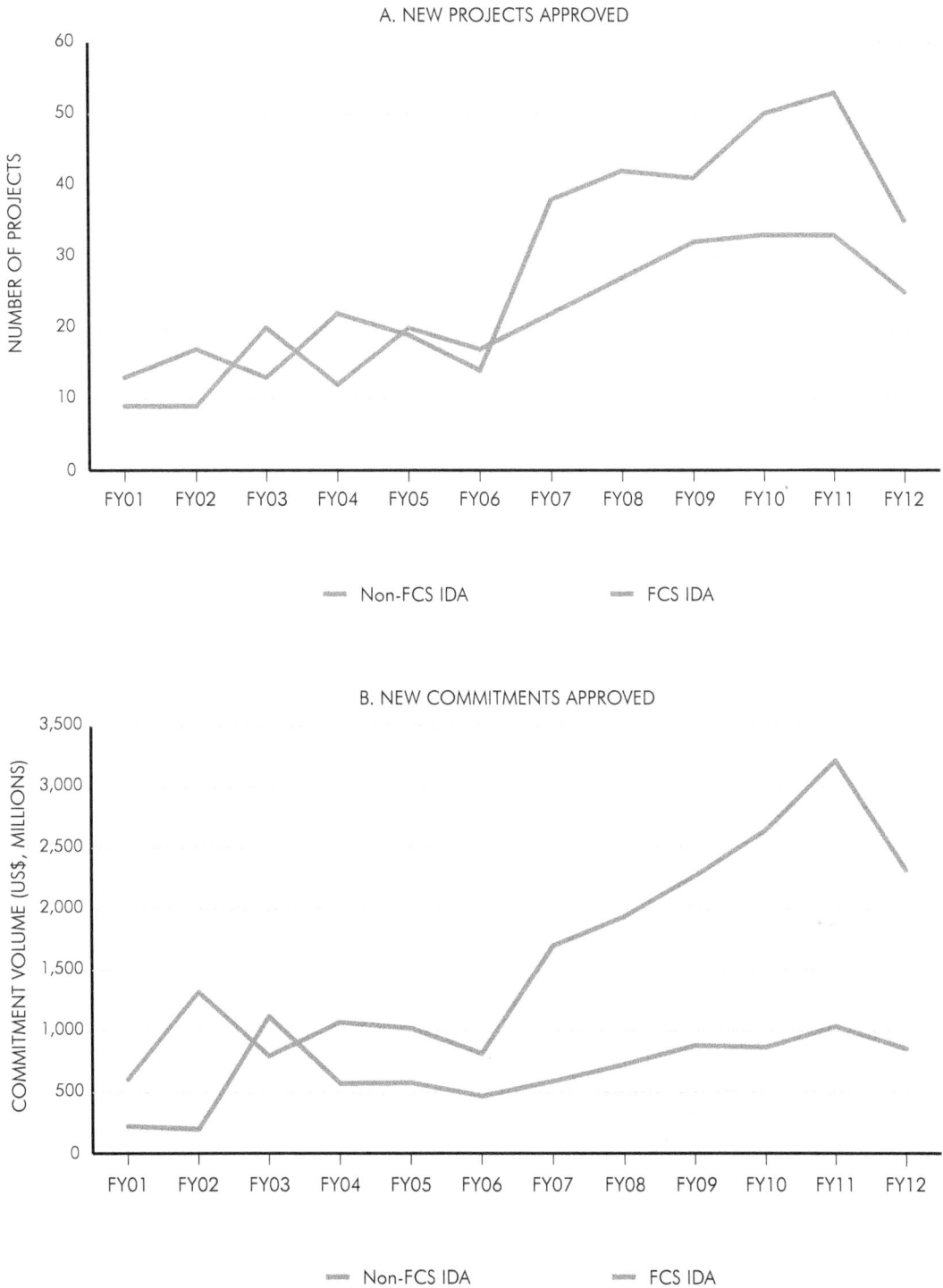

SOURCE: Business Warehouse.

World Bank Group collaboration has already shown progress in Côte d'Ivoire where a multiyear, comprehensive, joint IMF and Bank Group effort to address financial sustainability issues in the country's power sector paved the way for a large power investment in FY13. IFC invested $125 million and mobilized an additional $225 million for the expansion of the Azito Thermal Power plant, while MIGA is providing breach of contract cover to the project's equity investor and lead sponsor for $116 million. Following its expansion, Azito is expected to add about 140 megawatts to its capacity and, at 430 megawatts, become one of the largest independent power generators in Sub-Saharan Africa. Additionally, IFC is planning an investment in the expansion of Compagnie Ivoirienne de Production d'Electricité.

to combine advisory services (through support to feasibility studies) and investments to help develop bankable infrastructure projects in frontier countries, but thus far deployment of this instrument has been modest.

### INVESTMENT CLIMATE REFORM

The Investment Climate for private businesses in FCS is particularly challenging. Research indicates that the quality of investment climate matters for growth of firms and employment (Aterido et al. 2007; Dollar et al. 2005). The relevant literature suggests generally low productivity and high indirect costs and business-environment-related losses are depressing the productivity of African firms relative to those in other countries. While this analysis was not specifically undertaken for FCS countries, these effects are likely to be exacerbated in the FCS context. The high cost of production in turn negatively affects the profitability of private firms in FCS by inhibiting their growth and potential to create employment (Eifert et al. 2005).

IFC and the World Bank have focused their support to PSD mainly to reform business laws and regulations and procedures, build capacity in ministries and the judiciary, and facilitate FDI. The Bank Group's approach included some countries where both the World Bank and IFC were active in investment climate reform, or either the Bank or IFC took the lead in supporting reform.

Investment climate reforms are necessary but not sufficient for PSD. The projects were broadly relevant to the challenges of the private sector in the country, although business regulation,

The telecommunications sector is one of the few to attract sizeable and early investment and to demonstrate high rates of growth in FCS, outside of the resource extraction. Telecom is considered a transformational sector due to its potential to spur growth, entrepreneurship, and the delivery of services.

Rapid increases in access to telephony were recorded even in countries with very difficult business environments, or with ongoing conflict, and a high incidence of poverty. For example, 38 percent of Afghanis and 34 percent of Sierra Leoneans had a mobile phone subscription in 2010, up from 4 percent and 14 percent, respectively, five years earlier. While the growth of mobile networks was largely driven by private investment, and accessibility increased in great part due to greater competition, IEG found that the speed of mobile penetration was faster in countries where the World Bank or IFC supported the information and communications technology (ICT) sector; and coordination was identified in IFC telecom projects as a main success driver. In Afghanistan, the World Bank, IFC, and MIGA coordinated efforts to support sector reform and private sector investments. This is starting to yield results: increased coverage by mobile operators, lower prices and more mobile applications, and increased use of ICT in public sector governance.

SOURCE: IEG 2011.

as discussed above, was not the top constraint to PSD in FCS as identified in World Bank enterprise surveys and through interviews conducted by IEG with stakeholders in the country case studies. However, investment climate reforms typically have a longer time horizon and are important for longer-term growth prospects of the economy. There is a need for phasing and sequencing (and sufficient flexibility in implementation) of such support based on a timely diagnostic of the most urgent needs and constraints that would differ from the immediate aftermath of conflict versus longer-term issues. A post-conflict engagement also needs to consider possible negative effects that large-scale assistance programs may have in supplanting the private sector.

Results of IFC and Bank support for investment climate reform have been mixed. Implementation of investment climate reforms lagged, due to weak capacity, political economy issues, and internal Bank Group limitations; limiting the impact on improvements in business environments. Even where laws progressed, implementation of reforms and application of the law in practice was challenging, requiring longer time horizons and implementation support, in part due to the low capacity of local administration. This is true in particular for IFC Advisory Services (AS) projects, which are typically limited in duration, constrained by funding, and do not address public sector reform issues. Projects that focused on a few key priority issues and provided hands-on support to local institutions (as in South Sudan) had a better chance of succeeding. There is a need for more programmatic and phased approaches and closer collaboration among the Bank and IFC to ensure sustainability of reform efforts.

Results for IFC's assistance to public-private dialogue (PPD) have been mixed. PPD is dependent on political stability and consensus, often lacking in FCS. The Sierra Leone Business Forum was not self-sustained and ceased operations once funding from IFC ended. In Nepal, investment climate reform is being carried out in phases. During the first phase, the Nepal Business Forum was established, but the objective of introducing reforms to four procedures was achieved with delays. However, IEG has found the objective to promote public-private dialogue around private sector reforms an appropriate instrument to bring the government and the private sector together in discussions of a country's future.

In several IFC AS projects reviewed by IEG, the project design and results frameworks did not reflect the realities of FCS. Projects with narrowly defined objectives and longer time horizons tended to be more effective. Evaluations also indicated a need for a strong team in the field for effective implementation. Data are often not available or reliable enough for effective results measurements; projects need to consider how to develop appropriate results framework and incorporate monitoring and evaluation capacity building in project design.

## ACCESS TO FINANCE

The Bank Group helped to establish commercially oriented microfinance institutions and supported institutions that were lending to small and medium enterprises (SMEs). The Bank's lending to financial sector development in FCS was $270 million, 69 percent of which was in Afghanistan. IFC's support to the financial sector was small compared with IFC's global focus on financial intermediation (9 percent of IFC commitments in FCS). IFC contributed to the establishment of, or supported, small and micro finance institutions in Afghanistan, Cameroon, the Democratic Republic of Congo, Haiti, Nepal, and Yemen, in some cases providing access to finance for the first time to this market segment. MIGA also supported a micro finance institution in Afghanistan (see Box 6.3).

In Afghanistan, the early activities of the Bank Group supported the micro finance industry and contributed to significant growth in the subsector. The Bank supported the transformation and funding of the Microfinance Investment Support Facility for Afghanistan (MISFA) as an apex microfinance institution with nonlending technical assistance and two lending operations. IFC supported the First Microfinance Bank of Afghanistan, which has been highly successful in extending microloans and reaching its financial benchmarks. MIGA also supported one of the microfinance institutions in Afghanistan (BRAC). Both started off as implementing partners of MISFA. The Bank Group complemented its support to microfinance institutions with knowledge and advisory projects, including for financial infrastructure and skills development in the financial sector. Overall, Bank Group support for the financial sector in Afghanistan was an example for effective coordination and synergies.

SOURCE: IEG 2012a.

IFC's support also catalyzed the development of two of the three active microfinance institutions in the Democratic Republic of Congo. The integrated delivery of advisory projects with investments was considered crucial in helping the start-up of operations, including to support the establishment of the bank and capacity building of its staff as well as to support the development of market segments such as finance for women or SMEs lending.

IFC's SME Venture Fund, created in FY10 to provide risk capital in low-income countries, is active in five FCS and has begun to disburse funds to investee companies. Although it is too early to access the financial performance of the investee companies, the funds' main challenges have been the lack of good investment opportunities in the targeted SMEs segment, inability to raise additional funds to supplement IFC's investment in the Fund, investee quality and integrity, and limited exit strategies from investments. Fund managers indicated that the combined delivery of investments with advisory services and a hands-on approach to training and support were factors of success, as was having a strong country presence.

MIGA's Small Investment Program (SIP) has been relevant to support smaller size manufacturing, agribusiness, and services projects typical for FCS. MIGA's early engagement, focus on projects in relevant sectors, and use of an innovative instrument in Sierra Leone (a master agreement with an equity fund) have been relevant to developing SMEs and were supportive of the growth and jobs agenda.

Operational results of SIP projects have been poor. While IEG has not concluded evaluations of MIGA SIP projects in FCS, indications from the review of SIP guarantees in Afghanistan and Sierra Leone are that almost all of their MIGA-supported projects have struggled financially and operationally, and some have failed. This demonstrates the riskiness of doing business in FCS. While several projects in Afghanistan were affected by security risks, the weak results were driven mainly by commercial reasons. Projects encountered low demand for their services; poor access to infrastructure; weak management capacity; poor choice of local partners; underestimation of constraints and operating costs; and lack of knowledge of local markets. MIGA offers SIP guarantees at a capped premium, but the costs associated with underwriting and supervising a SIP guarantee can be significant, requiring more intensive support to guarantee holders and follow-up supervision of projects sensitive to environmental and social effects.

## SKILLS DEVELOPMENT

Bank Group support for skills development has been limited and remains insufficient to address long-term human capital constraints. The labor force in FCS, particularly countries emerging from conflict, is often characterized by a "lost generation" of youth without any formal education or training, which contributes to continued fragility. Bank support to programs for basic and professional skills development has increased in recent years. The Bank did not support skills development in FCS between FY01 and FY06 but had eight projects ($82 million) between FY07 and FY12. However, there is no comprehensive strategy in this area which systematically explores linkages with private sector needs to enhance employment prospects. In Sierra Leone, the country program focused on short-term jobs rather than addressing long-term human capital constraints, limiting the employment of Sierra Leoneans in private sector investments.

IFC's product for providing business skills training to SMEs, Business Edge, has been perceived as effective by some participants and sponsors especially where it was rolled out in conjunction with local sponsors and better adapted to local partners. Others felt it was too standardized and not appropriately tailored to the needs and capacity of the FCS environment, as it targeted primarily formal companies and entrepreneurs, rather than the more informal and rural firms that dominate FCS economies.

## EXTRACTIVE INDUSTRIES

FCS economies are highly dependent on extractive industries. Natural resources, comprising extractive industries and forestry, accounted on average for 28.5 percent of gross domestic product (GDP) in FCS, with a trend that broadly mirrored commodity prices. The largest source of revenues was from oil. In some FCS, natural resources dominate the economy, such as in Angola and the Republic of Congo where they contributed over 60 percent of GDP. Natural resource rents and the inequitable distribution of benefits from resource extraction have been a major driver of fragility and conflict in FCS (Collier 2006). Countries that are not FCS are less dependent on natural resources, although their share of GDP from natural resource extraction also grew from 3.7 to 7.1 percent between 2000 and 2011 (Figure 6.3).

FIGURE 6.3  Total Natural Resources Revenues

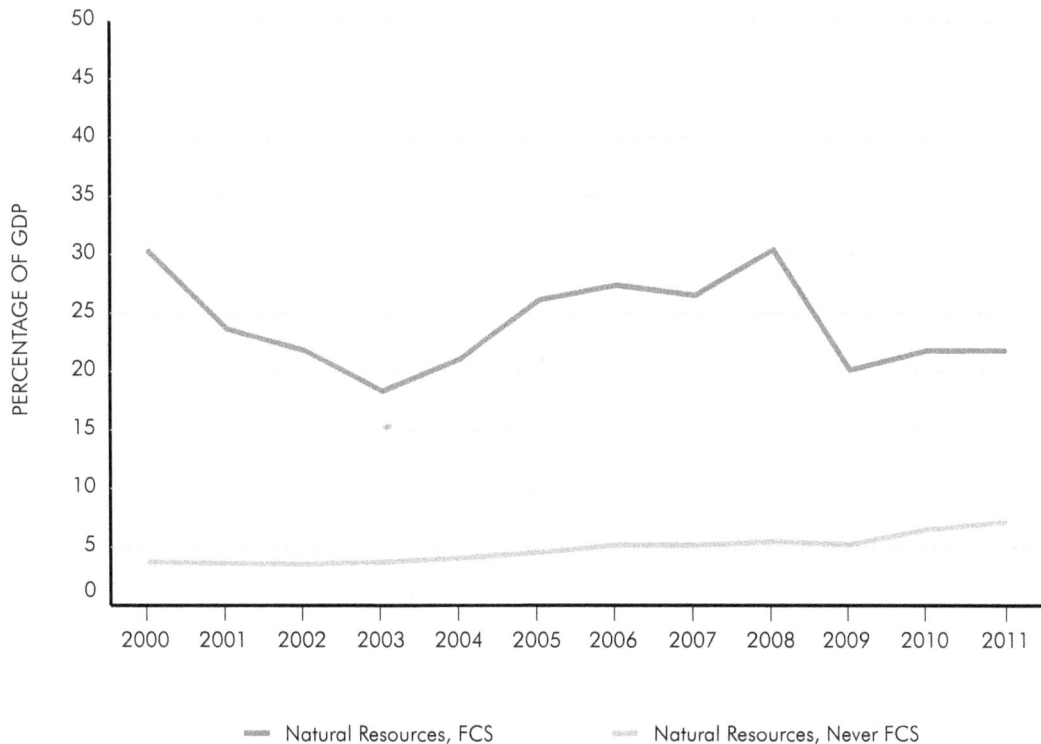

SOURCE: World Development Indicators.
NOTE: Country group data are weighted by gross domestic product (GDP) valued at purchasing power parity (PPP) as a share of country group GDP. Bangladesh is dropped from the Never FCS universe as an outlier because of the size of GDP in PPP terms. Number of observations: FCS, 28; Never FCS, 27.

World Bank Group assistance in extractive industries has focused on reforming the regulatory environment to improve governance and transparency in concessions and revenues, increase investment in these sectors, and enhance revenue management and investing of revenues for development purposes. Reforms to improve the capture of resource revenues and invest them in human, physical, and social capital, discussed in chapter 4, are critically important for the jobs and growth agenda in FCS (Boakye et al. 2012). The large volume of revenue from extractive industries can also have a potentially negative impact on the economy (Dutch disease[3]). The implications of these risks are more acute for FCS. IFC and MIGA have supported private investments in extractive industries selectively, based on the presence of acceptable sponsors. The sector was significant for IFC, accounting for one-fifth of IFC's commitments in FCS.

The Bank Group has only recently begun to assist countries with leveraging their investments in high-value extractive sectors for local development and sustained growth. The high-capital intensity that characterizes this sector has not created many direct jobs in FCS; in many cases it has involved the development of enclave economies with limited linkages to the local economy and employment opportunities. Most Bank Group operations in FCS have not paid much attention to leveraging the investments in extractive industries to create spillovers in the economy. These are key challenges for promoting inclusive growth and jobs in FCS. The Bank Group has initiated analytical work in Afghanistan on the development of resource corridors around mining investments, including multimodal infrastructure and linked industries. Liberia and Sierra Leone are also trying to leverage the mining sector to foster services and other industries aimed at increasing benefits for the local economy. In the Democratic Republic of Congo, however, a similar growth poles[4] project is being initiated but is targeted at regions that are not conflict-affected. These efforts to support local economic development are very recent and their impacts on the ground are not yet evident.

The lack of transparency in the sector made it challenging for IFC and MIGA to engage in direct investments even though extractive industries were attracting foreign direct investment because of high returns. Extractive industries are among the few sectors attracting foreign direct investment and there is a role for IFC and MIGA in supporting these companies which would likely meet their standards and sustainability policies and also support linkages projects with local communities and SMEs to increase local benefits from mining. In an IFC investment in a mining company in the Democratic Republic of Congo, the government revoked the sponsor's concession during a dispute. This demonstrated the riskiness of engaging in the mining sector in a volatile and low governance environment such as the Democratic Republic of Congo and led IFC to suspend new operations in the country. The Chad–Cameroon pipeline project jointly supported by IFC and the Bank was also affected by poor governance.

The IFC investment was financially successful and its involvement helped require the private sector partners to adhere to IFC's environmental and social policies. A MIGA-supported project experiencing local conflict heightened the need for the agency to include security and conflict risks in its due diligence (CAO 2005).

AGRICULTURE

Agriculture is the largest real sector in FCS and Never FCS IDA countries, accounting for about one-fourth of GDP on average in these country groups but for a much larger share of employment in FCS. Agriculture in FCS, and in IDA countries overall, is dominated by small-scale private enterprises that employ a large proportion of the national labor force (Table 6.1). The sector is critical for future growth in production and for employment. It is also significant for food security in FCS. Household surveys have shown that growth in the agricultural sector is more effective in reducing poverty among the poorest groups than among other groups in rural areas because the poorest groups are closely involved with growth in the agricultural production and gain directly and immediately from its growth (Christiaensen et al. 2010). Bank Group support for agriculture has not been commensurate with its potential impact on

TABLE 6.1  Characteristics of the Agricultural Sector in IDA Countries
(2000–2011, by percentage)

| Characteristic | Always FCS | Partial FCS | Never FCS |
|---|---|---|---|
| Agriculture's Share of Total GDP | 30 | 23 | 23 |
| Agriculture's Annual Growth of GDP | 2–3 | 5–6 | 2–5 |
| Incidence of Poverty in Rural Areas | 57 | 38 | 54 |
| Access to an All Season Road | 5–90 | 5–90 | 12–60 |
| Agriculture's Share of Total Employment | 40–70 | 30–60 | 30–80 |

SOURCE: World Development Indicators, FAOSTAT data.

employment, poverty reduction, and food security in FCS, and there have been significant gaps in strategic analysis and customizing agricultural interventions to the transition phase.

Agriculture remains important in Always FCS but performance suffered.[5] The average growth rate of agricultural production and cereal yields is lower in Always FCS compared with Never FCS. Productivity has changed very little and in many FCS it has declined. Access to markets is a major constraint in all FCS because of weak rural roads and inadequate market information systems.

World Bank assistance programs in agriculture in FCS generally lacked a sector strategy. Emergency projects during the post-conflict period correctly focus on rehabilitation, but they need to be implemented in the context of a medium- to longer-term strategy which links to the emergency investments. Assessments of country proposals submitted for financing to the Global Agriculture and Food Security Program also showed that the poorest countries had the least ready investment plans and country proposals. The World Bank Agricultural Action Plan has no strategy for FCS. It states only that the Bank can assist FCS through "strengthening institutions in fragile countries, including participation in community-driven agricultural development and natural resource management projects" (World Bank 2013a).[6] The National Solidarity Program in Afghanistan generated short-term benefits for rural communities, but in the absence of complementary strategic investments in agriculture, it did not provide the basis for longer-term sustainable development (Beath et al. 2012).

Agriculture projects in FCS countries were often a continuation of previous programs and had the hallmarks of business as usual without adaptation to FCS contexts and needs. Core agriculture investments such as support for rehabilitation of agricultural production and productivity, drought management, horticulture and livestock, and land administration projects made up 37 to 79 percent of the total Agriculture and Rural Development portfolio depending on the FCS grouping, while irrigation accounted for 7 to 19 percent[7] and infrastructure, which excludes rural roads, 1 to 3 percent (Table 6.2). In Always FCS almost 55 percent of the portfolio was allocated to community-driven development (CDD) projects, of which the National Solidarity Program in Afghanistan alone accounted for $1.45 billion (58 percent of all CDD projects in IDA countries).

Lack of clarity on land rights can be a major cause of conflict, fragility, and stagnation in rural areas, and is a major constraint to private sector engagement. In Sub-Saharan Africa, which accounts for 76 percent of Always FCS, only 10 percent of rural land is registered which leaves the rest susceptible to various types of land grabbing and misallocation (Byamugisha 2013). The lack of formal registration of land has also led to underinvestment in the agricultural sector. The Bank has assisted only two FCS countries with land policy issues and

TABLE 6.2 Share of Bank Assistance to IDA Countries for Agriculture and Rural Development (FY00–12, by percentage)

| Subsector | Always FCS | Partial FCS | Never FCS | Total |
|---|---|---|---|---|
| Infrastructure | 0.9 | 0 | 0.8 | **0.7** |
| Community-Driven Development | 55.3 | 2.4 | 14.7 | **24.7** |
| Agriculture | 37.3 | 78.8 | 74.4 | **64.5** |
| Irrigation | 6.6 | 18.9 | 10.1 | **10.1** |
| **TOTAL** | **100.0** | **100.0** | **100.0** | **100.0** |

SOURCE: Business warehouse.
NOTE: Some totals do not add up due to rounding.

three with project investments on land administration approved since FY01; only one of these (Guinea-Bissau in FY06) was in Sub-Saharan Africa.

Outcomes of Bank-financed agriculture projects in FCS have improved in FY07–12 compared with FY01–06. However, the main focus of these projects was to address the immediate impact of conflict on agriculture (such as emergency rehabilitation) rather than the sector's broader constraints, including weak rural institutions and agricultural policy. Support to the agricultural sector has not displayed a viable transition strategy from emergency rehabilitation to longer-term sustained growth in the sector.

IFC assistance to FCS in the agricultural sector remained very modest. A recent World Bank report on agribusiness in Africa states, "Agribusiness can play a critical role in jump-starting economic transformation through the development of agro-based industries that bring much needed jobs and incomes" (World Bank 2013b: xiv). IFC could help FCS develop and improve market structures and value chains for agricultural products, and facilitate the transfer of simple technology and skills in the sector. However, investment support by IFC for agriculture, forestry, and fisheries in FCS amounted to $25 million, just over 1 percent of support to FCS during FY01–12. IFC AS for agribusiness was a small share of all AS by IFC in FCS during FY05–12. MIGA, like IFC, has found support to agribusiness and fisheries projects in Afghanistan and Sierra Leone to be complex and difficult to implement.

## Conclusions

The Bank Group lacks a strategic and effective framework for inclusive growth and jobs in FCS. During the period FY01–12 the Bank did not have a deliberate approach for job creation in FCS, and country programs broadly assumed that job creation would result from economic growth. In the FCS context, a focus on employment would have been particularly pertinent given the disruptions of civil war and the potential to contribute to social cohesion. Although an emphasis on investment climate reform to foster growth is necessary, it is not sufficient to foster job creation. First, investment climate reforms typically take a long time to bring about improvements in the business environment conducive to higher investment, growth, and ultimately employment generation. The long time horizon is amplified in FCS due to the low capacity and governance environment. Second, economic growth in the short run can be driven by capital intensive sectors (such as mining) without much employment generation. Resource rich countries were the fastest growing economies both in FCS and non-FCS. Third, other sectors and value chains face a range of constraints that tend to be more acute in FCS and need to be overcome in order to trigger inclusive growth and job creation.

The Bank has focused activities directly targeted to employment mainly on short-term jobs through projects supporting CDD, social funds, and public works programs over the period FY01–12. However, as discussed in chapter 5, such efforts were short term and did not aim to address long-term employment and employability.

Most analytical work to diagnose the constraints to the development of specific sectors has not been followed up by the design of relevant interventions. Agriculture and, in some countries, tourism are two sectors with strong potential to generate jobs in FCS. Over the last few years, there has been considerable analytical work to diagnose the constraints that impede the development of these sectors; however, the translation of this work into operations is still at an early stage.

The tracking of Bank Group support to job creation has been hampered by weak monitoring and evaluation frameworks. There are few evaluations of programs for job creation, and capturing indirect jobs through results frameworks is challenging. IFC and MIGA support to private investments has contributed to direct and indirect jobs, but tracking such impacts has shortcomings. IFC has tracked the total direct employment in the companies it has invested in through the Development Outcome Tracking System, but the system does not allow an attribution of incremental employment generation to IFC. The 2012 IFC jobs study provided insights into how IFC and the World Bank Group can further strengthen the employment-creation effects of their activities. However, tracking of jobs created by IFC interventions is not yet fully embedded in its monitoring system.

There is a need for an inclusive growth and jobs strategy for FCS derived from a cross-sectoral approach that can be translated into sequenced and prioritized interventions that take advantage of potential synergies across the Bank Group. Bank Group support has focused on investment climate reforms, which are necessary but not sufficient for private sector development. Infrastructure constraints and land rights have not been adequately addressed, and synergies across the Bank Group are lacking. Fragmented interventions reduce the potential effect on long-term employment generation. More systemic approaches to job creation and private sector development that foster spillover effects from resource extraction have emerged only recently.

## Endnotes

[1] Data were not available for Kosovo and Tuvalu.

[2] World Bank enterprise surveys have some methodological limitations, including that they typically cover only formal companies. The results may therefore not be representative in light of the large informal sector in fragile countries.

[3] Dutch disease refers to the appreciation of a country's exchange rate caused by the sudden inflow of foreign exchange, most often associated with the discovery of natural resources crowding out other tradable sectors in the economy (Corden and Neary 1982).

[4] The central idea of the growth poles theory is that economic development, or growth, is not uniform over an entire region, but instead takes place around a specific pole (or cluster). This pole is often characterized by core (key) industries around which linked industries develop, mainly through direct and indirect effects. Core industries can involve a wide variety of sectors, such as extractive sectors. Direct effects imply the core industry purchasing goods and services from its suppliers (upstream linked industries) or providing goods and services to its customers (downstream linked industries). Indirect effects can involve the demand for goods and services by people employed by the core and linked industries supporting the development and expansion of economic activities such as retail (Rodrigue et al. 2013).

[5] Countries with the largest agriculture sector in terms of GDP among FCS were Liberia (67.1 percent), Sierra Leone (54.2 percent), the Democratic Republic of Congo (49 percent), and the Lao People's Democratic Republic (37.7 percent), most of this taking the form of subsistence agriculture.

[6] The World Bank Group Agriculture Action Plan 2013–2015 (World Bank 2013a), paragraph 72, underlines the continued relevance of themes that emerged from the WDR on Agriculture in 2008, namely raising agricultural productivity and its resilience; linking farmers to markets and strengthening value chains to improve market access and trade; facilitating rural and nonfarm income changes; reducing risk, vulnerability, and gender inequality; and enhancing environmental services and sustainability. While there is little doubt that these themes are important to FCS countries, they were not systematically addressed by the Bank in FCS in 2000–2012.

[7] In the Always FCS group, all of the irrigation investments were in Afghanistan.

# References

Aterido, Reyes, Mary Hallward-Driemeier, and Carmen Pages. 2007. "Investment Climate and Employment Growth: The Impact of Access to Finance, Corruption and Regulations Across Firms." IZA Discussion Papers 3138, Institute for the Study of Labor, Bonn, Germany.

Beath, Andrew, Fotini Christia, and Ruben Enikolopov. 2012. "Randomized Impact Evaluation of Afghanistan's National Solidarity Programme: Final Report." MIT, Harvard, New Economic School, February 14, 2012. http://e-gap.org/wp/wp-content/uploads/20120220-BCE-NSP-IE-2FU-PAP.pdf.

Boakye, Daniel, Sebastien Dessus, Yusuf Foday, and Felix Oppong. 2012. "Investing Mineral Wealth in Development Assets." Policy Research Working Paper (WPS6089), World Bank, Washington, DC.

Byamugisha, Frank F. K. 2013. *Securing Africa's Land for Shared Prosperity: A Program To Scale Up Reforms and Investments. Africa Development Forum Series.* Washington, DC: World Bank.

CAO (Office of the Compliance Advisor/Ombudsman). 2005. "CAO Audit of MIGA's Due Diligence of the Dikulushi Copper-Silver Mining Project in the Democratic Republic of the Congo." Washington, DC: International Finance Corporation/Multilateral Investment Guarantee Agency.

Christiaensen, Luc, Lionel Demery, and Jesper Kuhl. 2010. "The (Evolving) Role of Agriculture in Poverty Reduction: An Empirical Perspective." UNU WIDER Working Paper No. 2010/36, World Institute for Development Economic Research, Helsinki, Finland.

Collier, Paul. 2006. "Economic Causes of Civil Conflict and Their Implications for Policy." Oxford University Press, April 2006. http://users.ox.ac.uk/~econpco/research/pdfs/EconomicCausesofCivilConflict-ImplicationsforPolicy.pdf.

Commission on Growth and Development. 2008. *The Growth Report: Strategies for Sustained Growth and Inclusive Development.* Washington, DC: World Bank.

Corden, W.M., and J.P. Neary. 1982. "Booming Sector and De-Industrialization in a Small Open Economy." *Economic Journal* 92 (368): 825-848.

De Vries, Hugo, and Leontine Specker. 2009. *Early Economic Recovery in Fragile States. Priority Areas and Operational Challenges.* The Hague: Clingendael Institute.

Dollar, David, Mary Hallward-Driemeier, and Taye Mengistae. 2005. "Investment Climate and Firm Performance in Developing Economies." *Economic Development and Cultural Change* 54 (1): 1–31.

Eifert, Benn, Alan Gelb, and Vijaya Ramachandran. 2005. "Business Environment and Comparative Advantage in Africa: Evidence from the Investment Climate Data." Working Paper 56, Center for Global Development, Washington, DC.

Foster, Vivien, and Cecilia Briceño-Garmendia, eds. 2010. *Africa's Infrastructure: A Time for Transformation.* Washington, DC: World Bank.

IEG (Independent Evaluation Group). 2011. *Capturing Technology for Development. An Evaluation of World Bank Group Activities in Information and Communication Technologies.* Washington, DC: World Bank.

Leo, Benjamin, Vijaya Ramachandran, and Ross Thuotte. 2012. *Supporting Private Business Growth in African Fragile States: A Guiding Framework for the World Bank Group in South Sudan and Other Nations.* London: Center for Global Development.

Porter Peschka, Mary. 2011. "The Role of the Private Sector in Fragile and Conflict-Affected States." Background Paper, World Development Report 2011, World Bank, Washington, DC.

Rodrigue, Jean-Paul, Claude Comtois, and Brian Slack. 2013. *The Geography of Transport Systems*. 3rd ed. London: Routledge, Taylor & Francis Group.

World Bank. 2011. *World Development Report 2011: Conflict, Security, and Development.* Washington, DC: World Bank.

____. 2012. *2012 World Development Report on Gender Equality and Development.* Washington, DC: World Bank.

____. 2013a. *World Bank Group Agriculture Action Plan 2013–2015.* Washington, DC: World Bank.

____. 2013b. *Growing Africa: Unlocking Potential Agribusiness.* Washington, DC: World Bank.

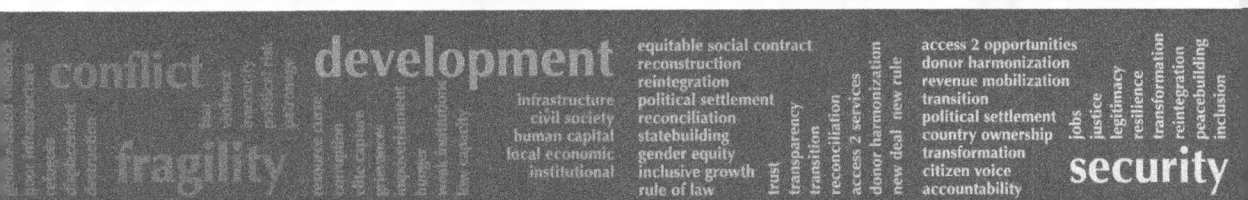

conflict development equitable social contract reconstruction reintegration infrastructure political settlement civil society reconciliation human capital statebuilding local economic gender equity institutional inclusive growth rule of law

trust transparency transition reconciliation access 2 services donor harmonization new deal new rule

access 2 opportunities donor harmonization revenue mobilization transition political settlement country ownership transformation citizen voice accountability

jobs justice legitimacy resilience transformation reintegration peacebuilding inclusion

fragility security

# 7   Tackling Gender Disparities in FCS

## CHAPTER HIGHLIGHTS

- In several conflict-affected countries, women and girls have been deliberately targeted to humiliate, intimidate, punish, and forcibly displace members of a community or ethnic group.

- Most of the demobilization, disarmament, and reintegration programs were not gender-sensitive and focused primarily on ex-combatants, with few programs for victims of violence.

- There was a lack of targeted programs for economic empowerment of women in fragile and conflict-affected states affected by gender-based violence.

Gender issues merit special attention due to the differentiated impact of conflict on men and women. Conflict situations produce different needs, coping strategies, and unique challenges. Conflicts may cause displacement or increases in the number of female-headed households. Disruption of household economies may compel women to become part of the workforce. Conflict situations may also provide them with new opportunities. Due to the impact of armed conflicts on civilians since the 1990s, acts of sexual violence and other forms of torture or mutilation have gained attention. In Sierra Leone, between 50,000 and 64,000 internally displaced women were sexually attacked by combatants. In the Democratic Republic of Congo more than 200,000 women and children have been raped since 2008.[1]

In several conflict-affected countries, women and girls have been deliberately targeted to humiliate, intimidate, punish, and forcibly displace members of a community or ethnic group.[2] High rates of sexual and gender-based violence may also persist in post-conflict settings before judicial and law enforcement systems are rebuilt.[3] New research commissioned by the Australian Agency for International Development highlights the urgent need for increased action to prevent sexual violence during conflict and after crises, and concludes that despite extensive efforts at the policy level, implementation of conflict and crisis related-sexual violence initiatives on the ground remains very limited (AusAID 2013).

The links between gender and FCS issues are emphasized in recent World Bank documents prepared for the International Development Association (IDA) Sixteenth and Seventeenth Replenishments (IDA16, IDA17) and in the 2012 World Development Report on (WDR) on gender equality and development (World Bank 2012b). Gender was one of the special themes for IDA16, where the Bank made a corporate commitment to strengthen efforts to integrate a gender perspective in IDA's support to fragile and conflict-affected countries (IDA 2012: 6). The special themes paper for IDA17 also states, "efforts are ongoing to better integrate gender into IDA's support to FCS" through gender-informed country strategy documents (country assistance strategies [CASs] and Interim Strategy Notes [ISNs]) and operations. However, there is lack of clarity on what "gender informed" entails.

The 2011 WDR on conflict states, "involving women in security, justice, and economic empowerment programs can deliver results and support longer-term institutional change," particularly given the context of the large number of female-headed households in violence-affected communities where women may engage in economic activity out of necessity (World Bank 2011: 258).

The 2012 WDR on gender emphasizes the role of women in peace-building and states that the needs and concerns of women (and their vulnerability) during conflict can help align policy priorities for the post-conflict reconstruction agenda. It also finds that women's representation

**TABLE 7.1** Unequal Legislation Discriminating against Women in Case Study Countries

| Legislation | Country Name |
|---|---|
| **1. Strengthening State Capacity** | |
| No nondiscrimination clause covering gender or sex in the constitution. | Yemen, Rep. |
| Customary or personal law is valid source of law under the constitution. | Congo, Dem. Rep.; Liberia; Sierra Leone; Yemen, Rep. |
| **2. Strengthening Citizens' Capacity** | |
| A married woman cannot travel outside her home the same way as a man. | Yemen, Rep. |
| For property acquired during the course of a marriage, there is no legal presumption of joint ownership between the husband and the wife. | Liberia, Nepal, Sierra Leone, Yemen, Rep. |
| If a spouse dies, the surviving spouse, regardless of gender, does not have equal inheritance rights to the marital home. | Yemen, Rep. |
| A woman's testimony does not carry the same evidentiary weight in court as a man's. | Yemen, Rep. |
| Adult married women need permission from their husbands in order to initiate legal proceedings in court. | Congo, Dem. Rep. |
| **3. Promoting Inclusive Growth and Jobs** | |
| A married woman cannot open a bank account in the same way as a man. | Congo, Dem. Rep. |
| A married woman cannot get a job or pursue a trade or profession in the same way as a man. | Cameroon; Congo, Dem. Rep. |
| A married woman cannot register a business in the same way as a man. | Congo, Dem. Rep. |

SOURCE: IFC Women, Business, and the Law database, accessed January 30, 2013.

in peace and reconstruction processes is very low. A review of 24 peace processes between 1992 and 2010 reported females to be 2.5 percent of signatories and 7.6 percent of the negotiating parties (World Bank 2012a: 308).

Unequal legislation and dual legal systems discriminate against women in FCS. The disproportionate impact of conflict on women is further exacerbated in several FCS by unequal legislation and the coexistence of dual legal frameworks (formal and customary law). An analysis of the country case studies shows that all six of the nine country case studies for which data was available (Cameroon, the Democratic Republic of Congo, Liberia, Nepal, Sierra Leone, and Republic of Yemen) have legislation discriminating against women (Table 7.1). Customary laws are often patriarchal and limit women's voice, and may restrict economic opportunities for women as they are not allowed to open a bank account, pursue a job, or register a business in the same way as a man.

This evaluation analyzes Bank Group engagement on gender issues in FCS IDA countries at two levels: Bank Group treatment of gender at the country strategy level and Bank Group focus on gender at the project level.[4]

## Bank Strategy on Gender in FCS/CAS Analysis

The majority of CAS documents reviewed recognize gender disparities but not necessarily in a fragility and conflict context.[5] The primary focus is on gender gaps in the health and education sectors, but the effects of conflict on women are not taken into consideration. The assistance strategies do not address the targeting of women as a tactic during armed conflict or gender-based targeting during the recovery period.

Most of the CASs now recognize gender disparities in varying degrees. Gender challenges and disparities were recognized by Afghanistan, Cameroon, Nepal, Solomon Islands, and Yemen throughout the review period but were not mentioned in the initial strategy documents for the Democratic Republic of Congo, Liberia, Sierra Leone, and Timor-Leste dating from the early 2000s (Table 7.2). On the whole, gender issues have been receiving more attention in the CAS for FCS since 2006. The IDA16 requirement of integrating gender in 100 percent of the CAS has further contributed to this trend.

The Bank's analytical work has contributed to a national dialogue on women in some countries. Gender-related analytical work has influenced country level gender dialogue in some of the case study countries (Afghanistan, Nepal, and Yemen). In Nepal the Bank's analytical work on gender contributed to agreement on a 33 percent quota for women in the Parliament. In Yemen, the CAS FY06–09 reported that the Bank's analytical work

TABLE 7.2 Snapshot of Gender Focus in Case Study Country-Level Diagnostics (FY01–12)

| Country | Majority of CASs mention gender disparities | CAS follow-up commitment to gender assessment | CAS with gender-integrated strategy or cross-cutting theme | Gender AAA[a] | Women targeted in war | Extreme legal discrimination in country[b] | CGA influence on programs | CGA influence on gender dialogue |
|---|---|---|---|---|---|---|---|---|
| Afghanistan | Yes | Yes | Yes | Yes | Yes | NA | Yes | Yes |
| Cameroon | Yes | Yes | No | No | No | Yes | No | No |
| Congo, Dem. Rep. | Yes | No | Yes | NA | Yes | Yes | No | No |
| Liberia | Yes | Yes | Yes | Yes | Yes | Yes | No | No |
| Nepal | Yes | Yes | Yes | Yes | No | Yes | Yes | Yes |
| Sierra Leone | Yes | Yes | Yes | NA | Yes | Yes | No | No |
| Solomon Islands | Yes | Yes | Yes | No | No | NA | No | No |
| Timor-Leste | Yes | Yes | Yes | NA | No | NA | No | No |
| Yemen, Rep. | Yes | Yes | Yes | Yes | No | Yes | Yes | Yes |

NOTE: AAA = analytical and advisory services; CAS = country assistance strategy; CGA = country gender assessment.
a. Dates for AAA: Afghanistan (2005), Liberia (2007), Nepal (2005), and Yemen (2005). b. Assessment is based on information contained in the IFC Women, Business, and the Law database.

contributed to developing a National Gender Strategy approved by the prime minister. When timely analytical work has been accompanied by attention to gender inclusive approaches in programs across the thematic areas it has been effective in conflict-affected countries.

Most of the gender-related analytical work in IDA countries has been conducted in countries that were not fragile or conflict affected. There were fewer gender assessments in Always FCS than in other IDA countries (Table 7.3). About 60 percent of the country gender assessments

TABLE 7.3 Gender-Related AAA in IDA Countries (2000–2012)

| Type of AAA | Economic and Sector Work | | Technical Assistance | |
|---|---|---|---|---|
| | Number of Countries with Gender ESW | Total Number of Gender ESW | Number of Countries with Gender TA | Total Number of Gender-Related TA |
| Always FCS | 5 | 5 | 4 | 7 |
| Partly FCS | 6 | 10 | 2 | 7 |
| Never FCS | 17 | 24 | 9 | 10 |
| **TOTAL** | **28** | **39** | **15** | **24** |

NOTE: AAA = analytical and advisory services; ESW = economic and sector work; FCS = fragile and conflict-affected states; IDA = International Development Association; TA = technical assistance.

and related analytical work was in Never FCS. The Bank's database lists gender assessments conducted for Cameroon, the Democratic Republic of Congo, and Sierra Leone, but documents were not traceable.

No specific trend is observable across countries in the extent to which gender is mainstreamed in projects. In Afghanistan and Nepal, the assistance strategies successfully influenced the Bank's project portfolio (Box 7.1 and 7.2.) on integrating gender across many sectors throughout the evaluation period. In Sierra Leone this does not appear to be the case. The 2005 CAS mentions gender issues in health, education, and social protection. While health and education projects benefited girls, there was little follow-through on social protection with the Ministry of Social Welfare, Gender, and Children's Affairs.

**BOX 7.1** The Bank's Achievements on a Rugged Path
to Gender Equality in Afghanistan

The Bank's Education Quality Improvement Projects I and II emphasize girls' education through improved access and recruitment and training of female teachers.

The Basic Package of Health Services program addressed gender issues both directly, by providing maternal and child health services, and indirectly by creating a significant number of jobs for women as community health workers and community midwives.

Bank assistance led to economic empowerment of women. Support for the Microfinance Investment Support Facility for Afghanistan led to the creation of a microfinance industry 70 percent of whose clients are women; and the Horticultural and Livestock Project enhanced female incomes since women are the majority of poultry producers.

The National Solidarity Program had mixed results for women with increased involvement in income generating activities, but little asset ownership or voice at village level.

The Bank contributed to the dialogue on gender through an FY05 Country Gender Assessment and two subsequent technical assistance activities. The Afghanistan National Development Strategy (2008–2013) committed to gender equality through the three pillars of security; governance, rule of law, and human rights; and economic and social development, and formulated a National Action Plan for Women in Afghanistan.

SOURCE: IEG 2012a.

# World Bank Support on Gender Issues at the Project Level

A gender analysis at the project level was conducted for the nine case study countries. Emphasis on gender issues was analyzed across three themes of the FCS evaluation: building state capacity, building capacity of citizens, and promoting inclusive growth and jobs. Table 7.4 provides a summary of results from the six case study countries and the three country program evaluations in FCS.

TABLE 7.4  Gender Sensitivity in Selected Sectors and Subsectors in FCS Case Study Countries (FY00–12)

| Countries | Health Projects | Education Projects | DDR or Reparations Programs | CDD Programs | Inclusive Growth and Jobs |
|---|---|---|---|---|---|
| Afghanistan | Yes | Yes | Not Applicable | Yes | Yes |
| Cameroon | Yes | Yes | Not Applicable | Yes | No |
| Congo, Dem. Rep. | No | Yes | No | No | No |
| Liberia | No | No | No | No | Yes |
| Nepal | Yes | Yes | Yes | Yes | Yes |
| Sierra Leone | Yes | No | No | Yes | No |
| Solomon Islands | Yes | Not Applicable | Not Applicable | Yes | No |
| Timor-Leste | Yes | No | Not Applicable | Yes | No |
| Yemen, Rep. | Yes | Yes | Not Applicable | Yes | No |

NOTE: Not applicable implies no Bank projects were financed for the category. CDD = community-driven development; DDR = demobilization, disarmament, and reintegration; FCS = fragile and conflict-affected states.

## BUILDING STATE CAPACITY

There is a lack of gender-sensitive actions in state-building in FCS. The focus on gender and the role of women in state-building is very limited across the case study countries. No country projects considered encouraging the role of women in state-building as peacemakers, negotiators, national level politicians, or public administrators. There was little action on training or reservations for women in government, with the exception of Nepal which designated quotas for women in Parliament and encouraged and monitored women's participation in public employment. Involving women in the process of state-building allows their needs to be prioritized especially in the post-conflict context. The participation of women in drafting the National Constitution in Yemen (in progress) is a good example. Having a clear agenda for the Ministry of Gender could also help. Most of the case study countries had a ministry of gender, but it tended to be sidelined by other ministries and had very small budgets further limiting its effectiveness.

## BUILDING CAPACITY OF CITIZENS

Several health and education projects of the Bank had a clear gender focus but lacked prioritizing in the FCS context. For health projects, this was particularly relevant in countries where women had special health care needs as a consequence of being targeted or attacked during armed conflict. An analysis of World Bank health projects in Sierra Leone shows that the focus has primarily been on maternal and child health, HIV/AIDS, malaria, tuberculosis, and the provision of affordable health services at primary health care centers. While significant achievements were made through some of these projects, there was no health care program to address needs of communities disproportionately affected during armed conflict. The Bank did not address the post-conflict needs of war victims with amputated limbs or other disabilities, and did not address post-traumatic stress and psychosocial counseling needs of women who were victims of sexual violence as a result of the conflict,[6] a situation worsened by the low doctor-patient ratio.

Overall the Bank's project portfolio emphasized girls education, mostly at the primary school level, through increased access and thereby increased primary school enrollment rates in FCS (based on case study countries). Increased enrollment of girls in school was seen in Afghanistan, Cameroon, Nepal, and Yemen. There was little emphasis on secondary and college-level education for women and girls.

The Bank funded a Peace Support Project (FY08) in Nepal with a gender-sensitive approach providing cash benefits to widows of conflict-affected families who are particularly burdened and disproportionately affected as a consequence of war.

Community-driven development projects like the Rural Water Supply and Sanitation Project and the Poverty Alleviation Fund empower and provide economic benefits to women in geographically remote and rural areas. Women are active members of the Water Supply and Sanitation User Committee and manage revolving funds for livelihoods programs.

The International Finance Corporation's public-private dialogue set up a Women's Entrepreneurship Development Fund in collaboration with the Nepalese government for businesswomen to overcome collateral related constraints and improve women's access to credit.

The Bank's analytical work on gender contributed to the national dialogue and led to a 33 percent quota for women in the national Parliament and earmarking of local government funds to finance activities targeted at women and children.

The Bank project portfolio did not distinguish between special education needs that may arise for FCS versus non-FCS. In general, the Bank gave little emphasis to "second chance" education and adult education which becomes more relevant in an FCS context where conflict may have forced boys and girls to drop out of school, reducing their prospects for acquiring employable skills in a post-conflict phase.

Most of the demobilization, disarmament, and reintegration (DDR) programs were not gender sensitive. Country case studies revealed that the Bank's engagement in DDR programs in FCS has been limited. Only one of four DDR programs in the cases study countries were gender sensitive. The rest focused primarily on ex-combatants. In the absence of post-conflict programs focusing on war-affected communities and victims of violence, the civilian population (particularly women) felt the perpetrators were being compensated (with the DDR program) rather than the victims of the war. No gender component was found in the DDR and reparation programs in Liberia and Sierra Leone—countries where women were deliberately targeted during armed conflict (Box 7.3). Women were largely excluded from the Democratic Republic of Congo's Emergency Demobilization and Reintegration Program (FY04) and the

DDR component of Sierra Leone's Community Reintegration and Rehabilitation Project (FY03). An exception was seen in Nepal's Peace Support Program which adopted a gender-sensitive approach by targeting widows and providing them cash payments as part of the reparations program since they were particularly burdened and disproportionately affected as a result of the war. Including women in such programs can facilitate a smoother social and economic transition in a post-war society, along with restoring government services in areas that were affected by the war.

CDD projects may involve women in different stages of the project cycle, but actual benefits to women are mixed across the CDD portfolio in FCS. For example, Afghanistan's National Solidarity Program, a regional flagship, resulted in increased involvement of women in income-generating activities but few gains in asset ownership. But there are some success stories. The 2013 impact evaluation reports that the program durably impacts the participation of women in local governance and increases men's acceptance of female participation in political activity and local governance (Beath et al 2012). In Nepal, the Bank adopted a gender-sensitive CDD approach through the Poverty Alleviation Fund (PAF) FY04. During field visits by Independent Evaluation Group staff, women at PAF sites reported participating in bridge construction, managing revolving funds for a livelihoods program resulting in social empowerment, seeing a rise in wages, and putting an end to exploitation by previous employers who were often rich land-owning farmers. In Sierra Leone, the Bank's second major post-war CDD program, the National Social Action (FY03) project involved women from the community as they prioritized health facilities and schools.

## PROMOTING INCLUSIVE GROWTH AND JOBS

The Bank did not have a long-term strategy for employment in FCS, which also affected women. An increase in literacy rates for women has not been followed by skills development or vocational training programs that could translate into employment. Employment generation for women in FCS comes from short-term employment in public works programs such as Sierra Leone's National Social Action Project or the Youth Employment Support Project. The Youth Employment Support Project provided temporary employment to about 18,000 youth of which 36.4 percent were women (Namara 2012), with a project-end target of 23,500 beneficiaries (about 77 percent achievement).

The Adolescent Girls Employment Initiative (AGEI) focuses on economic opportunities for women. The trust-funded AGEI is being piloted in eight low-income countries[7] that pose tough environments for girls. Each program is tailored to the country context, with the goal of helping adolescent girls and young women succeed in the labor market. Nepal and Liberia have seen success in implementing the AGEI by offering economic opportunities to adolescent girls. However, AGEI is a small scale program reaching 2,500 girls in Liberia and 3,500 girls in Nepal.

The International Finance Corporation (IFC) has addressed gender issues in FCS by providing access to credit for smaller businesses through programs like the Conflict Affected States in Africa (CASA) Initiative.[8] In the Democratic Republic of Congo, Liberia, and Sierra Leone, this initiative assists small business entrepreneurs, especially women, with access to credit, and in some cases such as the Democratic Republic of Congo, training to build and enhance management skills. IFC has also worked on regulatory reform to ease access to credit in some of the CASA countries. In Nepal, IFC has used public-private dialogue, and worked with the Nepal Business Forum to address challenges faced by women, such as the lack of collateral that restricts access to credit and restrictive laws that pose barriers for women who want to be commercially active. This work led the Nepalese government to set up a Women's Entrepreneurship Development Fund for businesswomen
to overcome collateral related constraints and improve women's access to credit.

There was no targeting of female-headed households in employment programs after cessation of armed hostilities. Female-headed households often have a higher chance of falling into poverty during armed conflict. Targeting can help them emerge from the poverty trap.

The impetus to provide women access to finance remained limited in FCS countries, but the few microfinance programs that exist were effective in benefiting women. Even though the total number of microfinance projects in FCS was limited, women did participate as beneficiaries in them. In Afghanistan, women were involved in microfinance and microbusiness through Bank-supported projects. In Sierra Leone, women were office bearers of bank accounts on behalf of their fishing or agricultural cooperative as it was a requirement of the Rural Development and the Private Sector Development project. Women also formed the majority of microfinance clients in Yemen where the Social Fund for Development supported 10 microfinance programs providing financial services (loans, savings) to low-income clients, especially women, focusing on improved living standards and increased income and economic activity (World Bank 2010: 13).

## Conclusions

The Bank has not responded adequately or in a timely manner to conflict-related sexual violence against women. Assessing whether women were targeted deliberately during armed conflict or faced extreme legal discrimination in the country could help determine whether gender-based violence should be prioritized in the Bank's country strategies and operations. An analysis of gender violence in the FCS case study countries shows that four of nine countries (Afghanistan, the Democratic Republic of Congo, Liberia, and Sierra Leone) could have benefited from greater sensitivity to this area.

Economic empowerment of women was not a focus of Bank support to FCS. The scale of gender-based violence can help determine whether programs require gender targeting or mainstreaming. For example, if there is a significant increase in the number of female-headed households after a conflict, programs like skills training, reparations, and access to finance may be more relevant for women rather than cash-for-work programs that may not create economic opportunities for women to join the workforce, especially in sectors such as road construction or mining which are male-dominated.

### Endnotes

[1] Data are from UN Women, Conflict-Related Sexual Violence, http://www.unifem.org/gender_issues/women_war_peace/conflict_related_sexual_violence.html.

[2] Data are from UN Women, Facts & Figures on Peace and Security, http://www.unifem.org/gender_issues/women_war_peace/facts_figures.html.

[3] The World Bank has made efforts to prevent sexual violence and provide treatment to victims through multi-donor trust funds like the Statebuilding and Peacebuilding Fund and the Learning on Gender and Conflict in Africa Program, but the scale of these efforts is extremely small with funding of about $12 million across seven countries in Africa.

[4] Chapter 7 is based on a background paper, "Gender Issues in FCS," that was commissioned for the evaluation and is available on request.

[5] Sierra Leone did not address the needs of women and children in the post-conflict period but eventually included gender disparity issues in the CASs.

[6] Severe needs for women were identified in field visits by IEG staff to the Western Area Rural District and Port Loko District in Sierra Leone and in a meeting with the Ministry of Social Welfare, Gender, and Children's Affairs.

[7] The eight AGEI countries are Afghanistan, Haiti, Jordan, the Lao People's Democratic Republic, Liberia, Nepal, Rwanda, and South Sudan.

[8] For more information visit the IFC's CASA Initiative website: http://www.ifc.org/wps/wcm/connect/region__ext_content /regions/sub-saharan+africa/advisory+services/strategicinitiatives.

## References

AusAID (Australian Agency for International Development). 2013. "Risk and Incidence of Sexual Violence in Conflict and Post-Conflict Zones." A Systematic Review Policy Brief, AusAID, Canberra, Australia.

Beath, Andrew, Fotini Christia, and Ruben Enikolopov. 2012. "Randomized Impact Evaluation of Afghanistan's National Solidarity Programme: Final Report." MIT, Harvard, New Economic School, February 14, 2012. http://e-gap.org/wp /wp-content/uploads/20120220-BCE-NSP-IE-2FU-PAP.pdf.

IDA (International Development Association). 2012. "Progress Report on IDA Support to Fragile and Conflict-Affected Countries." IDA16 Mid-Term Review, IDA Resource Mobilization Department Concessional Finance and Global Partnerships, October 2012, World Bank Group, Washington, DC.

Namara, Suleiman. 2012. "Sierra Leone—Youth Employment Support: P121052—Implementation Status Results Report: Sequence 05." World Bank, Washington, DC.

World Bank. 2010. "Yemen—Third Social Fund for Development Project." Implementation Completion and Results Report, ICR 000001330, World Bank, Washington, DC.

____. 2012a. *World Development Report 2013: Jobs.* Washington, DC: World Bank.

____. 2012b. *2012 World Development Report on Gender Equality and Development.* Washington, DC: World Bank.

conflict development fragility security

equitable social contract
reconstruction
reintegration
infrastructure    political settlement
civil society    reconciliation
human capital    statebuilding
local economic    gender equity
institutional    inclusive growth
rule of law

access 2 opportunities
donor harmonization
revenue mobilization
transition
political settlement
country ownership
transformation
citizen voice
accountability

equitable social contract
trust transparency transition reconciliation access 2 services donor harmonization new deal new rule
jobs justice legitimacy resilience transformation reintegration peacebuilding inclusion

# 8  Bank Group Inputs and Processes

## CHAPTER HIGHLIGHTS

• The assumption that the Country Policy and Institutional Assessment, designed primarily as an instrument to determine allocations under the performance-based allocation system, works equally well for FCS classification has proved to be problematic in recent years with the emergence of new drivers of fragility and conflict.

• The World Bank has enhanced its capacity to engage in FCS through significant increases in administrative budgets and in-country staff resources.

• The unit cost for project preparation in Always FCS in FY12 was 9 percent higher than in Never FCS IDA countries.

• The unit cost per project for supervision in Always FCS in FY12 was 18 percent higher than in Never FCS IDA countries.

• Technical assistance, financed predominantly by trust funds, registered an exponential increase since FY01 by 504 percent in the Always FCS IDA countries.

• There is a need to clarify the Bank Group's role on security and justice; the evaluation found demand for specialized services such as public expenditure reviews of the security sector conducted in partnership with United Nations agencies but little demand for Bank work on justice from clients or country departments.

- The IFC deploys its standard instruments with little adaptation or product innovation in FCS contexts.

- IFC performance incentives are not yet aligned with its strategy to increase engagement in FCS.

This chapter discusses the internal drivers and classification system for fragile and conflict-affected states (FCS) as well as the human and financial resources of the World Bank Group deployed to support assistance programs. Results for FCS International Development Assistance (IDA) countries are compared with those for non-FCS IDA countries in the light of the commitments made by Bank management to enhance its support. More recently, the International Finance Corporation (IFC) and the Multilateral Investment Guarantee Agency (MIGA) have also signaled their intention to focus on the FCS. Findings and data on IFC are included in this chapter. Data on institutional inputs and incentives are not available for MIGA, which does not have any field offices in client countries.

## The Relevance of Fragility and Conflict to FCS Classification

Classification of countries as FCS should be expected to draw attention to the relevance of fragility or conflict drivers to the Bank Group's strategy and operational work. The classification itself, however, is not based on an analysis of fragility or conflict. It uses the Country Policy and Institutional Assessment (CPIA) ratings as a proxy indicator of fragility. The assumption that CPIA, designed primarily as an instrument to determine allocations under the performance-based allocation system, works equally well for FCS classification has proved to be problematic in recent years with the emergence of new manifestations of fragility and conflict.

The FCS classification derived primarily from CPIA ratings has not been consistent with actual fragility and conflict risks in many countries. The World Bank draws up the FCS list, based on an agreement reached at the beginning of the IDA Fifteenth Replenishment with other multilateral development banks, as countries having a harmonized average CPIA rating of 3.2 or less. The only exceptions are countries with a United Nations (UN) or regional peacekeeping or peace-building mission during the past three years. In reality, the characteristics of fragility and conflict appear to have evolved from those prevalent in low-income countries that are driven by ethnic or tribal divides, natural resource capture, or military coups to include fragility arising from dissatisfaction and the demand for political change in lower- and upper-middle-income countries. The FCS list did not include any of the Arab Spring countries, or Mali, because they were over the CPIA threshold, and the list does not consider underlying causes of conflict or political instability. Nepal was excluded from the list during its decade of conflict and was only added in 2010 after the Comprehensive Peace Agreement, when a UN mission was deployed. Cameroon has been on the FCS list during four of the last 10 years and has moved in and out of the list twice based on CPIA ratings, although the underlying fragility and political risks remain acute and unchanged. Because

Cameroon's CPIA rating is above the 3.2 threshold, the country team still does not treat it as a fragile and conflict-affected state. Unless the CPIA criteria change, countries such as Nepal and Sierra Leone will graduate from the list of fragile countries although risks persist.

Compiling country-level data on fragility and conflict from available sources, the evaluation identified 16 countries that could have been added to the FCS list during the past decade. Five criteria for fragility were considered: political coup, conflict and violence, social exclusion and ethnic diversity, refugee inflows, and conflicts in neighboring countries. Several countries with internal conflicts (like Nepal and Sri Lanka) were also excluded from the list during their conflict years. As the Bank evolves toward more robust analyses of fragility and conflict, and seeks to develop country assistance strategies that are more relevant and responsive to fragility and conflict, a more robust approach to classification will be necessary. This could be done by expanding the list of indicators, supplementing the CPIA-based classification with other instruments, or substituting another instrument for classification purposes.

The Bank Group has developed additional indicators to assess fragility and conflict risks, but they are not currently used to develop the FCS list. The Bank Group relies on Post-Conflict Performance Indicators (PCPI) to inform the allocation of resources to countries eligible for IDA's exceptional allocations to post-conflict and reengaging countries. This set of indicators, which includes indicators of conflict, is currently used by the Bank to determine the size of exceptional allocations to countries deemed eligible for this support and are only applied ex-post, after countries have been deemed eligible for exceptional allocations (Box 8.1), rather than to determine if countries should be eligible for exceptional allocations. The PCPI instrument has added a conflict dimension to other indicators that resemble CPIA indicators. The use of explicit indicators of conflict and violence is thus not new but for this to be a useful tool for classification, such indicators would need to be applied ex-ante to all countries with fragility or conflict risks as part of a new or modified system for FCS classification.

## Management Commitments to Enhance Bank Support to FCS

In 2007, the World Bank made several commitments and changes to enhance the effectiveness of its support to the FCS. The aim was to make operational procedures more appropriate for FCS circumstances and to ensure the Bank is investing adequately in the quality of the staff and support required to make projects work in challenging environments. Early reforms were outlined in the March 2007 paper, "Strengthening the World Bank's Rapid Response and Long-Term Engagement in Fragile States" in which Operations Policy and Country Services (OPCS) identified the importance of supervision and noted that additional staff time was required to work effectively in fragile environments (World Bank 2007). This necessitated an increase in FCS field presence given the limited representation of posted

**BOX 8.1** Post-Conflict Performance Indicators Framework

During IDA replenishment negotiations in 2001–2002, the World Bank established an allocation framework to provide post-conflict countries access to IDA resources in addition those they receive under the regular performance-based allocation system. The Post-Conflict Performance Indicators (PCPI) framework was developed as a key instrument for this approach.

The PCPI measures the quality of a country's policy and institutional framework to support a successful transition and recovery from conflict as well as to foster sustainable growth, poverty reduction, and the effective use of development assistance. PCPI scores play a major role in determining the allocation of IDA resources to post-conflict countries and, starting in 2002, reengaging countries as well.

The PCPI is organized into four clusters:

• Economic Management and Structural Policies

• Social Inclusion and Human Development

• Governance

• Post-Conflict Risk

The first three clusters are used to assess the performance of all countries eligible for IDA special allocations. The Post-Conflict Risk cluster is designed to assess progress in areas that are particularly relevant in a post-conflict context. These include security, management of conflict and recovery, and peace building.

The PCPI partially overlaps with CPIA ratings. The overall PCPI score falls between 1 and 6. A PCPI score of 5-6 is broadly consistent with a CPIA rating scale of 3-3.5. However, the PCPI clusters provide a more in-depth and post-conflict relevant examination of some CPIA dimensions. The framework reflects an emerging consensus that development challenges in post-conflict and other fragile situations require a deep understanding of the links between the security, political, economic, and social spheres.

officers in these countries. A commitment was also made to increase support from back-line staff to FCS. The 2007 paper also made commitments to recruit high-quality talent and increase remuneration allowances for FCS postings. Additional career incentives were to be introduced by increasing the visibility and value of FCS field postings. This was to be complemented by better management of lessons learned in fragile environments, clearer guidelines on operational flexibility, and greater network support where required.

## Human Resources in FCS

Organizational capacity has been an important issue for the Bank in FCS in recent years. In response to the 2006 evaluation of the Low-Income Countries Under Stress (LICUS) Initiative by the Independent Evaluation Group (IEG), which identified organizational capacity as a major constraint to implementation, OPCS prepared a paper in 2007 on "Strengthening the World Bank's Rapid Response and Long-Term Engagement in Fragile States." The paper committed the Bank to addressing issues of organizational capacity in FCS and outlined a range of institutional reforms designed to improve Bank performance (World Bank 2007). These included the provision of more and better-organized staff support through increased field presence, callable sector capacity, institutional back-up, cross-country sharing of lessons, and incentives to attract top-performing staff to work in these difficult environments.

The first of the OPCS reforms sought to address an increase in the field presence in FCS. Broad agreement on the limitations of the mission model for working in fragile states led to consultations with country directors and country managers on increasing staff presence in country offices. Among fragile states 68 percent of countries had either no internationally recruited staff or only one in the field. The OPCS paper committed to lifting the field presence to ensure adequate local knowledge and understanding of the fragility context in which the Bank was working. There was an initial commitment to an additional 30 staff in LICUS or near-LICUS field offices.

The second and third reforms were focused on getting the right type of specialized capacity to provide extended mission support when required. A callable roster of staff and consultants was to be set up and deployed when required with FCS experience. In addition, work programs of the technical networks were to be adjusted to respond to FCS demands on legal and fiduciary functions, operational procurement, and strategy support.

The fourth reform was to make changes to the incentive system to attract high-quality staff to work in FCS. The commitment was to instigate proactive recruitment through making customized offers, grading country managers in FCS at the same level as counterparts in other countries, and revisiting promotion criteria with networks to better recognize the skills acquired in FCS. A guaranteed short-listing process was also to be introduced to facilitate better options for reentry of staff from their field assignments. In addition, new extended assignment benefits were introduced in 2008 for FCS staff. The rationale for these changes was to make FCS assignments more workable for staff with families and broaden the pool of those applying for positions.

**FIGURE 8.1** Increase in GE+ Staff in FCS Country Offices (FY06–12)

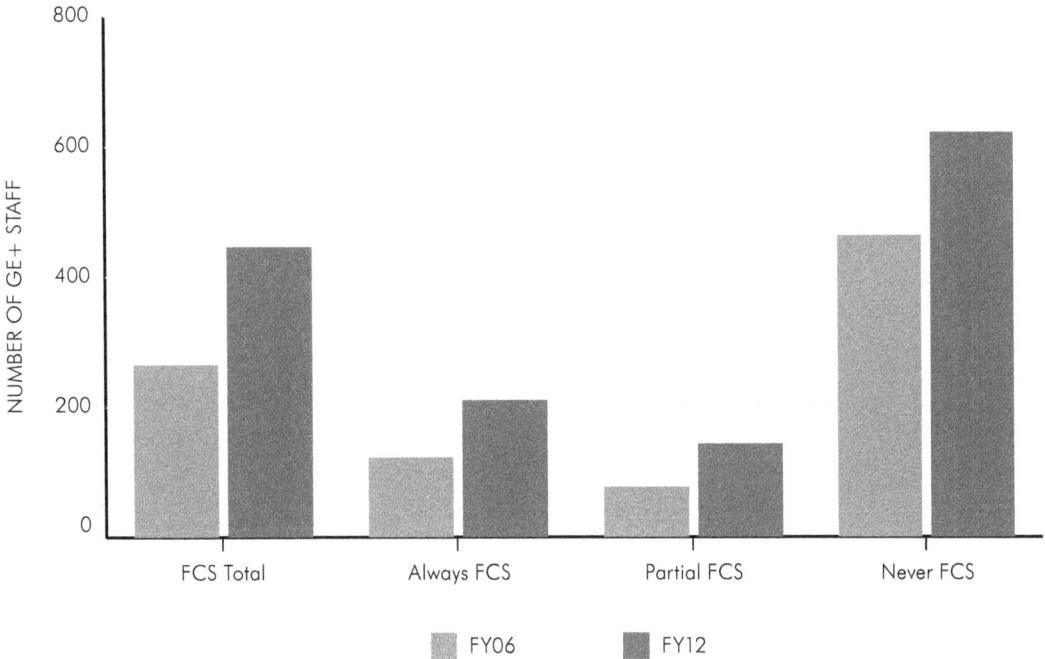

SOURCE: HR Analytics data of the World Bank.
NOTE: Total FCS figures include countries excluded from the Always and Partial lists that are used for broader analysis of data in the evaluation.

These reforms were to be implemented to ensure the Bank had a stronger organizational structure to address the challenges of working in FCS. This IEG evaluation looks at the progress, if any, against this commitment and gauges the impact of these changes on the performance of the Bank in FCS.

STAFF NUMBERS

World Bank staff numbers in FCS have increased considerably since 2006. In all IDA FCS, there has been a 68 percent increase from 265 GE+ level staff in FY06 to 446 GE+ level staff in FY12 (see Figure 8.1).[1] In comparison, GE+ staff increases in the IDA countries that were Never FCS have risen only 34 percent from 463 to 621. This shows that additional human resources have been deployed in IDA FCS in keeping with management's commitment. In addition, the only two FCS countries that previously had no Bank staff (Kiribati and Solomon Islands) now have GE+ staff based in the country resulting in a Bank presence in all FCS countries.

FIGURE 8.2 Number and Percentage Increase in GE+ Staff (FY06–12)

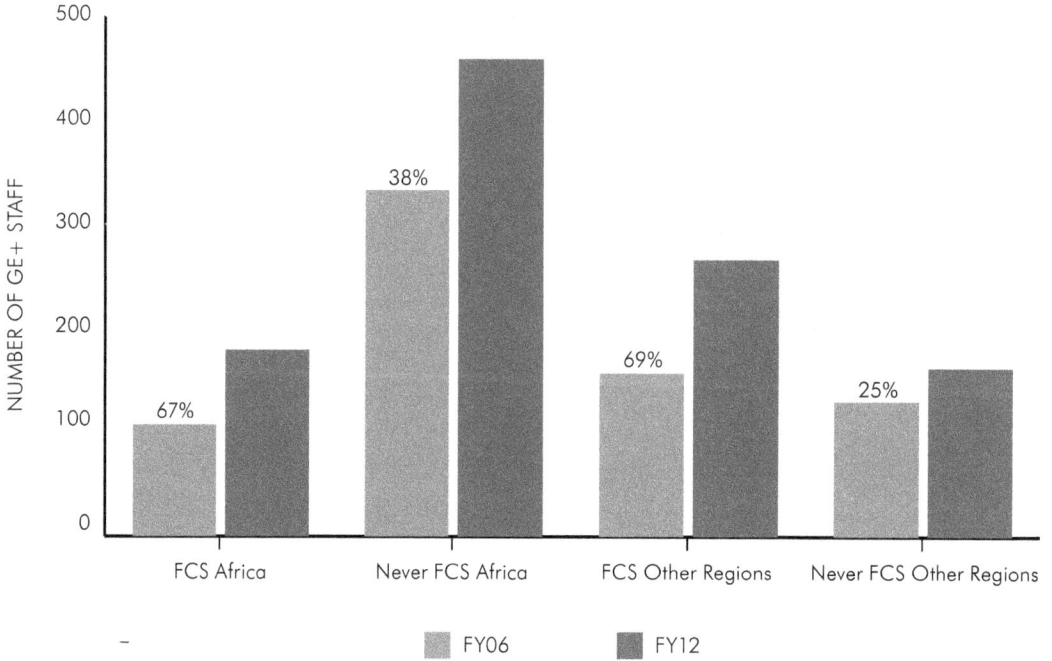

SOURCE: HR Analytics data of the World Bank.
NOTE: The percentage above the bars refers to the percentage increase from FY06 to FY12.

While the staff increases in FCS are considerable, there are notable regional and country-specific differences. The increases have been consistent between the FCS in the Africa Region and FCS staff in other Regions (see Figure 8.2), but this differs from the trend for the remaining IDA countries. In the Africa Region, countries which were Never FCS absorbed the majority of additional GE+ staff, while all other IDA countries only increased their levels by 25 percent. The increases in GE+ staff numbers have been steady over time (see Figure 8.3) indicating that the commitment to increase human resource capacity has been addressed in FCS both in the Africa Region and other Regions over time.

However, staff increases in FCS have been concentrated in a few countries. The top eight FCS countries accounted for 63 percent of the increase, five countries accounting for 46 percent of the increase. The high growth FCS countries are equally split with four countries in Africa and four in other Regions. This shows a targeting of resources to particular FCS countries, the growth being higher in countries where the country director is based than in other FCS country offices, and some case study countries still lacked staff capacity. The upgrading of country managers in FCS to the level of those in other countries is to be commended.

FIGURE 8.3 Number of GE+ Staff in FCS Africa versus FCS in Other Regions (FY06–12)

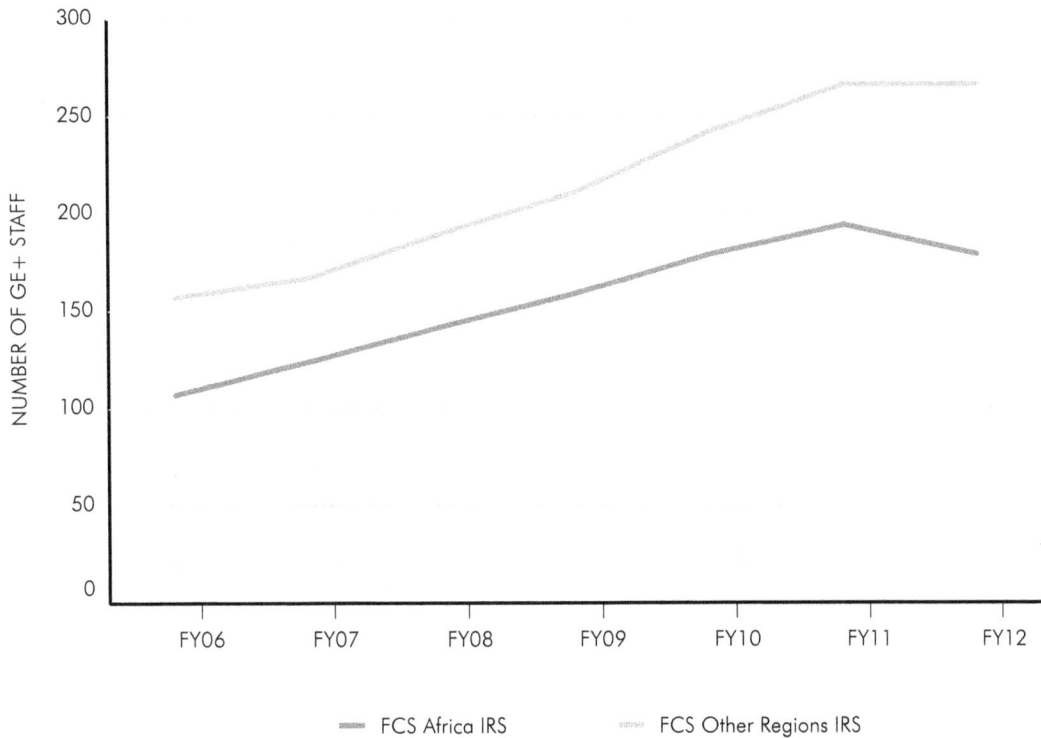

SOURCE: HR Analytics data of the World Bank.
NOTE: IRS = internationally recruited staff.

## NATURE OF STAFFING

The regions have also focused on the seniority and diversity of their staff, increasing internationally recruited staff by 150 percent (from 26 to 66) in FCS Africa and by 100 percent (from 41 to 80) from FY06 to FY12 in other Regions (Figure 8.4). This indicates that the 2008 human resources policies of the Bank led to decentralization of skilled Bank staff, and there is now a broader skill set contributing to the Bank's work in FCS.[2]

There has been a significant increase in female representation in FCS. In FY07 only eight FCS country offices had female GE+ staff. By FY12, more than 18 of the 32 FCS country offices had female GE+ staff. Similarly, in FY07 women made up only 15 percent of the total GE+ staff in FCS offices; by FY12 this figure had increased to 30 percent. It is noteworthy that 51 percent of all new international hires to FCS between FY07 and FY12 were female. This compares favorably with other IDA countries where only 30 percent of additional international hires were female. The improvement in the gender balance and diversity of staff in FCS has been a positive outcome of the 2007 human resources reforms.

FIGURE 8.4 International and Locally Recruited Staff in FCS (FY06–12)

NUMBER OF GE+ IN FCS AFRICA VS. FCS OTHER REGIONS, FY06–12

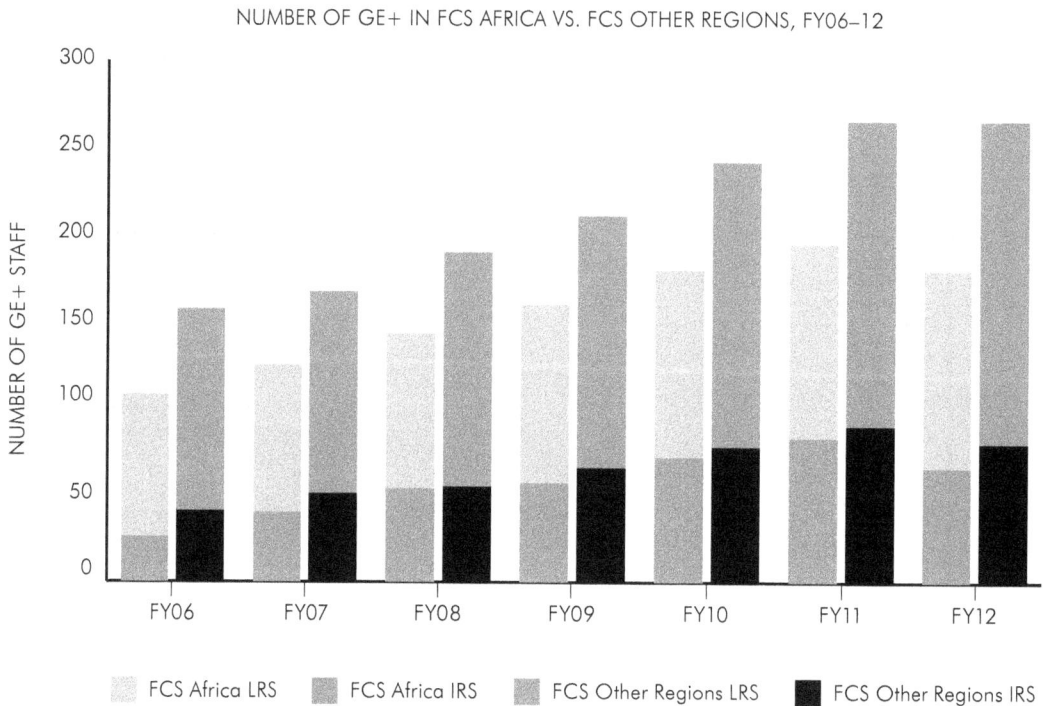

SOURCE: HR Analytics data of the World Bank.
NOTE: FCS = fragile and conflict-affected states; LRS = locally recruited staff; IRS = internationally recruited staff.

## DIFFICULTY IN RECRUITING AND RETAINING STAFF

Another objective of the human resources reform was to get specialized capacity at the right time and to institute good practice mechanisms and systems for capturing lessons among staff. While there is some evidence from the case study countries that specialized capacity has been called on for individual program tasks, and in the preparation of country assistance strategy (CAS) documents in the post 2011 World Development Report (WDR) period, there were few examples to indicate it had been institutionalized. Results from the IEG staff survey, conducted for this evaluation in the fourth quarter of FY13, was less positive about the support from headquarters and other regional offices than about the support from country office staff. There was little evidence from any of the case study countries that formal systems to capture lessons learned was prevalent, and few staff were aware of specific guidelines for working in FCS.

FIGURE 8.5 Views of Bank Staff Working on FCS Issues about Human Resources Incentives

WHEN WORKING ON A FCS COUNTRY, WHAT HAS BEEN YOUR EXPERIENCE IN EACH OF THE FOLLOWING HUMAN RESOURCE MATTERS?

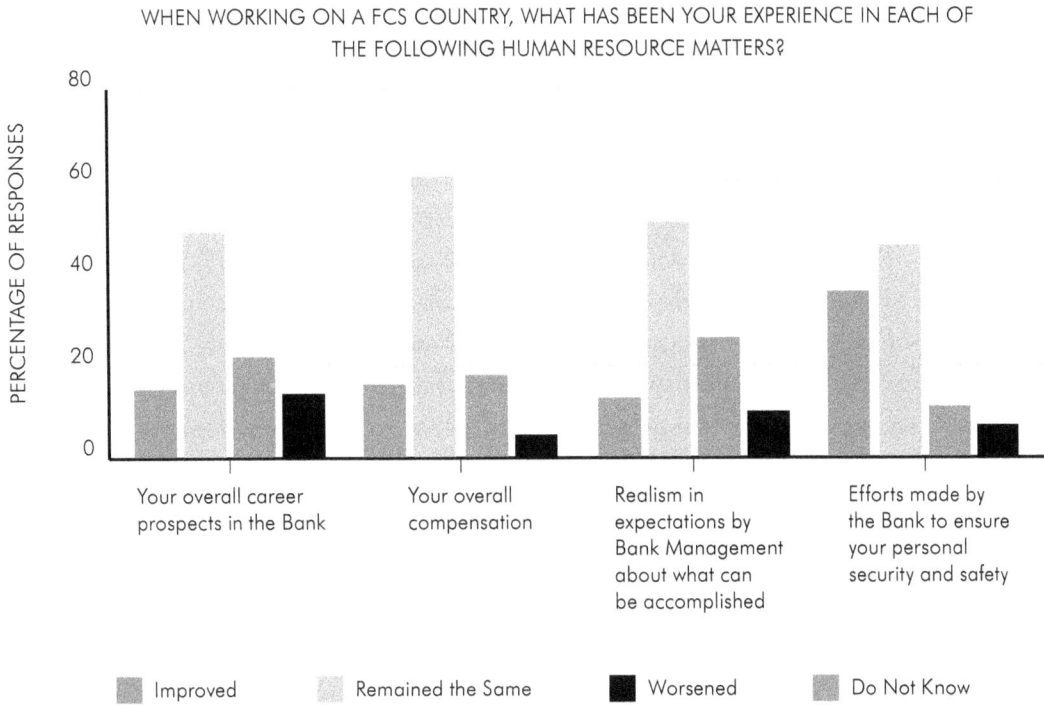

SOURCE: IEG FCS staff survey, 2013.

Staff remain unconvinced that financial incentives alone were the determinant in attracting seasoned Bank Group staff and managers to FCS postings. Most in-country Bank staff reported working in FCS because of the interesting assignment; none mentioned financial incentives as a determinant for taking on the position. In several case study countries, IEG found a large number of contractual staff (many of whom were young and inexperienced) who were there to gain the experience they value, and there continues to be a reliance on headquarter-based task team leaders in smaller country offices. The case study findings were further reinforced by staff survey results, where staff was more positive about the efforts to ensure their security and safety than about other incentives or the realism of management expectations (Figure 8.5).

Analysis of the data showed little change in the quality of international staff posted across all FCS in terms of years of experience in the Bank. There has been an increase in the number of senior level staff posted in FCS country offices (GH-level staff increased by 26 and GI-level staff by 5). This represents a 103 percent increase in the seniority of FCS field staff including country managers.

The other historical concern related to FCS staffing is the long-term opportunity and career prospects for those working in isolated and difficult operational conditions. Staff posted to FCS country offices are concerned about the opportunities they have when they return to headquarters or complete their posting. Human resources policies introduced to address these concerns, including mandatory interview inclusion for returning FCS staff applying for jobs at headquarters, are not perceived as adequate. Most staff feel that this incentive does not supplant the benefit of being deployed in large offices engaging regularly with multiple projects and senior staff, and having access to important networks that often do not reach the FCS country offices. Despite the aggregate results on deployment of more and experienced staff to FCS country offices, interviews with staffs from the case study countries indicate that they remain unconvinced about the effectiveness of human resources policies and career incentives or their ability to successfully transition back into positions at headquarters at the end of their field posting. In contrast, in other organizations, taking a post in a difficult environment such as FCS would be high profile and career enhancing rather than detrimental.

## The Role of the Center on Conflict, Security and Development

The Center on Conflict, Security and Development (CCSD) was established by the World Bank in 2011 to strengthen corporate support to the FCS agenda. The evaluation found evidence of different forms of support mobilized and provided by the CCSD to the country teams in FCS. It has successfully raised the profile and visibility of Bank Group support to FCS and established a community of practice for FCS work. Feedback from UN partners at headquarters indicates an improvement in the relationship at the corporate level. Beginning with the intensive engagement in preparation of the 2011 WDR, the UN-World Bank Partnership appears to be one that is valued mutually.

At the country level the feedback is more mixed but that seems to be more dependent on the personalities of the country management and the nature of the operational engagement by the country teams—more collegial where it is complementary and more fractious where overlapping activities or competition over resources lead to rivalries. The role of personalities is difficult to assess objectively, but the change in relationships when individuals arrive or depart is quite noticeable. CCSD could help to clarify with its UN counterparts the respective roles and boundaries of work on governance and rule of law, where the relationship with the United Nations Development Programme is unclear and uneasy.

FIGURE 8.6 Views of Bank Staff about the Role of the Center on
Conflict, Security and Development

TO WHAT EXTENT HAS THE CENTER FOR CONFLICT, SECURITY AND DEVELOPMENT
BEEN EFFECTIVE IN...?

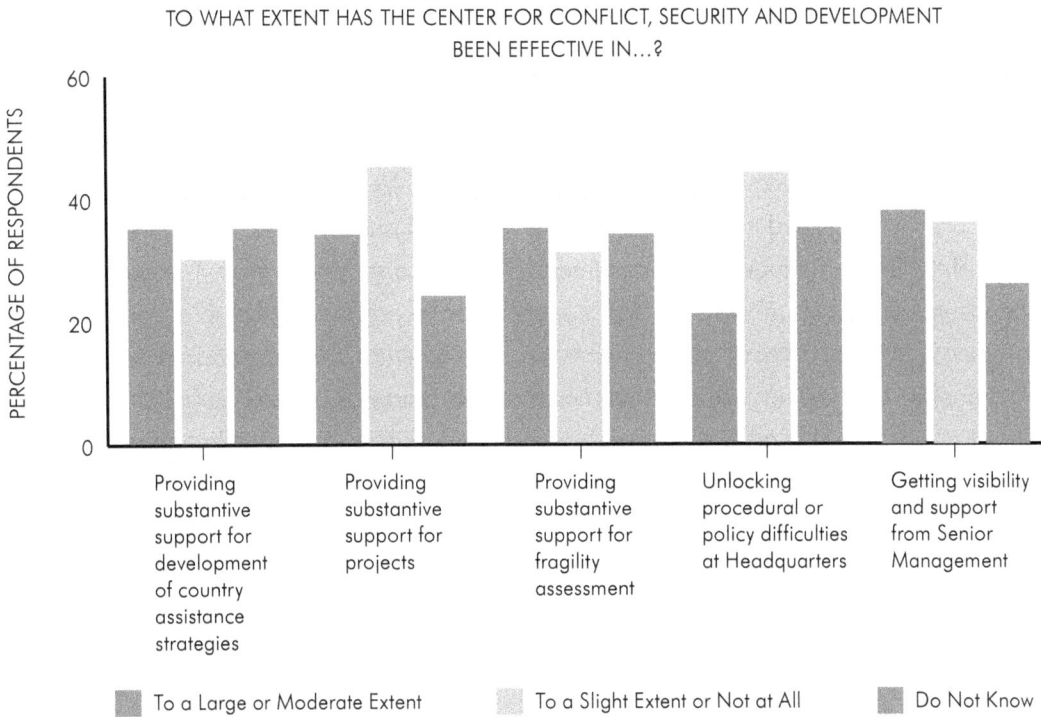

To a Large or Moderate Extent          To a Slight Extent or Not at All          Do Not Know

SOURCE: IEG FCS staff survey, 2013.

The survey of Bank staff working on FCS issues found the CCSD to be relatively more effective in getting visibility and support from senior management and in providing substantive support for CAS development and fragility assessments. Support for projects was reported to be somewhat less effective, and its role in unlocking procedural and policy difficulties at headquarters was reported to be less effective (Figure 8.6). CCSD seems to be aware that its initial focus on country assistance strategies and corporate partnerships needs to expand to operational support. One positive development during FY13 is the formal establishment by CCSD of an implementation support team to provide rapid operational help to task teams working in FCS. If task teams reach out to this support team, and they are able to demonstrate their problem-solving ability, this perception could change. At the same time, feedback from staff suggests that there is room for greater outreach to some of the staff who have voluntarily joined this community of practice and for greater attention to some barriers they still face.

# World Bank's Administrative Budgets in FCS

As part of the evaluation the World Bank's administrative budget, expenditures from FY01–12 were analyzed for all IDA-only countries, including the Always and Partial FCS, and the comparator non-FCS country groups. The budget analysis focused on expenditures for overall client services and the operational expenses on project preparation (lending), supervision and implementation support (supervision), and analytical and advisory activities (AAA), which was further subdivided into economic and sector work (ESW) and technical assistance (TA). Budget data were divided into two time periods, FY01–06 and FY07–12, to understand the effects of the 2007 management commitments to enhance support in FCS. The operational expenditures on project preparation and supervision were adjusted further to account for the increase in the number of lending operations over time (for a more complete description of the analysis and findings see appendix M). Financial data was adjusted for inflation by converting nominal U.S. dollars into constant 2011 U.S. dollars, and contributions from the Bank's budget and trust funds were analyzed separately. The country groupings are the same as for the FCS evaluation.

FIGURE 8.7 Operational Budgets in Always FCS (FY01–12, 2011 constant US$, millions)

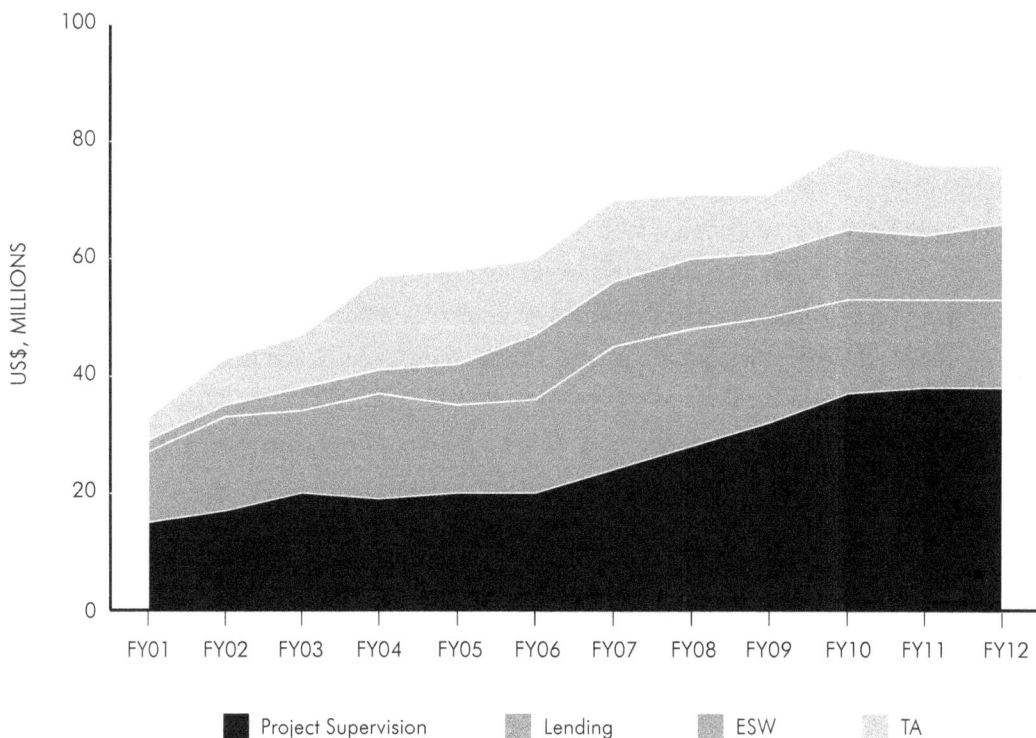

SOURCE: World Bank databases.
NOTE: ESW = economic and sector work; TA = technical assistance.

The main insight from the analysis is that the Bank has redeployed administrative budgets for country and operational expenditures in favor of FCS IDA countries compared with non-FCS countries; in real terms preparation and supervision expenditures per project have increased since FY07 in the Always FCS countries. More specific findings from the budget analysis (appendix M) for the period are summarized below:

- Operational expenditures in IDA countries have shifted with substantial increases for supervision and economic and sector work, particularly in FCS IDA countries; technical assistance registered even larger increases in all three country groups.

- Supervision expenditures for the Always FCS countries as a group increased by 151 percent from FY01–12, and by FY12 they had grown to almost half of the operational budget in that country group (Figure 8.7). The corresponding increase in Partial FCS was 125 percent, and in the Never FCS IDA countries it was 59 percent.

- Technical assistance, financed predominantly by trust funds, registered an exponential increase since FY01 by 504 percent in the Always FCS, 352 percent in Partial FCS, and 171 percent in Never FCS IDA countries. Among the Always FCS IDA countries, the largest increase occurred during FY06–07, while in Partial and Never FCS the largest increase occurred in FY09–10.

- The unit cost for project preparation (lending coefficient) increased by 7 percent in Always FCS IDA countries compared to the base values in FY07, but decreased by 23 percent and 13 percent respectively in the Partial FCS and Never FCS IDA countries; however the increase in Always FCS follows a decline of 31 percent in the lending coefficient from FY01–06 (see appendix H).

- The unit cost for project preparation in Always FCS in FY12 was 9 percent higher than in Never FCS IDA countries.

- The unit cost per project for supervision (supervision coefficient) increased by 20 percent in Always FCS IDA countries compared to the base values in FY07, while it decreased slightly in Partial FCS and Never FCS.

- The unit cost per project for supervision in Always FCS in FY12 was 18 percent higher than in Never FCS IDA countries.

- The average size of operations in FCS IDA fell by one-third, from $30 million to about $20 million, while in non-FCS IDA countries it increased marginally to $44 million. Adjusting for the size of operations, in FY12, the lending cost in the Always FCS was $13,200 per $1 million in new lending.

- Budgetary resources for lending per million dollars in commitment volume increased marginally in FCS during the FY07–12 period but decreased by 36 percent in Partial FCS and 26 percent in Never FCS (where average project size increased). Budgetary resources for supervision per million dollars in commitment volume increased by 55 percent in Always FCS during the FY07–12 period but had a more modest increase of 8 percent in the Never FCS group.

In conclusion, there is ample evidence that the World Bank has enhanced its capacity to engage in FCS through significant increases in administrative budgets and in-country staff resources. Portfolio performance in FCS has improved since 2001 compared to other IDA countries. As discussed in previous chapters, the outcome ratings for operations exiting the Bank's portfolio during FY01–12 provide evidence that the FCS now perform better than non-FCS. Improvements in the portfolio performance in FCS both for investment lending and policy-based lending indicate the potential for scaling up Bank support to FCS.

## Business Model, Product Mix, and Incentives at IFC and MIGA

IFC deploys its standard instruments with little adaptation or product innovation in FCS contexts; its conventional products may not be conducive to work with the largely informal economies of FCS. IFC and MIGA have shown little adaptation and innovation in their product mix and processes in FCS to respond to the different capacity and needs of the private sector and higher country and sponsor risks. Support to venture capital funds is small in scale and nascent, and does not meet the needs for high-risk early investments in small and micro enterprises. Harnessing the large potential for growth and employment generation in FCS would require more hands-on and sustained support to local entrepreneurs, providing advice, training, and coaching in addition to financial support. IFC may have a limited role in this nonconventional sphere, given its cost structure, business model, and product mix as a development financier. An IEG survey also highlighted the limited adaptation of IFC and MIGA projects to the conditions and constraints in FCS; Advisory Services were viewed as better adapted. The weak capacity environment and sponsor issues underline the need for systematically combining investments (and guarantees) with tailored technical assistance to strengthen the capacity of sponsors and clients to not only adhere to IFC's and MIGA's policy mandates, but also to upgrade lacking business skills. The higher country and sponsor risk in FCS would imply a review of IFC's and MIGA's risk tolerances.

IFC and MIGA have begun to implement some adaptations to their products to FCS contexts. IFC's five-year Conflict Affected States in Africa Program, a trust fund to finance advisory services, was perceived by stakeholders as relevant and additional. It contributed to generating more advisory projects and diversifying the portfolio in its target countries, FCS in Africa, but fell short in fostering product innovation to adapt advisory services offerings to FCS specific needs (Dahlberg 2012). MIGA has recently launched the Conflict-Affected and Fragile Economies Facility with the objective of catalyzing private capital flows to FCS and has used the Small Investment Program to support smaller investments in FCS.

## STAFFING

IFC has increased its staffing in FCS as part of internal reforms intended to align its organizational structure, processes, and incentives with its strategic priorities. In particular, IFC's reorganization, Vision 2010, launched in FY07, aimed to bring it closer to its clients through decentralization (IEG 2012). Accordingly, staff numbers in FCS have increased since 2006, albeit from a very low base, considering IFC was a more centralized institution prior to Vision 2010. Staffing in FCS doubled from 64 in FY06 (of which 6 in Always FCS) to 124 (of which 45 in Always FCS) by FY13. However, the increase in FCS (94 percent) was greater for IDA countries that are not FCS (131 percent). IFC has also expanded the number of country offices in FCS from 8 in 2006 to 20 in 2013, most of the increase being in Always FCS. Offices in Always FCS are small (average of 2 staff) compared to offices in Partial FCS or those in IDA non-FCS.

Most of the staff in FCS are from IFC Advisory Services. The staff increase in FCS has mostly been locally hired staff for Advisory Services. Advisory Services staff account for 63 percent of the FCS staffing compared with 53 percent in all IDA countries in FY13. Hiring in FCS is driven by direct hires rather than reassignment of existing IFC staff.

While field presence has increased, IFC has not yet fully aligned its human resources policies and incentives in FCS with those of the World Bank. While IFC follows the same compensation guidelines as the World Bank for staff posted in FCS, it has not implemented policies intended to foster career progression of FCS staff. IEG interviews indicated the difficulty of attracting quality staff to work in FCS offices. Staff also noted that local pay scales have not been commensurate with attracting local talent to IFC positions. A large proportion of the IFC and MIGA staff responding to the IEG survey also reported that they did not experience an improvement in human resource incentives.

IFC performance incentives are not aligned with supporting its strategy of increasing engagement in FCS. IFC manages its strategic objectives through several instruments, including its corporate scorecard. Although IFC has added indicators such as the number of projects supported in IDA countries to its scorecard, business volume remains a key performance metric in corporate and departmental scorecards (IEG 2013). This creates a disincentive for departments to support investments and advisory services operations in FCS, as these tend to be smaller in size and involve more complex appraisal and design due to opaque market and sponsor information and the presence of weaker sponsors. IFC notes the lower relative profitability of its portfolio in FCS, driven by higher expenses and risks. Development outcome ratings for investments and advisory services are also part of the scorecards; performance of investments in FCS is relatively weak. In short, doing business in FCS works against staff's volume and productivity indicators. MIGA has experienced similar challenges due to the often smaller size and high complexity of underwriting projects in FCS. IFC has also linked staff performance awards, such as the Long Term Performance Award, to developmental results and financial results for investment projects. However, because projects in FCS on average are smaller and riskier and more uncertain in terms of their developmental and financial performance, this creates a disincentive for staff to take on projects in FCS. Developing performance metrics adjusted to risks and conditions in FCS could help encourage a more risk-tolerant institutional culture.

## Endnotes

[1] GE+ staff refers to all the technical and managerial staff in the World Bank. The paper analyzes changes in GE+ staff deployment only since IEG's 2006 evaluation of LICUS countries and the OPCS paper emphasized the need for experienced and highly qualified staff in FCS contexts.

[2] The utilization of Face-time data (number of days of staff commitment by project) for this evaluation was abandoned given the lack of time series data. Data on Face-time are currently only available for two years, which does not allow meaningful comparison of trends in FCS.

# References

Dalberg. 2012. *IFC: Conflict Affected States in Africa Mid-Term Review*. Final Report. Washington DC: International Finance Corporation.

IEG (Independent Evaluation Group). 2012. *The Matrix System at Work: An Evaluation of the World Bank's Organizational Effectiveness*. Washington, DC: World Bank.

____. 2013. *Results and Performance of the World Bank Group*. Washington, DC: World Bank.

World Bank. 2007. "Strengthening the World Bank's Rapid Response and Long-Term Engagement in Fragile States." Operations Policy and Country Services, March 30, 2007, World Bank, Washington, DC.

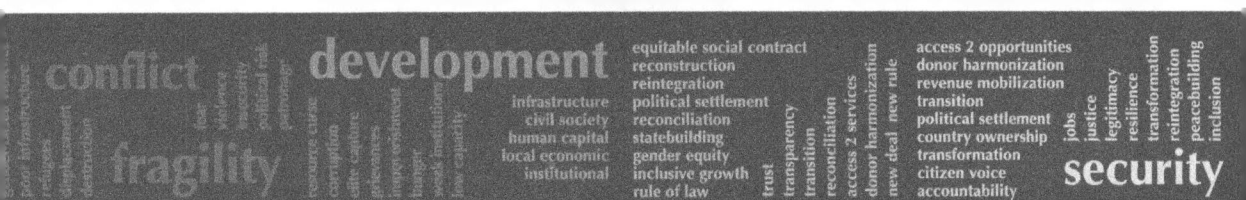

conflict development equitable social contract access 2 opportunities
reconstruction donor harmonization
reintegration revenue mobilization
infrastructure political settlement transition
civil society reconciliation political settlement
human capital statebuilding country ownership
local economic gender equity transformation
fragility institutional inclusive growth citizen voice
rule of law accountability security

# 9

# Aid Flows and Donor Coordination

## CHAPTER HIGHLIGHTS

- The share of overall ODA flows in IDA-only countries has changed in favor of fragile and conflicted-affected states, however, the share of IDA flows to FCS remains much lower than that to non-FCS IDA countries.

- Since 2002, overall ODA per capita to FCS has exceeded per capita ODA to other IDA countries, and ODA to FCS continued to grow.

- Despite the exceptional allocations that supplement performance-based allocations, FCS IDA-only countries still receive less ODA per capita from IDA than countries that are not FCS.

- Multi-donor trust funds are more than a source of finance in FCS and play a central role in donor coordination, policy dialogue, and institution building.

- Multi-donor trust funds with active involvement of recipient governments, clear governance protocols and responsibilities, and complementarity with Bank country programs, as in Afghanistan and Liberia, were more effective than those in Haiti and Sudan.

This chapter analyzes the evolution of official development assistance (ODA) to fragile and conflict-affected states (FCS) and summarizes the findings from IEG's review of multi-donor trust funds (MDTFs) in FCS. Developing countries, especially FCS, continue to rely heavily on ODA to address their short-term financing needs and support policy reforms toward inclusive growth and poverty reduction. In parallel, MDTFs have grown in importance as a modality of support and exceed IDA flows to Bank-administered programs in FCS. Donor coordination has improved at the corporate and country level, but at the program level successes in some areas have been tempered by difficulties in others.

## Official Development Assistance to FCS

The share of overall ODA has changed in favor of FCS, but the share of International Development Association (IDA) flows to FCS remains much lower than to nonfragile countries. Prior to the year 2000, aggregate aid to FCS was much less than aid to nonfragile countries. The increase in ODA to FCS over the past decade has resulted in aggregate ODA disbursements to FCS catching up with ODA to nonfragile countries by 2010.

Since 2002, overall ODA per capita to FCS has exceeded per capita ODA to other IDA countries, and it continued to grow. Per capita ODA to FCS surpassed ODA to non-FCS in 2002 and has more than doubled over 2001–2011. But IDA provided more per capita ODA to non-FCS than to FCS during this period (Figure 9.1). In 2011, FCS received $27.1 billion in overall ODA, disbursements from IDA being about $1.5 billion. Over the same period, ODA from the European Union to FCS grew much more rapidly and in 2011 was more than $2.5 billion, half of its assistance to the IDA-only countries.

The increase in ODA to FCS was primarily driven by growth in bilateral aid from Development Assistance Committee (DAC) countries. DAC countries were the most significant contributor of aid to IDA countries as a whole and to FCS in particular. DAC assistance to FCS increased by more than 250 percent, compared with a 40 percent increase to non-FCS. By 2011, the FCS were receiving 53 percent of aid from DAC countries, compared to 30 percent in 2000. DAC assistance has in effect reversed the trend of performance-based allocation of aid to low-income countries.

Multilateral aid to FCS also grew much faster than aid to other IDA countries, but the increase in financing by IDA was slower than that for all multilaterals. Multilateral aid to FCS increased by 170 percent over 2000–2011, compared to 70 percent increase for non-FCS. Among the multilateral agencies, the contribution of European Union (EU) institutions to FCS was 70 percent more than IDA's disbursements in 2011 (Figure 9.2).

FIGURE 9.1 Overall per Capita ODA to IDA Countries (2011 constant prices)

## A. OVERALL ODA

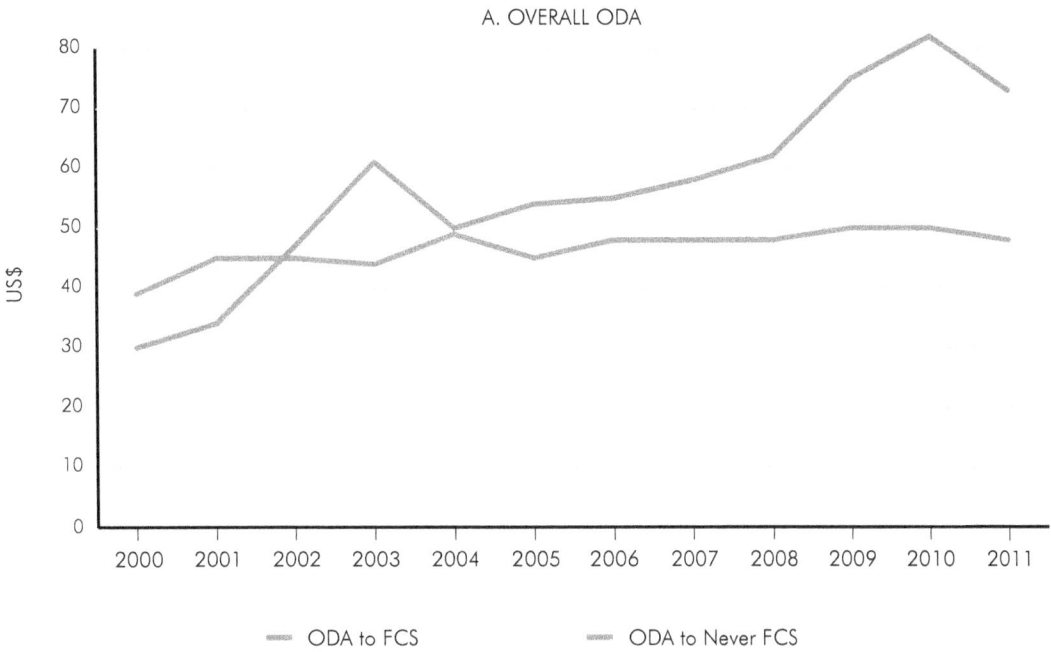

ODA to FCS ▬▬▬    ODA to Never FCS ▬▬▬

## B. IDA FINANCING

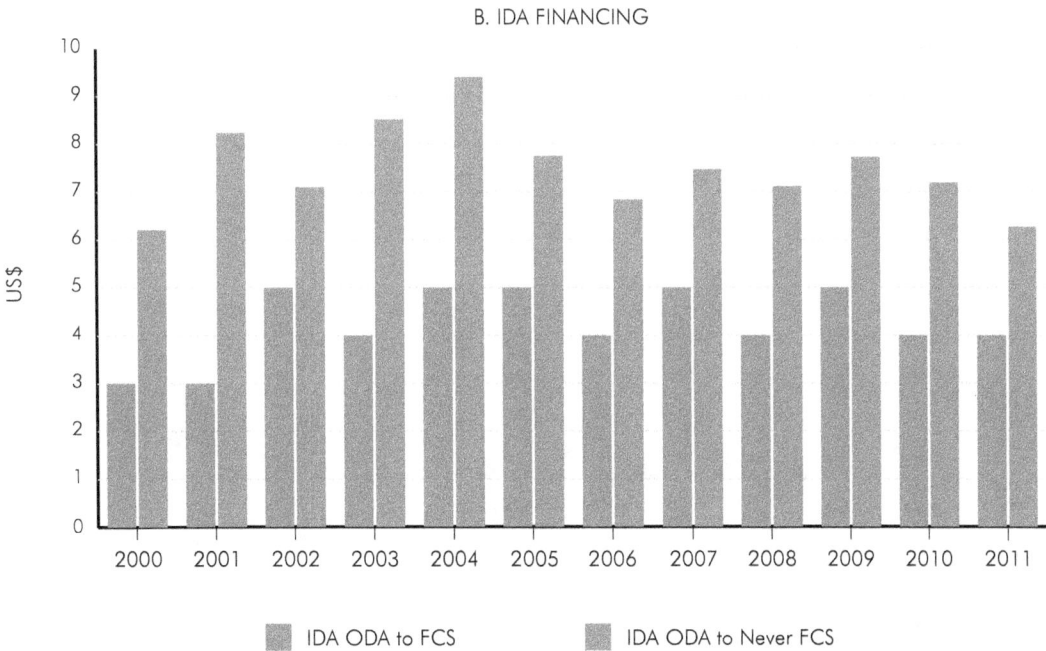

IDA ODA to FCS ▪    IDA ODA to Never FCS ▪

SOURCE: OECD database.

FIGURE 9.2 ODA Disbursements to IDA FCS (2011 constant prices)

A. ALL DONORS, DAC COUNTRIES, MULTILATERALS

B. IDA, EU INSTITUTIONS, AFDF

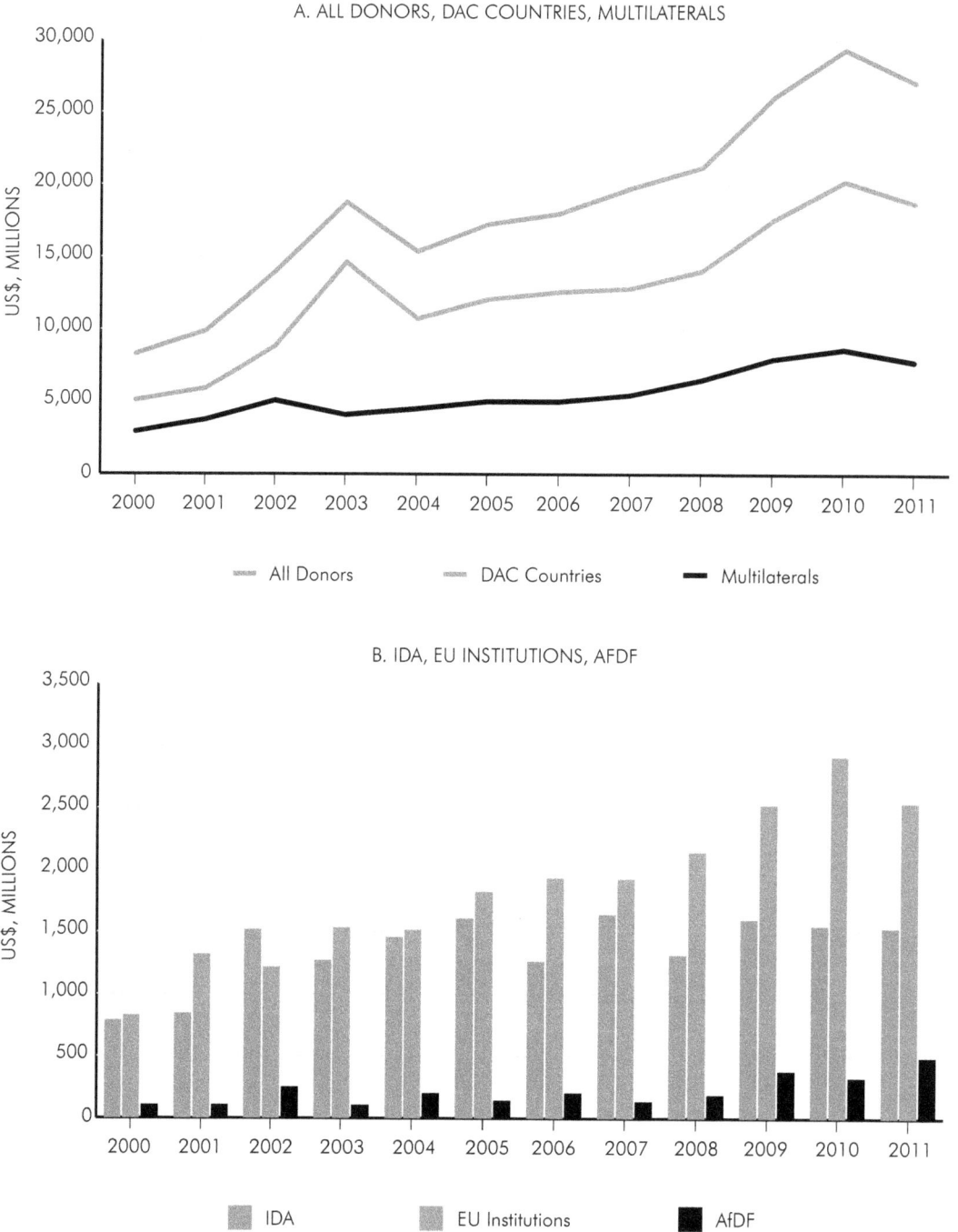

SOURCE: OECD database.
NOTE: AfDF = African Development Fund; DAC = Development Assistance Committee; EU = European Union; FCS = fragile and conflict-affected states; IDA = International Development Association; ODA = official development assistance.

FIGURE 9.3 Share of ODA Disbursements to FCS IDA Countries in Total ODA

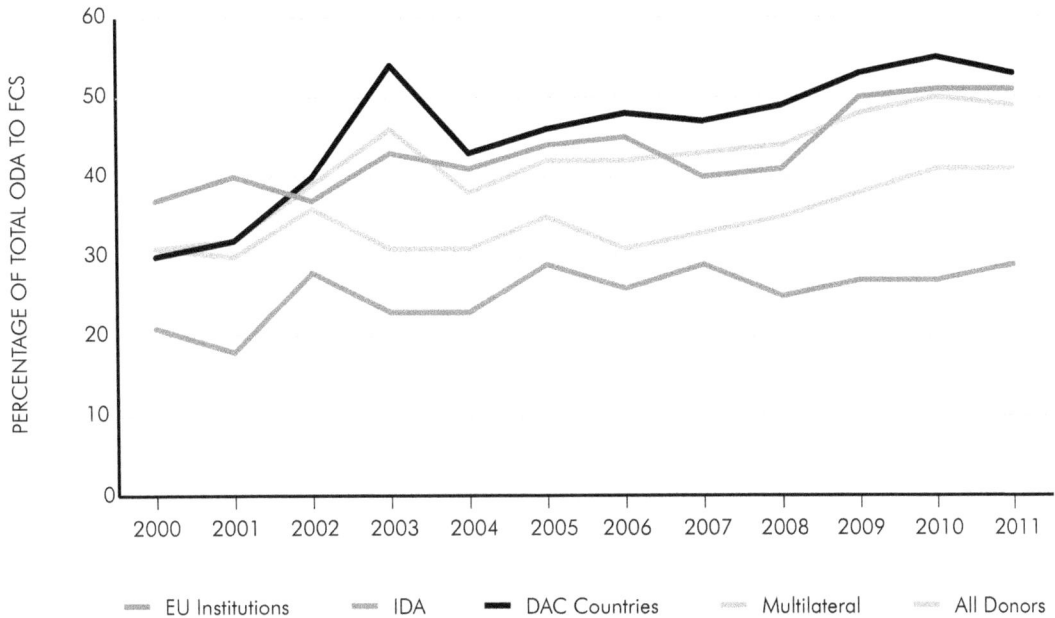

**FIGURE 9.3** Share of ODA Disbursements to FCS IDA Countries in Total ODA

SOURCE: OECD database.

ODA from all donors to FCS reached 50 percent of the total ODA to IDA-only countries in 2010, while the share of ODA from all multilateral agencies to FCS remained around 40 percent in 2011 (Figure 9.3). The share of EU assistance to FCS increased to 50 percent of its aid to all IDA countries while the share of IDA's ODA to FCS is under 30 percent of its assistance to IDA-only countries. Including blend countries, IDA to FCS remains about one-sixth of total IDA assistance. Despite exceptional allocations to post-conflict and re-engaging countries that supplement performance-based allocations, the FCS still receive less ODA per capita from IDA than countries that are not fragile.

There was significant variation among donors in ODA to FCS. Among bilateral organizations, France, Germany, Japan, United Kingdom, and the United States have historically been the highest contributors to FCS and to non-FCS (Figure 9.4). ODA from these donors to FCS increased in 2006–2011 relative to 2000–2005. Other major donors, such as Australia, Canada, and non-DAC countries (which include Brazil, China, India, the Russia Federation, and South Africa) increased their development aid to FCS very substantially in 2006–2011. China's aid increased by nearly 30 percent annually during 2004–2009, and China intended to provide concessional loans of $10 billion to Africa in 2010–2012 (OECD 2012). Another example is India which recently established its own global aid agency with an estimated budget of $15 billion for 2012–2017, a large share of which is going to FCS.

FIGURE 9.4 ODA by Major Donors (2011 constant prices)

A. MAJOR DONOR CONTRIBUTIONS TO NEVER FCS

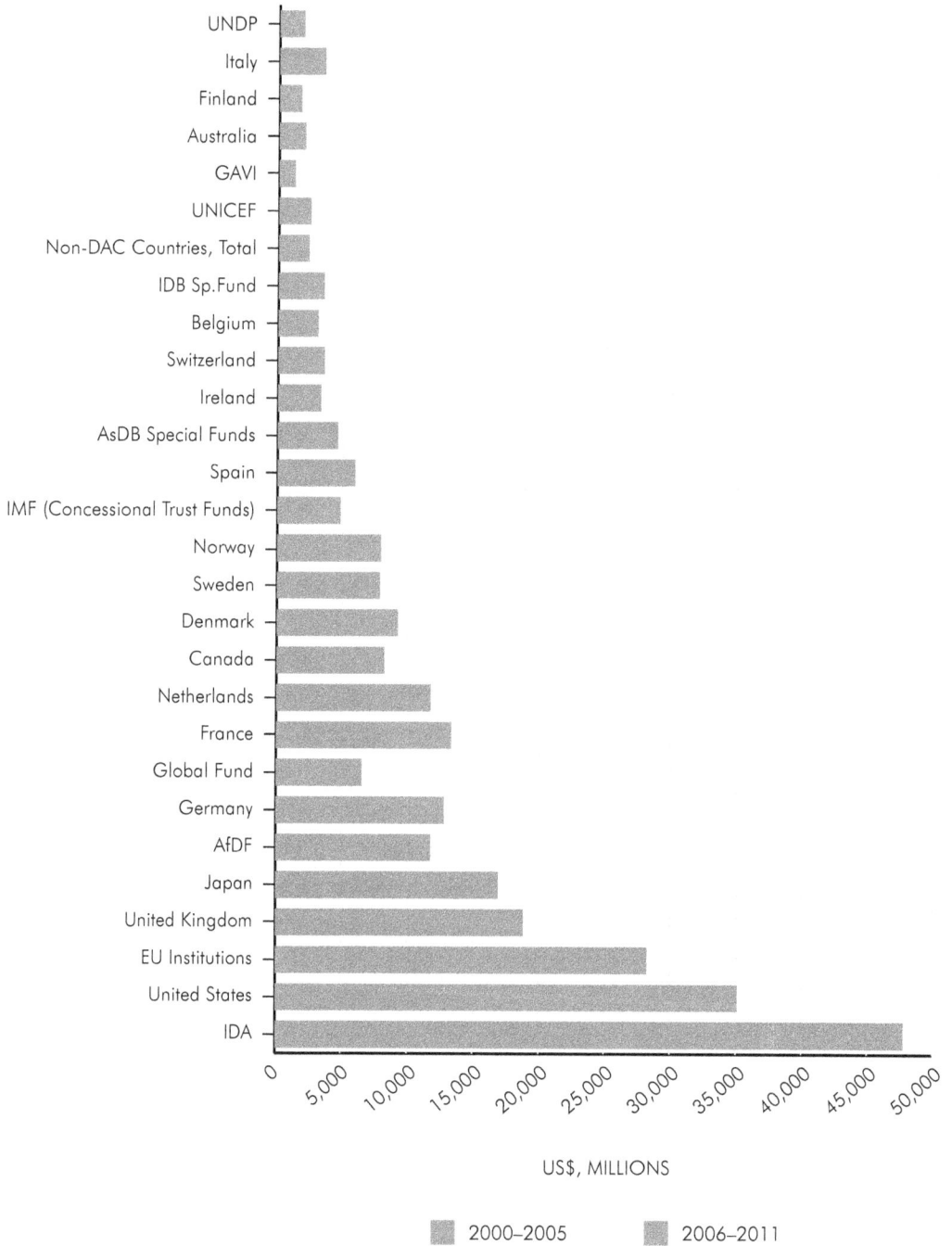

US$, MILLIONS

■ 2000–2005     ■ 2006–2011

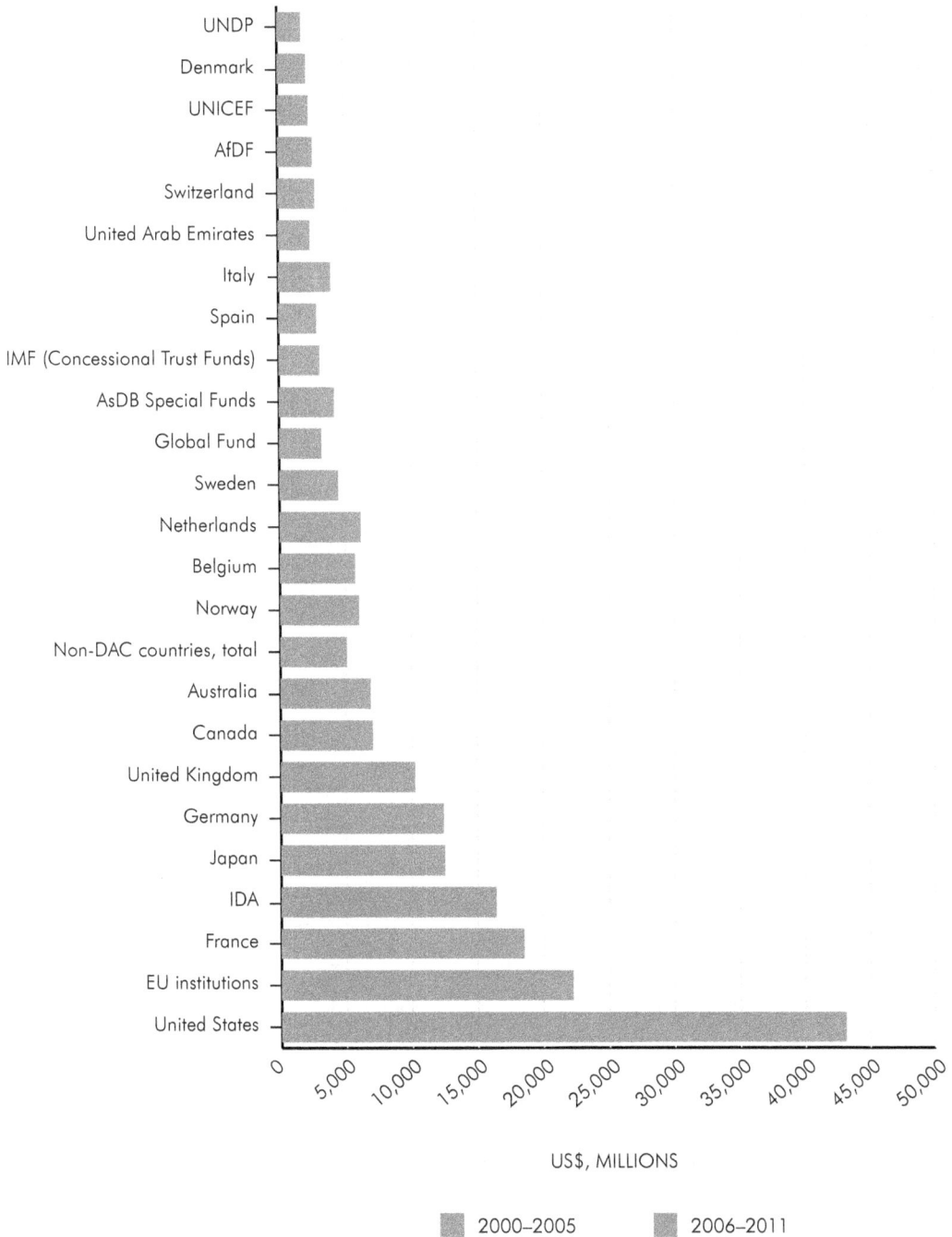

B. MAJOR DONOR CONTRIBUTIONS TO FCS

US$, MILLIONS

■ 2000–2005　■ 2006–2011

SOURCE: OECD database.
NOTE: AfDF = African Development Fund; ADB = Asian Development Bank; DAC = Development Assistance Committee;
EU = European Union; GAVI = Global Alliance for Vaccines and Immunizations; IDA = International Development
Association; IDB Sp. Fund = Inter-American Development Bank Special Operations Fund; IMF = International Monetary
Fund; UNDP = United Nations Development Programme; UNICEF = United Nations Children's Fund.

ODA destinations have changed since 2000 with growing donor interest in post-conflict and disaster-affected countries. Among FCS, the highest aid receivers during 2006–2011 were Afghanistan ($34 billion), the Democratic Republic of Congo ($17.6 billion), Sudan ($13.1 billion), Haiti ($8.5 billion), Cameroon ($6.5 billion), and Côte d'Ivoire ($6 billion). While Afghanistan, the Democratic Republic of Congo, and Haiti received support from many donors, Cameroon and the Democratic Republic of Congo received significant share of ODA from France, reflecting close ties between these countries. Geographic proximity was also relevant, the United Arab Emirates being a major donor to the Republic of Yemen, while Australia was the most important bilateral donor to Solomon Islands and Timor-Leste.

In per capita terms, small countries and islands attracted the largest concessional resources. Solomon Islands had the highest ODA among FCS, while Tuvalu was the top aid receiver among the nonfragile countries (Table N.13). On average, allocations to small islands that were FCS received less aid than those that were not fragile (Tuvalu had nearly four times more ODA than Solomon Islands). In contrast, among other FCS, the countries that have been fragile for many years tended to receive higher volumes of aid per capita.

Among the nine case study countries, aid has been well targeted to Always FCS. Five of the six countries that were always FCS—Afghanistan, Liberia, Sierra Leone, Solomon Islands, and Timor-Leste—received higher per capita ODA than the Partial FCS group. Out of these nine countries, Solomon Islands received the highest average annual ODA per capita ($641), followed by Timor-Leste ($273), Liberia ($228), and Afghanistan ($171).

## The Role of Multi-Donor Trust Funds in FCS

MDTFs play a key role in providing essential financing and targeted support to FCS. The ability of MDTFs to quickly mobilize resources and support recovery efforts prior to countries building formal partnership arrangements makes them an important tool in FCS and a necessary bridge to longer-term development. As part of the FCS evaluation, an assessment of the World Bank's management of MDTFs in FCS was undertaken, looking at the six largest country-specific and the two largest multicountry trust funds.[1] The Independent Evaluation Group (IEG) evaluation of trust fund support for development found that Bank-administered MDTFs exceeded IDA as a source of finance in FCS where they play a vital role in supporting countries to rebuild and establish basic services after periods of conflict or disaster (IEG 2011b). The Bank is a well-respected partner and often the preferred custodian for these funds, but there has also been frustration at Bank performance and processes. The review focused on evaluating the performance of MDTFs as a development tool in FCS rather than looking at the results of individual projects funded through the trust funds. In addition to the large MDTFs in FCS, the reconstruction MDTF in Haiti was included to see how it compared with trust funds more closely aligned to conflict situations.

## THE MDTF CASE STUDIES

The Sudan and Timor-Leste trust funds were set up as post-independence arrangements to fill a gap prior to IDA funds being available to support public services. The Afghanistan and Liberia trust funds followed protracted periods of conflict and helped rebuild services and infrastructure. The West Bank and Gaza trust fund was established to prepare the region for self-government, and the Haiti trust fund was an international response to the 2010 earthquake. In countries such as South Sudan that are not yet IDA eligible, MDTFs help to set up government systems and provide essential services. The review grouped together the Multicountry Demobilization and Reintegration Program (MDRP) and the Transitional Demobilization and Reintegration Program (TDRP) as a multicountry trust fund designed to respond to the security needs of Africa's Great Lakes region, while the Statebuilding and Peacebuilding Fund (SPF) is included as a multicountry trust fund designed to provide strategic funding to catalytic programs in FCS.

In the case study countries, the MDTF commitments have been larger than the IDA allocations (Figure 9.5), except where the trust fund had a single purpose (e.g., infrastructure in Liberia and reconstruction in Haiti). The MDTFs provided over $7.5 billion in funding over the last 10 years, more than 70 percent of it to Afghanistan. They are an important cofinancing tool for a variety of projects. Financial management received the highest share ($2.8 billion); agriculture and rural development had the largest number of projects (22).

## MULTI-DONOR TRUST FUND FOCUS

MDTFs work best when they fit the country context and are strategically linked to the broader donor agenda. Where trust funds were attuned to the specific fragility issues in the country (or region) they have been more successful. In Liberia, the MDTF was set up to respond to a particular government priority. It had a simple structure and clear focus and dealt with the capacity limitations in the country at the time. Where trust funds had open-ended objectives, they have struggled to maintain relevance and deliver against their original mandate. In the case of South Sudan, the trust fund was large and complex, with a large cohort of actors. This made management difficult and the trust fund was unable to deal adequately with significant capacity limitations[2] in the government and with the overwhelming needs outlined in the development plan.

FIGURE 9.5 Total Amount of Funding from IDA and Trust Funds per Economy (US$, millions)

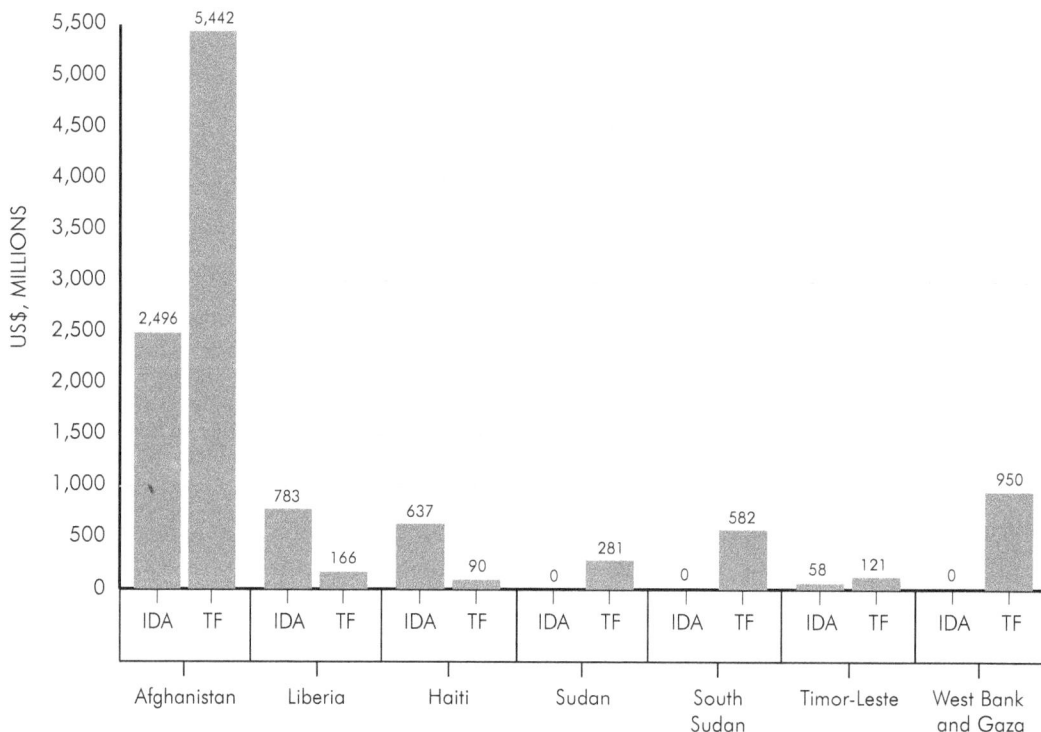

SOURCE: World Bank databases.
NOTE: IDA = International Development Association; TF = trust fund.

MDTFs work best when they are central to the Bank's country strategy and are linked to the Bank's portfolio. MDTFs have played a complementary role in the Bank's portfolio. MDTFs in Afghanistan and Liberia have successfully established links between IDA allocations and trust funds. In Liberia, IDA funds were used to design and prepare initial project proposals while the trust fund was being set up. In Afghanistan, IDA funds were used to pilot programs, which the trust fund helped to scale up. In Timor-Leste trust funds were used to prepare for a longer-term IDA program. In Africa's Great Lakes region, the MDRP was used to deliver a demobilization, disarmament, and reintegration (DDR) program that complemented other Bank work in the region and the SPF is supporting operationalization of the 2011 WDR (Box 9.1).

The MDRP was a regional response to the peace agreement in the Democratic Republic of Congo. It was an innovative DDR trust fund that identified the multi-country nature of the problem and set up a mechanism to deal with it. This was succeeded by the TDRP with a broader mandate to consolidate the results of the MDRP and provide emergency financing for future DDR requirements. These trust funds were a multi-partner coordinated response to DDR that was the most appropriate approach to a regional conflict and offered an effective mechanism for mobilizing and coordinating financial resources and harmonized support.

The SPF supports a wide range of small projects (averaging $2.7 million) and, as acknowledged in its 2012 mid-term review, serves as a catalytic and flexible resource to support operationalization of the 2011 WDR. While SPF projects have shown that they can be innovative and support conflict-sensitive policy, there is only limited evidence that they have informed Bank country strategies, and the current monitoring and evaluation of projects tracks implementation progress rather than outcomes. Recent work in response to the recommendations of the mid-term review is addressing this issue with a new monitoring and evaluation framework focused on the objectives of the SPF in addition to the objectives of individual projects.

## GOVERNANCE OF MDFTS AS AN AID MECHANISM

Trust funds worked best where there was an active government voice to direct donor support. This requires government ownership, including influence over its governance arrangements, and an explicit link to the country's development plan. Where the recipient government was given authority to articulate direction (as in Afghanistan and Liberia), the MDTFs were better able to respond to operational issues. Strong government engagement, robust debate, and clear reporting protocols allowed decision makers to avoid ad hoc demands.

This was not always the case. In Haiti and South Sudan,[3] the trust funds were affected by special interest priorities and were less able to focus on building core government capacity. MDTFs have played a useful role in providing stable and predictable financing in circumstances where there was pressing demand for recurrent costs such as in Afghanistan, Timor-Leste, and West Bank and Gaza (IEG 2010, 2011a, 2012). These MDTFs were also able to identify the most pressing investment priorities and finance gaps in development plans.

Crafting the right approach in these circumstances is important to avoid disparities becoming entrenched. In Timor-Leste this was illustrated by the growing resentment toward overseas advisers and in Afghanistan in the unsustainable public service salaries.

Having a structure with clear governance protocols and demarcated responsibilities was central to successful trust fund arrangements. Where the decision-making process was straightforward and coordinated by a management committee of limited size, projects were relevant, better prepared, and complementary to MDTF goals and best able to adapt to changes in context. Where the trust funds were encumbered with multiple reporting lines, various committees and constant requests from donors, progress was slow. In Afghanistan and Liberia, donor roles were clearly specified in the governance arrangements, while in Haiti and South Sudan more flexible management arrangements complicated governance and caused friction between the various parties.

These messages resonate with the findings of a recent review of UN–World Bank partnerships (Demetriou and Morrison 2013). The review found that effective cooperation in MDTFs (e.g., Iraq), projects and programs (e.g., Cambodia Local Governance and Service Delivery) can often be based on parallel, independent funding streams for Bank and UN activities, bound together by common reporting systems and other mechanisms for strong mutual accountability, particularly within a framework that supports and strengthens government leadership.

## MDTF PERFORMANCE

MDTFs have much to offer as a delivery mechanism, but implementation delays can have a negative impact on the reputation of the Bank and cause donor frustration. In most cases, these issues have been the result of unreal expectations about what can be delivered and the speed with which structures and systems can be built. This was particularly apparent in South Sudan where the broad mandate and unrealistic requests stifled the long-term success of MDTF projects. Haiti too faced delays. The Bank was criticized for overpromising and underdelivering. Most of the MDTFs made good progress once the systems and protocols were in place, but getting projects underway takes time. The Bank needs to be more explicit about the length of time it takes to become operational. Donors need to be more realistic in their expectations on results and impact.

Overall, the ability of the various trust funds to report on fund specific issues has been poor. Regular reporting on the progress of projects is adequate but there is little evidence that the specific objectives of the trust funds or the higher objectives of donor harmonization, capacity building, and government system strengthening are being monitored or evaluated. This has limited the ability of the trust funds to adequately measure their success and was particularly relevant to the multicountry funds such as the SPF, which has not adequately examined the catalytic effects of its programs. Quarterly reports of project status were the primary source for measuring trust fund performance. Independent reviews are the only other source of trust fund performance, and these were limited by the lack of data and MDTF documentation.

Transition arrangements for MDTFs are often poorly conceived and do not adequately respond to recipient country needs. Both in interviews with trust fund staff and in the documentation, transition issues appear to have been left until the fund was winding down. There was little discussion about how the trust funds fit into the long-term strategy plans, nor how the funding gap might be filled in the longer term. This was apparent in Timor-Leste where performance in the post-conflict period was good, but the longer-term outcomes were marginal.

MDTFs are essential in the funding of critical recovery activities in FCS and necessitate trust fund structures that foster rather than hinder donor cooperation. In each of the case studies, the Bank was seen as a responsible and trusted partner who had the necessary skills and proficiency to deal with complex financial management and program arrangements. However, careful consideration of the trust fund structure is essential to avoiding inefficiencies and conflict between agencies. In Haiti, the structure of the trust fund as a Financial Intermediary Fund required all implementing partners to comply with the operating procedures of the Bank often with significant delays. In South Sudan, Bank procedures were identified as a factor in the poor performance of the MDTF and caused friction between partners. Establishing separate trust funds with joint representation on management boards (e.g., in Afghanistan) was an effective harmonization approach, as was the allocation of specific sector roles to different partners (e.g., Timor-Leste partnership with the Asian Development Bank).[4]

In most cases, MDTFs have not received adequate senior management attention except where there have been problems, as in South Sudan, or the funding is so large, as in the Afghanistan Reconstruction Trust Fund, that it has significant reputational risk. More effective incorporation of trust funds into Bank work and appropriate incentives are required to make trust fund work more visible and important to senior staff. Without the high-level engagement and recognition, trust funds struggle to find high-caliber staff to work with them, and the skill set required remains undervalued.

Knowledge, skills, and understanding of MDTFs are undervalued in the Bank. Trust fund financing has now eclipsed IDA money in many FCS. This is not reflected in the caliber and quality of trust fund staff. External staff brought in to work on trust funds may be technically proficient but have also contributed to delays in operations due to limited knowledge of Bank systems and procurement processes, causing frustration among donors. There have also been issues with the retaining and sharing of knowledge among those working or planning to work on MDTFs. And internal management of the knowledge such as partnerships and donor relations acquired in working with trust funds is not formally retained or disseminated by Bank units, reducing the Bank's ability to transfer lessons across trust funds to make them a more effective development instrument.

## Donor Coordination

Donor coordination in FCS occurs at multiple levels—corporate, country, MDTF, and program. Partnerships at the corporate level are manifested in continued support for IDA and in high-level dialog with the UN. At the country level, FCS who are coming out of conflict often have a heavy UN presence for peacekeeping and helping countries arrive at a political settlement. In countries where lingering security remains a concern, partnerships with organizations like the North Atlantic Treaty Organization that play a leading role in security have become more necessary over the past decade. At the trust fund level, as discussed above, MDTFs are an important vehicle for donor coordination but are also a product of donor collaboration. MDTFs can be a highly effective tool for government engagement, harmonization, strategic alignment, and the security of financial flows, but these outcomes require thoughtful structures and skillful management to ensure the process is not compromised by unrealistic expectations and poor programming.

At the corporate level, both in preparing the 2011 WDR and during subsequent implementation, the relationship between the World Bank Group and the United Nations appears to have improved. This new spirit of partnership is manifested in more frequent contacts at the highest level, including joint statements issued (UN and World Bank 2008) and a joint mission by the UN Secretary-General and the World Bank President to the Democratic Republic of Congo, Rwanda, and Uganda resulting in a commitment of $1 billion in Bank Group financing for regional development priorities. The Bank's partnership with the UN in FCS is also visible in regular contact and collaboration between the Bank's Center on Conflict, Security and Development and UN agencies, which is furthered by the UN–World Bank Fragility and Conflict Partnership Trust Fund.

At the program level, partnerships are equally essential but the results are uneven. Significant challenges remain at the country and operational level, and consequently a recent review of the UN–World Bank partnership concludes that progress in strengthening the overall partnership in FCS has been mixed. Attempts to promote closer Bank–UN partnerships through high-level agreements have generally been unsuccessful. There continues to be wide variation at the country level in the nature and extent of partnership, and relationships are still primarily determined by the personalities involved. Furthermore, institutional differences and constraints, insufficiently understood, are a challenge for both. The continuing lack of "inter-operability" between Bank and UN systems remains a challenge for the cross- or joint financing of projects. Despite the 2011 WDR priority on security, justice, and jobs, except for a few examples (such as the Liberia Security Sector Public Expenditure Review), there has been little joint work between the UN and the Bank in these areas and little Bank activity at all in security and justice (Demetriou and Morrison 2013).

Collaboration with donors interested in certain sectors, such as those leading to the Millennium Development Goals, is more ubiquitous. In countries where bilateral donors have financed small, stand-alone projects, the on-budget support provided by IDA has sometimes been perceived as a threat, as in the health sector in Yemen, where some agencies felt overwhelmed by the scale of IDA financing. A more difficult challenge arises when other donors are collaborating with each other but the Bank is an outlier. Nepal is a case in point where the Bank declined to join with eight partner agencies and the United Nations Development Programme (UNDP) in supporting the Local Government and Community Development Program. The Bank also withdrew its support from the Nepal Peace and Development Strategy 2010–2015[5] supported by 13 development partners over relatively minor differences in language referring to the ongoing political dialog and because of the perception that it was led by the UN systems in Nepal, adversely affecting the Bank's relations with the donor community.

The Bank's relationship with the UNDP is particularly challenging. In Afghanistan, UNDP administers the Afghanistan Law and Order Trust Fund, since UNDP has a comparative advantage in the political dialog and security sectors, while the Bank administers the Afghanistan Reconstruction Trust Fund. This is a good example of symbiosis with explicit boundaries between the two. However, in the case study countries, IEG also found several examples of rivalry with UNDP. In Afghanistan, the Bank and UNDP have put forward two alternative models of local governance, neither of which has been wholly adopted by the government. In Nepal, the Bank has been dismissive about the years of investment by UNDP and other bilateral agencies in local government. In Haiti, the nature of the trust fund has created competition between World Bank and UNDP. At least some of these tensions could have been avoided.

# Conclusions

The analysis of ODA flows reveals how donor flows have changed since 2000 in favor of FCS. While IDA allocations have moved in the same direction, the share of IDA lags noticeably behind that of DAC donors and EU institutions. ODA has privileged a few countries, especially small island states and countries that have persisted on the FCS list. However, not all countries affected by conflict received the same degree of donor support, and resource endowments and growth potential do not appear to have influenced aid allocations.

MDTFs with active involvement of recipient governments, clear governance protocols and responsibilities, and complementarity with Bank country programs were more effective. In Afghanistan and Liberia this was evident, while in Haiti and South Sudan the complexity of the arrangements and limited government participation led to weaker outcomes. In addition, the evaluation found trust fund skills were undervalued, Bank senior management engagement was limited, and while the reporting of MDTF output progress was covered, inadequate attention was given to the consideration of higher-order objectives.

## Endnotes

[1] A background paper on MDTFs was commissioned for the evaluation and covers these issues in more depth. The paper is available upon request.

[2] For a more detailed description of the issues, refer to the background paper on MDTFs that was commissioned for the report and is available on request.

[3] The Sudan MDTF was more successful due to stronger capacity of partners and is covered in more detail in an independent evaluation report (World Bank 2013).

[4] A third approach not covered in this review is the two-window model used in Iraq which was referred to by a number of interviewees.

[5] This report produced jointly by 13 development agencies and published by the United Nations Resident and Humanitarian Coordinator's Office, Nepal can be found at http://un.org.np/report/pds-2010-2015.

# References

Demetriou, Spyros, and Mary Morrison. 2013. "Review of the United Nations—World Bank Partnership in Fragile and Conflict-Affected Countries." Unpublished paper, United Nations–World Bank Fragility and Conflict Partnership Trust Fund, New York.

IEG (Independent Evaluation Group). 2010. *The World Bank Group in the West Bank and Gaza, 2001–2009.* Washington, DC: World Bank.

____. 2011a. *Timor-Leste Country Program Evaluation, 2002–2011.* Washington, DC: World Bank.

____. 2011b. *Trust Fund Support for Development.* Washington, DC: World Bank.

____. 2012. *Afghanistan Country Program Evaluation, 2002–11.* Washington, DC: World Bank.

OECD (Organisation for Economic Co-operation and Development). 2012. *Evaluating Peacebuilding Activities in Settings of Conflict and Fragility: Improving Learning for Results,* DAC Guidelines and References Series, OECD Publishing. doi: 10.1787/9789264106802-en.

UN (United Nations) and World Bank. 2008. "United Nations–World Bank Partnership Framework for Crisis and Post-Crisis Situations." Statement signed by Ban Ki-moon, secretary-general, United Nations, and Robert Zoellick, president, World Bank on October 28, 2008, New York City. http://siteresources.worldbank.org/EXTLICUS/Resources/UN-WBFramework.pdf.

World Bank 2013. *Independent Evaluation of the World Bank Administered Multi-Donor Trust Fund in Sudan: Final Evaluation Report.* Washington, DC: World Bank.

conflict development

equitable social contract
reconstruction
reintegration
infrastructure   political settlement
civil society   reconciliation
human capital   statebuilding
local economic   gender equity
institutional   inclusive growth
rule of law

access 2 opportunities
donor harmonization
revenue mobilization
transition
political settlement
country ownership
transformation
citizen voice
accountability

fragility

security

# 10 Conclusions and Recommendations

The World Bank Group has made significant efforts in understanding fragility and conflict drivers and in enhancing its capacity to address these issues in some of the poorest and most challenging environments among its client countries. The response to the challenge of fragile and conflict-affected states (FCS) in International Development Association (IDA) only countries has included scaling up of investments and technical assistance, larger investment of staff and administrative budget resources since 2007, managerial attention leading to improvements in quality of the World Bank's portfolio, strategic commitments by the International Finance Corporation (IFC) and the Multilateral Investment Guarantee Agency (MIGA) to scale up their support to FCS, and the production of the 2011 World Development Report (WDR). The Bank Group also established the Center on Conflict, Security and Development (CCSD), a knowledge platform (i.e., the Hive), and a FCS community of practice. The evaluation finds the efforts and results to date to be commendable and moving in the right direction. A few key lessons have emerged from the evaluation:

- Country assistance strategies are more relevant and realistic when they integrate analysis of fragility and conflict drivers which often persist in FCS for many years, making it imperative that country teams draw on these analyses and adapt to them in the design and implementation of assistance programs.

- Bank Group operations in FCS are more resource intensive, but enhanced financial and staff resources and greater managerial attention can lead to better performance outcomes in FCS.

- Fragile and conflict-affected states are constrained by a lack of capacity, weak infrastructure and services, and social tensions that weaken the effectiveness of public sector reforms. To be effective, Bank Group support for state-building needs to be sustained through careful sequencing, better use of political economy analysis, and prioritization of long-term reforms. This is best achieved by a mix of predictable, programmatic budget support, investment projects, and technical assistance to build country capacity at national and subnational levels and country ownership for reforms.

- Community-driven development (CDD) programs have played an important role in providing local benefits and services in FCS. In the absence of attention to institutional and financial sustainability of CDD programs, the viability of community institutions and benefits will remain at risk.

- Inclusive growth and jobs has been constrained by the absence of clearly prioritized and sequenced support for a focused medium- to long-term strategy. It did not systematically develop the linkages and synergies across World Bank Group in critical areas, such as linkages between education, skills development, infrastructure, and private sector development. Many FCS lacked adequate analysis of the conflict and fragility drivers and of the binding constraints and opportunities for the private sector.

- Mainstreaming of gender in country programs is feasible in FCS, but in countries where the conflict affects women disproportionately, deliberately targeted programs by the Bank Group can help to address the social and economic consequences of conflict.

- When the private sector adapts its product mix—as it has done with microfinance—to the social and institutional conditions in FCS, it can provide services relevant to the needs of those countries.

- Multi-donor trust funds (MDTFs) are more than a source of finance in FCS and play a central role in donor coordination, policy dialogue, and institution building. MDTFs with active involvement of recipient governments, clear governance protocols and responsibilities, and complementarity with Bank country programs, as in Afghanistan and Liberia, were more effective than those in Haiti and Sudan.

## Operationalizing the 2011 WDR

In 2011, a paper by Bank management on operationalizing the 2011 WDR sought to identify the operational changes needed to align operations in FCS to the paradigm shift outlined in the WDR (World Bank 2011a). The paper listed six changes in the Matrix of Actions. A 2013 paper and Board presentation in March 2013 provided a management update on implementation of the 2011 WDR, pointing to an increasing number of Bank strategies

**TABLE 10.1 Progress Report on Operationalizing the 2011 World Development Report**

| Management commitments to operationalize the 2011 WDR | IEG findings | Assessment |
|---|---|---|
| Making FCS strategies more fragility focused | Progress evident in most recent strategies in all but one of the case study countries. | ++ |
| Strengthening partnerships on development, security, and justice | Partnerships established at the global level with the UN and bilateral partners, but little evidence of advances in Bank program on justice in-country, except for Justice for the Poor, which remains a marginalized research program, wholly dependent on trust funds. The proposed new Bank Anchor on justice remains unfulfilled. Partnerships on security in conflict countries predate the WDR. Conceptual clarity is needed on the Bank's role and comparative advantage in security and justice. | – |
| Increasing attention to jobs and private sector development (PSD) | The commitment to pay increasing attention on jobs and PSD has raised expectations in client countries but has not materialized. An effective framework for jobs in FCS is urgently needed. This should be a high priority, parallel to building state capacity in FCS. | – – |
| Realigning results and risks frameworks in FCS | Considerable debate exists around this topic, including with IEG, but impacts are not evident in most case study countries. Concrete decisions and actions are still awaited on a viable approach to balancing risks and results, which is evaluable. | +/– |
| Seeking less volatility in financing | This received attention in almost all of the case study countries and in the IDA17 discussions; actual results are awaited. | ++ |
| Striving for global excellence in FCS | The knowledge platform created and managed by CCSD (the Hive) provides ready access to global knowledge; a learning and networking event (FCS days) provided useful forum for exchange of global knowledge among FCS community of practice; and CCSD staff also provide substantive support to country teams on request. But the staff survey reveals these services are not well known and not fully appreciated; this remains work in progress. | + |

NOTE: The symbols mean: – – no progress; – little progress; +/– discussions ongoing; + some progress; and ++ substantial progress.

addressing drivers of fragility. The management update outlined the priorities to ensure performance continues to improve in FCS and reported on a more agile set of operational procedures for FCS, a stronger community of practice, and more resources on the front line. The update highlighted the healthy disbursement rates, the portfolio quality improvements, and the growth in supervision time in FCS. These improvements have led to an increase in the cost of doing business, but pointed to a change in the institutional culture where FCS plays a more prevalent role in the Bank's work. The report by management pointed to the five-point plan which built on the reforms outlined in 2007 and pledged to integrate country partnership strategies with fragility drivers; develop more agile operation policies; implement human resources reforms to get the best people; increase funding for state- and peace-building goals; and build a stronger community of practice. These actions were seen as central to the shift in operational performance in FCS.

Progress has undoubtedly been made in the two years since the 2011 WDR, but this effort needs to be sustained and in some areas even intensified. The evaluation finds that progress is more evident in four of the six areas identified, although they will need continued support over the next few years. Table 10.1 summarizes the status of each of the six areas and draws attention to the three that are conceptually and operationally still problematic. The findings are broadly consistent with management's own observations made at the IDA Seventeenth Replenishment deliberations in mid-2013, but they also identify conceptual, strategic, and operational areas that still need to be addressed.

Bank Group engagement in FCS is clearly a long-term agenda. Progress has been made in enhancing support to country teams and achieving greater Bank inputs and improvement in portfolio quality in the FCS, but at least at two levels more clarity and work are needed. First, at the conceptual level, there is a need to clarify the Bank Group's role on security, justice, and jobs. The 2011 WDR called for "strengthening legitimate institutions and governance for citizen security, justice, and jobs" (World Bank 2011b: 2). This does not, however, mean that the Bank Group has to take the lead on all three. The evaluation found demand for specialized services such as public expenditure reviews of the security sector conducted in partnership with UN agencies but little demand for expanded Bank work on security and justice from clients or country departments. It would be useful to clarify the specialized contributions the Bank can make based on comparative advantage, recognizing that other multilateral and bilateral agencies have a comparative advantage and mandate to engage more systematically in those areas. The evaluation concludes that, other than in clearly defined niche areas, partnerships are likely to be the principal means of engagement on security and justice. On the jobs agenda, there was unanimity among clients and development partners that the Bank Group needs to play a leading role, but there was also agreement that a workable jobs strategy for high-risk FCS environments has yet to be developed. Second, while considerable efforts have been made to undertake and draw on fragility and conflict analyses to formulate country assistance strategies (CASs), the insights and lessons have not yet been applied to Bank Group operations. More work needs to be done to flesh out the operational implications of the analyses, and IFC, MIGA, and World Bank country teams need to be made aware of, and made capable of, applying them. This is consistent with the results of the staff survey undertaken for the evaluation.

## Key Findings and Recommendations

Several challenges and constraints identified in this evaluation are yet to be overcome. The following key findings and recommendations are put forward with a view to strengthening these efforts.

With the evolution in the nature of fragility and conflict drivers over the last few years, the reliance on Country Policy and Institutional Assessment (CPIA) ratings to determine FCS status results in considerable errors of exclusion and inclusion in FCS classification. The Bank applies a set of Post-Conflict Performance Indicators to determine the size of exceptional allocations to countries deemed eligible for this support. However, these indicators are applied ex-post, after countries have been deemed eligible for exceptional allocations, rather than to determine if countries should be eligible for them. Indicators of conflict, violence and political instability are not currently used to identify fragile and conflict status.

- **The evaluation recommends that the Bank Group should develop a more suitable and accurate mechanism to define FCS status.** This would involve, at a minimum, integration of indicators of conflict, violence and political risks within the current system that serves as the basis for FCS classification.

Project level outcome ratings have improved in FCS. However, lack of realism and selectivity in most FCS country strategies evaluated has resulted in lower-outcome ratings for Country Assistance Strategy Completion Reports. Most FCS strategies have not been underpinned by systematic analysis of the drivers of fragility, conflict, and violence. Recent CAS documents in FCS make greater use of fragility and conflict analysis, but even so, FCS strategies do not include scenarios based on political economy and conflict risks with built- in contingencies to adjust objectives and results if risks materialize.

- **The evaluation recommends that country assistance strategies should be tailored better to FCS,** with clear articulation and monitoring of risks and contingencies of risks and scenarios up front and contingencies for rapid adjustment of strategic objectives, implementation mechanisms, and results frameworks if those risks materialize. This would enable formulation of more realistic country strategies and tailored performance assessments when risks that are monitored lead to changes in strategic objectives.

The Bank has made considerable effort on civil service reform, but there has been lack of traction due to political economy interests which weaken client ownership. In several FCS, Bank attempts to build capacity of the civil service reform have been adversely affected by the substitution of civil servants by externally-funded advisers who function as a "second civil service," the recruitment of civil servants to project implementation units implementing donor-financed projects, and the competition for skilled national staff among donor agencies and international nongovernmental organizations. These measures are often necessary to provide urgent humanitarian and reconstruction assistance and to rejuvenate the government and the economy in the immediate aftermath of conflict. However, in the medium term, unless they are absorbed within the public sector, they also weaken rather than strengthen the capacity of the civil service. Building sustainable civil service capacity is in keeping with the g7+ objective of aligning donor assistance with national programs and country systems under the New Deal.

Regular and predictable budget support has been found to be correlated with improvements in policy and institutional reforms, especially when the reforms have been complemented by related investment lending and technical assistance. Among the CPIA indicators, regular budget support is most highly associated with improvement in the ratings for governance reforms in public sector management.

- **The evaluation recommends that, to enhance state-building outcomes, the Bank should provide increased support to reform-oriented FCS for capacity building at national and subnational levels through predictable, programmatic budget support, complemented by technical assistance, and investment lending.** This would involve more systematic dialog with other development partners to reach agreement on measures to build capacity and sustain reforms.

CDD programs have been a major feature of Bank assistance to IDA FCS and have been effective in providing essential short-term development assistance to local communities. However, these programs have not evolved over time and institutional sustainability has not received adequate attention. In FCS these programs are still projectized and not joined up with local government, and do not receive regular fiscal transfers. Nor has the Bank instituted alternate financing and governance mechanisms to ensure their viability beyond the life of the projects supporting them. As a result, their institutional sustainability is questionable.

- **The evaluation recommends that the Bank should develop and implement a plan to ensure the institutional sustainability of the large volume of the community-driven development programs through which large volumes of investments have been channeled within FCS.** This could involve either more systematic linkages between CDD programs and local government organizations or the development of an alternative time-bound plan for financial and institutional sustainability of CDD programs.

Gender issues in FCS are often even more acute than in other IDA countries. Women are more vulnerable to gender-based violence and often face greater economic burden than in more stable societies. The Bank has been relatively effective in mainstreaming gender in IDA FCS within the health and education portfolios and in CDD projects. But gender analysis has often been delayed, and the Bank has not responded adequately or in a timely manner to conflict-related violence against women. The Bank Group as a whole has paid insufficient attention to legal discrimination against women and economic empowerment of women. Both conflict-related violence and legal constraints on business activities of women are more acute in the Africa Region.

- **The evaluation recommends that in post-conflict countries, programs addressing gender issues need to be more responsive to the conflict context and help the government address the effects of violence against women and the legal constraints on economic empowerment.** This would involve timely gender analysis in FCS to assess the effects of conflict and violence, and implementation of measures to address conflict-related violence against women and legal constraints against women's engagement in economic activities.

The 2011 WDR identified jobs as one of the priority areas to break the cycles of violence in FCS; however, Bank group support has not been effective particularly in creating long-term jobs in FCS. Direct World Bank support for job creation has been primarily in the form of short-term jobs through microfinance programs as well as public works, CDD, and demobilization, disarmament, and reintegration programs. Employment in agriculture, which absorbs 50 to 80 percent of the FCS workforce, has received inadequate attention, and the potential for leveraging natural resources management and migration toward job creation remains untapped.

World Bank Group support was not clearly prioritized and sequenced around a medium- to long-term agenda specifically focused on jobs and growth. It did not systematically develop the linkages and synergies across World Bank Group entities and activities for effective engagement by the Bank Group in FCS. The Independent Evaluation Group found a lack of Bank Group coordination in critical areas, such as linkages between education, skills development, infrastructure, and private sector development, weakened its effectiveness in achieving the Bank Group's poverty reduction objectives. Many FCS lacked adequate diagnostics of the conflict and fragility drivers and of the constraints and opportunities for the private sector, and even when diagnostics was available it was often not utilized by staff from other Bank Group entities.

- **The evaluation recommends that the World Bank Group should develop a more realistic medium- to long-term framework for inclusive growth and jobs in FCS and ensure synergies and collaboration across the three Bank Group institutions.** Such an approach should be based on sound country diagnostics of conflict and fragility drivers, and should address the main constraints and opportunities for job creation, including the role of the private sector. It should systematically explore linkages and synergies among Bank Group activities for job creation in order to accelerate progress toward the Bank Group's strategic goals of poverty reduction and shared prosperity.

The private sector in FCS countries presents different types of opportunities and business challenges to IFC and MIGA. IFC and MIGA have approached doing business in FCS in much the same way as in non-FCS countries even though sponsor quality is lower and capacity is weak; and project risks are higher than in IDA countries. IFC projects that integrated tailored capacity building for clients into project appraisal, design, and implementation of investments to account for the weak capacity environment tended to have a better chance of success. But IFC lacked the resources to offer firm-level capacity building to noninvestee companies which have the potential for local private sector development or future IFC financial engagement.

IFC and MIGA's products are not specifically tailored to needs and conditions in FCS. IFC's business model as a development financier may not be conducive to reaching private firms in FCS, which are on average smaller with weaker capacity and are more informal compared with other organizations. IFC and MIGA lack flexibility similar to the Bank's OP 8.0, and appraisal and approval processes are perceived as cumbersome and lengthy.

Staff incentives and performance measurement systems linked to project performance and volume targets are not aligned with increasing IFC engagement in FCS. Similarly, results measurement frameworks may not be fully adapted to FCS contexts. IFC has relatively few investment officers deployed to country or regional offices dedicated to working on FCS;

and MIGA has not developed specialized staff expertise with knowledge of FCS markets for business development and risk assessment and underwriting. Both IFC and MIGA have little specialized training and knowledge management products to support learning from experience and, over time, improving portfolio performance.

- **The evaluation recommends that IFC and MIGA should adapt their business models, risk tolerances, product mix, sources of funds, staff incentives, procedures, and processes to be more responsive to the special needs of FCS and to achieve their strategic priorities of increasing engagement in FCS.**

## References

World Bank. 2011a. "Operationalizing the 2011 World Development Report: Conflict, Security and Development." Working Paper DC2011-0003, prepared for a meeting of the Development Committee, April 16, 2011, World Bank, Washington, DC.

____. 2011b. *World Development Report 2011: Conflict, Security, and Development.* Washington, DC: World Bank.

# Bibliography

Acemoglu, Daron, and James A. Robinson. 2006. *Economic Origins of Dictatorship and Democracy.* New York: Cambridge University Press.

ADB (Asian Development Bank). 2010. "Asian Development Bank's Support to Fragile and Conflict-Affected Situations." Independent Evaluation Department, Special Evaluation Study, SES: REG 2010-45, ADB, Manila.

Bannon, Ian, and Paul Collier. 2003. *Natural Resources and Violent Conflict: Options and Actions.* Washington, DC: World Bank.

Barron, Patrick, and Adam Burke. 2008. "Supporting Peace in Aceh: Development Agencies and International Involvement." Policy Studies 47, East-West Center, Washington, DC.

Birdsall, Nancy, Homi Kharas, Ayah Mahgoub, and Rita Perakis. 2010. *Quality of Official Development Assistance Assessment.* Washington, DC: Brookings Institution and Center for Global Development.

Blundell, Arthur G. 2010. "Forests and Conflict: The Financial Flows That Fuel War." Background Paper for the 2011 World Development Report, World Bank, Washington, DC.

Bräutigam, Deborah, Odd-Helge Fjeldstad, and Mick Moore, eds. 2008. *Taxation and State-Building in Developing Countries: Capacity and Consent.* New York: Cambridge University Press.

Brooks, Jonathan. 2012a. *A Strategic Framework for Strengthening Rural Incomes in Developing Countries.* Paris: Organisation for Economic Co-operation and Development (OECD).

_____. 2012b. *Agricultural Policies for Poverty Reduction.* Paris: OECD.

Chapman, N., and C. Vaillant. 2010. *Synthesis of DFID Country Program Evaluations Conducted in Fragile States.* Evaluation Report EV 709. London: U.K. Department for International Development.

Cliffe, Sarah, Scott Guggenheim, and Markus Kostner. 2003. "Community-Driven Reconstruction as an Instrument in War-to-Peace Transitions." Conflict Prevention and Reconstruction Series Working Paper 7, Social Development Department, World Bank, Washington, DC.

Commission on Human Security. 2003. *Human Security Now: Protecting and Empowering People.* New York: Commission on Human Security.

Dani, Anis, and Arjan de Haan, eds. 2008. *Inclusive States: Social Policy and Structural Inequalities.* Washington, DC: World Bank.

DFID (U.K. Department for International Development). 2010. "Building Peaceful States and Societies. A DFID Practice Paper." DFID, London.

_____. 2012. "Results in Fragile and Conflict-Affected States and Situations." How To Note, February 28, 2012, DFID, London.

Gough, Ian, Geof Wood, Armando Barrientos, Philippa Bevan, Peter Davis, and Graham Room. 2004. *Insecurity and Welfare Regimes in Asia, Africa and Latin America: Social Policy in Development Contexts.* New York: Cambridge University Press.

IEG (Independent Evaluation Group). 2009. *Independent Evaluation of MIGA's Development Effectiveness—2009: Enhancing MIGA's Risk Mitigation in IDA and Conflict-Affected Countries.* Washington, DC: World Bank-MIGA.

Keefer, Philip. 2012. "Why Follow the Leader? Collective Action, Credible Commitment and Conflict." Policy Research Working Paper 6179, Development Research Group, World Bank, Washington, DC.

Kreimer, Alcira, John Eriksson, Robert Muscat, Margaret Arnold, and Colin Scott. 1998. *The World Bank's Experience with Post-Conflict Reconstruction.* Washington, DC: World Bank.

OECD (Organisation for Economic Co-operation and Development). 2008. "Evaluating Conflict Prevention and Peacebuilding Activities." Development Assistance Committee Factsheet, Organisation for Economic Co-operation and Development,Paris, France. www.oecd.org /dac/evaluationofdevelopmentprogrammes /dcdndep/39289596.pdf.

Operations Evaluation Department. 2012. *Evaluation of the Assistance of the African Development Bank to Fragile States.* Tunis-Belvedère, Tunisia: African Development Bank Group.

Robinson, James A. 2010. "From Community Driven Development to Community Driven State." Unpublished paper, Harvard University, Department of Government, Cambridge, Mass.

Scanteam. 2010. "Flexibility in the Face of Fragility: Programmatic Multi-Donor Trust Funds in Fragile and Conflict-Affected Situations." Report commissioned by the World Bank Operational and Country Services Fragile and Conflict-Affected States Group, July, Scanteam, Oslo, Norway.

Scott, James C. 1998. *Seeing Like a State: How Certain Schemes to Improve the Human Condition Have Failed.* New Haven, CT: Yale University Press.

World Bank. 1997. *A Framework for World Bank Involvement in Post-Conflict Reconstruction.* Washington, DC: World Bank.

Yang, Dean. 2008. "International Migration, Remittances and Household Investment: Evidence from Philippines Migrants' Exchange Rate Shocks. *Economic Journal 118* (April): 591–630.

# World Bank Group Assistance to Low-Income Fragile and Conflict-Affected States

Fragile and conflict-affected states (FCS) have become an important focus of World Bank Group assistance in recent years as recognition of the linkages between fragility, conflict, violence, and poverty has grown. Addressing issues of recurring conflict and political violence and helping build legitimate and accountable state institutions are central to the Bank Group's poverty reduction mission.

This evaluation assesses the relevance and effectiveness of World Bank Group country strategies and assistance programs to FCS. The operationalization of the *World Development Report 2011: Conflict, Security, and Development* (2011 WDR) is also assessed, to see how the framework has been reflected in subsequent analytical work, country assistance strategies, and the assistance programs. The evaluation framework was derived from the concepts and priorities articulated in recent WDRs, policy papers, and progress reports issued by Bank Group management, to draw lessons from FCS. The framework is organized around the three major themes emerging from the 2011 WDR: building state capacity, building capacity of citizens, and promoting inclusive growth and jobs.

The evaluation focuses on International Development Association (IDA)-only countries, which are deemed to have certain characteristics, such as very low average income and no access to private finance, making them eligible for special finance tools and programs. As the benchmark for measuring results, Bank Group performance is evaluated in 33 fragile and conflict-affected states against that of 31 IDA-only countries that have never been on the FCS list. Six new country case studies; analyses of Bank Group portfolios; human resources and budget data; secondary analysis of IEG evaluations; background studies including those on aid flows, gender, private sector development, and jobs; and surveys of Bank Group staffs and stakeholders are also included in the evaluation.

ISBN 978-1-4648-0218-8

SKU 210218

**WORLD BANK GROUP**

www.ingramcontent.com/pod-product-compliance
Lightning Source LLC
Chambersburg PA
CBHW082354270326
41935CB00013B/1616